MARKETS AND BAGMEN

Markets and Bagmen

Studies in the History of Marketing and British Industrial Performance 1830–1939

Edited by R. P. T. DAVENPORT-HINES

Gower

Published by
Gower Publishing Company Limited
Gower House
Croft Road
Aldershot
Hants GU11 3HR
England

Gower Publishing Company
Old Post Road
Brookfield
Vermont 05036
USA

British Library Cataloguing Publication Data

Markets and bagmen: studies in the history of
  marketing and British industrial performance
  1830–1939.
  1. Marketing — Great Britain — Case
  studies
  I. Davenport-Hines, R.P.T.
  658.8′00722   HF5415.12.G7

  ISBN 0 566 05066 8

Printed in Great Britain at the
University Press, Cambridge

Contents

Illustrations

Figures

Tables

Contributors

Richard Davenport-Hines was awarded a Ph.D. in history from Cambridge University in 1979, and has been a Research Officer at the Business History Unit, London School of Economics, since 1982. He has edited both the quarterly journal, *Business History*, since 1984 and a collection of essays, *Speculators and Patriots* (1986). A Fellow of the Royal Historical Society, he received the Wolfson Literary Prize in 1985 for his biography, *Dudley Docker*. He is currently writing a history of the Glaxo pharmaceutical group.

Francis Goodall graduated in geography from St John's College, Oxford in 1954, winning the Henry Oliver Beckit prize. After working for thirty years with British Gas and the National Health Service he was compulsorily retired, and joined the Business History Unit as an assistant to the *Dictionary of Business Biography*, to which he contributed several entries. He is now writing a Ph.D. exploring the relations between the gas supply industry and the manufacturers of gas appliances.

Edgar Jones was educated at Oriel College, Oxford where he read modern history, and his doctorate at Nuffield College was a regional study of the relationship between transport improvements and industrial development. He has contributed to several journals and to the *Dictionary of Business Biography*, and has written *Accountancy and the British Economy 1840–1980; the Evolution of Ernst & Whinney* (1981), and *British Industrial Architecture 1750–1939* (1985). He is currently completing the first volume of a history of Guest Keen & Nettlefolds which focuses on the iron, coal and engineering industries. He is the Hon. Treasurer of the Business Archives Council and has been an academic visitor at the Business History Unit since 1981.

Jonathan Liebenau has been a member of the Business History Unit since 1980, specialising in science-based industry, technical innovation, and the history of research and development. Since completing his doctorate in history and sociology of science at the University of Pennsylvania, he has written *The Formation of the American Pharmaceutical Industry* (1986), and articles on social studies of science, technology and medicine. He is currently writing a history of the British pharmaceutical industry and working on the history of pharmaceuticals internationally. A collection of essays edited by him on technology and British business will appear in this series.

Geoffrey Tweedale completed his Ph.D. in American economic history at the London School of Economics in 1984, having meanwhile worked on the University of Massachusetts' *Guide to the Study of United States History outside the US, 1945–80* (1985), and the Business History Unit's *Dictionary of Business Biography*. He is currently researching the interwar Sheffield steel industry.

Acknowledgements

The essays in this collection have all been contributed by members of the Business History Unit at the London School of Economics, and the authors are together indebted to Professor Leslie Hannah and to Dr Geoffrey Jones: to the former for his vivacity and enterprise as director of the unit since 1978, and to the latter for his staunch support and constructive aid when acting as temporary director of the unit when the essays were written in 1985. Above all this book could not have appeared without the tenacity and inexpugnable good nature of the real directors of the unit, Miss Susan Crawshaw and Mrs Alison Sharp.

Earlier versions of these papers were pre-circulated and discussed at a seminar, which comprised the authors together with John Armstrong, T. A. B. Corley and Professor Derek Oddy: to whom all the contributors are indebted not only for their patience and kindness in attending, but also for the sapience and discretion of their comments and criticisms.

For other information or help I am most grateful to Mr C. C. C. Bridge, Dr David Jeremy, Sir James Marshall-Cornwall, the Duke of Portland and Sir Kenneth Strong.

If it was suitable for this book to carry a dedication, it would be, in Saki's words, to 'Hugo, who was strong, good and beautiful, a rare type and not very often met with'.

R. P. T. Davenport-Hines

1 Introduction

R. P. T. Davenport-Hines

The six case-studies in this book are an attempt to contribute to the growing interest in the history of marketing exhibited by historians and economists. For manufacturing industry, as indeed for the business historians who write about it, marketing has too often been neglected: a recent speaker at Harvard Business School likened it to the dog in 'Silver Blaize', of which Sherlock Holmes remarked that the significant fact was that it did not bark.[1] These case-studies hold inherent interest, which will be enhanced by relating them to contemporary theoretical studies of marketing. This introduction does not offer a major synthesis of the history of marketing: instead a modest and tentative model is presented simply to stimulate discussion and draw together the themes of this collection.

A model taken from Kotler's textbook on the analysis, planning and control of marketing management and from Borden's seminal 'Note on the Concept of the Marketing Mix' is used in this introduction.[2] With the aid of these examples of marketing theory we can categorise the conclusions of the six case-studies and examine the theoretical implications. Although the match between historical methods and modern marketing theory is not perfect, the two approaches do have elements which are of value to one another.

Following Kotler, we can suppose that all marketing operations fall within one of five separate concepts, and that these in turn are subject to up to twelve different elements which together constitute the marketing mix. The five alternative marketing concepts for manufacturers are:

(1) the production concept
(2) the product concept
(3) the selling concept
(4) the marketing concept
(5) the societal marketing concept

The consumer preferences and managerial and other characteristics associated with these different marketing concepts are shown in Table 1.1, while Table 1.3 summarises the decisions and activities which are required of managers and

Table 1.1 To show the characteristics of the five alternative concepts of marketing for manufacturers

Concept	Consumer preference	Managerial charac-teristics	Other characteristics
Production	Consumers favour widely available products	Managers concentrate on high production efficiency & wide distribution coverage	
Product	Consumers want products distinguished by quality, performance or other characteristics	Product-orientated managers concentrate on quality or refinements, but may neglect market desires or pricing	Managers over-enamoured with technological superiority of product, especially if invention is involved
Selling	Consumers are hostile to product e.g. encyclopaedias; or operating in a buyer's market	Managers concentrate on hard-selling or aggressive promotion campaigns; business may suffer from over-capacity	Attain profits by sales volume
Marketing	Consumer preference needs may be inchoate or malleable	Managers determine the needs of specific or strategic markets, or targeted buyers, and concentrate on satisfying these more efficiently than competitors	Attain profits through customer satisfaction
Societal marketing	Consumer is potentially aware of ecological, medical or political implications of product (non-disposable bottles, high-carbohydrate processed food, South African sherry)	Managers determine market demand, and satisfy it more effectively than competitors, while preserving or enhancing the well-being of society or the consumer	

executive directors of industrial companies in meeting the twelve elements of the marketing mix.

The application of such terms to historical case-studies will repel or depress some readers, and are fraught with difficulties in instances where, for example, the marketing of Sheffield hardware or of woodscrews is traced over the course of almost a century. Nevertheless it does seem worthwhile to introduce historians to some of the concerns of economists, and indeed to test the validity of the latter's concepts in the more empirical world of historians. This introduction should, in part, be regarded as a *ballon d'essai*.

All of the case-studies in this collection concern goods and marketing conditions which have some congruence with Kotler's product concept. Woodscrews, pharmaceuticals, armaments and hardware each accord in some elements with the characteristics of the product concept, while both cocoa and engineering products for China conform entirely to the concept. Similarly none of the case-studies in this collection extends beyond 1939, and it is therefore not surprising that none of them represents an example of societal marketing, a concept which has only flourished since the 1960s. British and American pharmaceutical companies in the period of the late-nineteenth and early-twentieth centuries covered by Liebenau seem instead to have practised an amalgam of the product and marketing concepts. The market described by him in Chapter 4 is one in which consumer preferences were inchoate, pricing was a negligible factor and improvements in the efficacy or quality of the product were a keen preoccupation of managers.

Table 1.2 To show the applicability of the five marketing concepts to the manufacturers' products considered in this book

Production concept	Woodscrews
Product concept	Engineering products; cocoa; medicines
Selling concept	Armaments
Marketing concept	Hardware; medicines
Societal marketing concept	

The two clearest examples of the product concept are those of cocoa and engineering products. In the former case consumers wanted a tasty and nutritious drink, while the Rowntrees were product-orientated owner-managers with an occasionally erratic approach to some aspects of marketing, especially advertising. Prospective British engineering exporters to China, as detailed in Chapter 5, faced consumers with definite, if varied, demands, and a market of delicacy and sophistication. But instead of the careful and systematic scrutiny of local market desires that was required, the quasi-marketing organisation, the British Engineers' Association, indulged in truculent and somewhat confusing propaganda.

Woodscrews provide an example of the production concept in operation tempered by some divergences from Kotler's model. Nettlefolds' product dominated the British market for almost a century after 1870 and underwent few technical changes in that time. There was minimal organisational or structural innovation in their production, running over the course of a century into countless millions of screws; but the company's early success over its competitors would have been impossible without the higher productive efficiency which Nettlefold and Chamberlain obtained by introducing innovative American machinery. From the outset the Nettlefold woodscrew enjoyed massive distribution coverage by confining sales to wholesalers, whose loyalty could be fostered and retained more easily than tens of thousands of retailers. Among wholesalers' customers there seems to have been little product differentiation. Manipulation of discounts to wholesalers was the other cardinal feature in marketing the Nettlefold woodscrew. Although the company consistently emphasised the quality of its product, and refused to introduce cheaper lines or market inferior products under its own name, its managers were not product-orientated in Kotler's terms. There was little need for technological refinements of the product, and between 1850 and 1939 neither new technology nor new working practices made much impact on the productive efficiency originally derived from the United States. This fact, together with the use of discounts to ensure wide distribution through wholesalers, places woodscrew marketing firmly within the production concept.

The long and ultimately ignominious story of Sheffield's sales of hardware to the United States has many similarities to Kotler's marketing concept. The North American market was initially small, unsophisticated but characterised by a need for product specifications to be modified to meet individual consumer needs. The 'personal element' was important, and after 1860 questions of technology became less important than problems of marketing. Standardisation, backed by skilful advertising and distribution, became crucial in the United States market, but in the decisive period between 1870 and 1890 Sheffield traders proved notably deficient in each of them, as the British domestic market favoured multiplicity of patterns and types. Production and design alike were 'motley', accompanied by 'largely uncoordinated and poorly organised' marketing (pp. 65, 68). To succeed, the Sheffield manufacturers needed, among other things, to target specific buyers — specifically 'to tap the wealthier sections of the US community' (p. 74) — but in this they failed singularly. The pre-1860 recipes for attaining profits through customer satisfaction proved utterly unsuitable for changed tastes after the American Civil War.

Kotler identifies the selling concept as often occurring in a buyer's market, with businesses suffering from over-capacity, and in this there is some resemblance to the marketing of armaments described in Chapter 7. Arms manufacturers faced a monopsony market: governments were almost their only customers and often used their power ruthlessly against their private suppliers. The large and expensive arsenals of the manufacturers often had orders far beneath their capacity, and in the battle for overseas markets representatives of armaments companies were notoriously aggressive. All this conforms to Kotler's definition of the conditions for 'selling concepts', although it must be added that in many markets the 'product concept' is also applicable. Government procurement officers desired products distinguished by their destructive power or ballistic performance, and there were occasional cases of companies neglecting pricing or market needs because of infatuation with obtaining a technologically superb product.

This application of Kotler's criteria to historical case-studies suggests that although his concepts provide some useful standards by which to measure manufacturers' marketing performance, historical evidence tends to blur the distinctions which he has drawn. In particular several of the case-studies in this collection seem to contradict economists' perceptions of price elasticity and the relation between pricing and sales. This is not surprising in the case of armaments and pharmaceuticals: but it is striking in the instance of hardware, and can also be detected to some extent in the accounts of cocoa and woodscrews. Notwithstanding possible deficiencies in historical data or method, it does seem doubtful whether modern marketing theory is adequate to explain the diversity of the past.

Less negative conclusions however emerge from the use in a historical context of Borden's suggested elements of a 'marketing mix' for manufacturers. The elements of this mix are twelvefold:

(1) product planning
(2) pricing
(3) branding
(4) channels of distribution
(5) personal selling
(6) advertising
(7) promotions
(8) packaging
(9) display
(10) servicing
(11) warehousing and transportation
(12) market research and analysis

The decisions and procedures which they entail for manufacturers are shown in Table 1.3. Tables 1.4 and 1.5 attempt to evaluate the desirable and actual performance by manufacturers of cocoa, hardware, medicines, engineering products, woodscrews and armaments on the different ingredients of the marketing mix. Such evaluations are necessarily crude, but so long as they are not taken with excessive solemnity,[3] they do trace a useful pattern, and show the shortfall or otherwise between the perceived priorities for marketing success with various specified products, and the actual performance for these categories of the manufacturers studied in this book.

Valuable though the definitions and processes in Table 1.3 are, there are obstacles to their use in historical analysis. Chief among these is that they belong to the modern world, and that even when historians are conscious of them in their research, there is little surviving evidence into which they can be moulded. If it is desirable for historians to think in terms of Borden's definitions — and it does seem that the latter provide a needed element of stringency — it also has to be acknowledged that in many cases measurement or practical application, following Borden's mix, can only be factitious.

If anything is clear from the foregoing, it is that questions of marketing deserve more detailed and systematic research by historians. One bold effort is Stephen Nicholas's recent survey of British overseas marketing performance before 1914, with its credo

Table 1.3 To show the twelve elements of the marketing mix for manufacturers

Elements	Decisions and activities required
Product planning	Determination of product to be sold, including quality, design, quantities and potential market. Product research. Market research.
Pricing	Determination of price levels, including psychological aspects (e.g. odd/even). Determination of pricing policy (one or variable prices? Use of retail price maintenance?) Determination of profit margins.
Branding	Decisions on whether to market non-branded, individual brand or company brand. Securing and sustaining the co-operation of wholesalers/retailers/customers.
Channels of distribution	Decision on what channels to use: wholesalers, retailers or direct to customer. Securing and sustaining the co-operation of wholesalers/retailers/customers.
Personal selling	Decisions on methods to be employed by (1) manufacturer's organisation; (2) wholesalers; (3) retailers. Organisation, selection and training of sales force.
Advertising	Determination of expenditure and emphasis to be given to advertising. Determination of copy policy. Determination of mix of advertising between trade and consumers. Determination of media of advertising.
Promotions	Proportions in which they are to be directed at trade and consumers.
Packaging	Determine the importance of packaging. Formulate packages.
Display	Determine the importance of displays, and devise them.
Servicing	Determine the importance of servicing, and devise procedures.
Warehousing/transportation	Determine the importance of physical handling, and devise appropriate procedures.
Market research and analysis	Determine the importance of fact finding, and devise appropriate procedures.

that 'the lack of attention to marketing methods and techniques marks a serious omission in the debate on entrepreneurial failure', and its general exculpation of British manufacturers from charges of incompetence, insularity and complacent backwardness. Nicholas has ensured that future discussion of this topic will be conducted with considerably more stringency; but in such a wide-ranging study it is inevitable that some details will dissatisfy the specialist and that other considerations are neglected. Certainly several of the case-studies in this collection controvert

Table 1.4 To evaluate the potential importance and priorities of the twelve elements of the marketing mix to the manufacturers' products considered in this book

	Cocoa	Hardware		Medicine		Engineering products	Woodscrews	Armaments
		pre-1860	post-1860	USA	UK			
Product Planning	10	–	–	10	2	2	7	8
Pricing	6	4	3	1	3	5	9	8
Branding	10	6	5	3	4	5	7	8
Channels of distribution	3	2	2	8	6	8	7	2
Personal selling	4	1	8	8	2	7	6	8
Advertising	7	8	1	3	2	7	3	3
Promotion	4	–	–	4	6	8	3	9
Packaging	5	7	6	4	3	4	7	1
Display	4	5	7	2	3	5	5	5
Servicing	1	–	–	2	–	3	1	2
Wharehousing/ transportation	2	3	4	5	4	1	9	3
Market research & analysis	3	–	–	9	2	7	7	4

Note. I am indebted for these evaluations to the authors of the individual papers.

Table 1.5 To evaluate the actual performance by the manufacturers considered in this book on the twelve elements of the marketing mix

	Cocoa	Hardware		Medicine		Engineering products	Woodscrews	Armaments
		pre-1860	post-1860	USA	UK			
Product planning	5	8	5	9	2	1	5	6
Pricing	4	8	4	3	3	5	9	7
Branding	10	8	4	4	5	5	7	8
Channels of distribution	8	8	4	7	7	2	7	2
Personal selling	5	9	6	8	1	2	6	6
Advertising	4	6	3	5	5	2	3	2
Promotion	9	–	–	4	6	2	3	7
Packaging	5	5	4	5	3	2	7	1
Display	5	6	4	–	–	2	5	4
Servicing	1	–	–	3	–	2	1	2
Warehousing/transportation	4	7	6	5	4	5	9	2
Market research and analysis	6	–	–	7	2	2	4	4

Note. I am indebted for these evaluations to the authors of the individual papers.

Nicholas's conclusions and reinforce 'the traditional picture of the British industrialist employing amateurish marketing techniques and outdated selling institutions'.[4]

His survey is confined to overseas marketing, but a pressing need remains for comparative study of manufacturers' domestic marketing. Only in Chapter 4 of this collection, in which Liebenau compares pharmaceutical marketing techniques of Mulford and its competitors in the USA, and Wellcome and its rivals in Britain, is this attempted to any extent. Mulford is described as a pharmaceutical company engaged in efficient large-scale production, with standardisation of products. Apart from issuing pamphlets and promotional journals, Mulford's marketing relied on direct contact with customers through salesmen trained to provide scientific information in authoritative detail. As part of this emphasis on direct education, the company subsequently founded the Mulford School of Bacteriology and Immunology. Comparable British manufacturers practised less standardisation, and made other minor adjustments of technique suited to variations of local market: but overall the divergence was not great, and there is no pointed contrast in the efficiency or performance of the British and American firms. On both sides of the Atlantic companies were science-based and dealing in intellectually challenging new methods and products: there are implications in the work of most of Liebenau's co-authors that different conclusions would emerge from a comparative study of more traditional and less science-based manufacturers.

No evaluation of Britain's comparative performance in export marketing can ignore the role of the Chambers of Commerce abroad, which Dr Nicholas elides. When well-organised and intelligently led such chambers could provide valuable marketing opportunities, particularly for new products or expensive specialities, not only by their expert knowledge of potential local demand, but by introducing principals to local agents, and by organising exhibitions, demonstrations and other propaganda.[5] The facilities provided by British Chambers of Commerce abroad, the attitude of local merchants and the scope for pushing new products naturally varied among markets; but there is evidence that some British chambers lacked enterprise or competitive spirit in a way which retarded exports. In Spain, for example, where British machine-tools (mentioned by Nicholas) fell from a commanding market position in the 1890s to 'ignominious losses' before 1914,[6] there existed 'a strong feeling among British subjects abroad that by coming together they are merely introducing competition against themselves'. According to Sir Victor Wellesley, the commercial attaché at Madrid in 1908–10 and Controller of Commercial and Consular Affairs from 1916, a diplomat with constructive sympathy and understanding of the business community, British Chambers of Commerce abroad were 'very often got together for the glorification perhaps of one or two individuals' and did no serious business. When Wellesley toured Chambers of Commerce in England he was 'constantly' asked for names of reliable agents in Spain, and he regretted that there were 'very few' British Chambers of Commerce abroad in comparison with the French. In those which did exist Wellesley often found an excessively *laissez-faire spirit*' or 'a very strong disposition on the part of influential members against the Commercial Attaché visiting them at all' with new business propositions, lest the attaché introduced new competition or disturbed the status quo.[7] Similarly in the late 1920s, at a meeting of the principal British merchant houses in Peru when 'a lone voice suggested that a local British Chamber of Commerce was needed', one of the chief British merchants 'replied that it was *not* wanted, because it would "only increase competition"': there was 'no sign of dissent'.[8] This attitude was not universal but in some countries it hobbled export penetration, particularly in new products. There is need for more research on the contribution of British Chambers of Commerce abroad into overseas marketing, for they constitute a factor which cannot be ignored.

Another area for investigation is the social background and social status of bagmen. Gerry Rubin's recent account of nineteenth-century packmen and tallymen describes the 'vigorous pursuit' of 'a "status passage" from mid-nineteenth century packmen of allegedly questionable character to early-twentieth century credit drapers, joined together in trade associations', and identifies their 'quest for enhanced social status' with the promotion of 'more respectable business standards'.[9] Other speculation suggests that travelling salesmen in the late-nineteenth century commanded considerable respect among sections of the lower and middle classes, and perhaps even constituted an aristocracy of the *petit bourgeoisie*. By the 1930s however it seemed that bagmen enjoyed lower esteem from their social peers: they were perceived less as living independent and affluent lives, and more as degraded dependants living on the social margin. Travelling salesmen of the interwar period were associated with the world of Graham Greene, whereas a generation or two earlier they belonged to the novels of Victorian meliorists. Philip Larkin's salesman of agriculture 'dips and feeds', staying in 1929 at an ugly provincial hotel with 'ex-Army sheets' on the beds, comic pictures of hunting and the trenches on the walls, foul dinners 'from soup to stewed pears' and lonely bores drinking 'whisky in the Smoke Room', conveys all the dingy melancholy of the life.[10]

Perhaps in the period between 1880 and 1929 there was a comparative fall in earnings of bagmen which contributed to this apparent loss of esteem. Possibly there were other reasons. For overseas markets, at least, aristocratic bagmen became more popular, in the belief that their contacts and aplomb would succeed where big business was at stake. Lord Murray of Elibank going to Venezuela in 1912 on behalf of Lord Cowdray's oil interests, and his brother the Master of Elibank to Turkey in 1923 for Vickers, is one family example.[11] The dignification of certain sorts of bagmen may well have hastened the derogation of others. If companies turned to well-connected outsiders for the top representative jobs, this may have resulted in a fall in status at every other level in the sales hierarchy.

These ideas are conjectural. Nevertheless it is absurd to try to evaluate the marketing performance of British industry, either at home or abroad, without a clearer sense of the remuneration, social origins and popular perception of the bagmen who were responsible for the performance. The questions of status and performance are inextricably linked. Further research is essential in this area.

Nicholas cites a study of Vickers to justify his claim that in British armaments exports, 'success abroad was due in large part to the care spent grooming an expert sales force, to an extensive agent network to provide local intelligence, to generous credit, and to the willingness to set up factories inside the major foreign markets'.[12] As shown in Chapter 7 this view of Vickers needs modification, for their foreign factories were not a success,[13] and especially after 1918 the company repeatedly lost business through inability to provide credit, while their sales force deservedly had a mixed reputation. But in any case Vickers was by far the most efficient of the armourers at overseas marketing: companies such as Armstrongs, Birmingham Small Arms, or Coventry Ordnance lacked comparable salesmen, agency arrangements, credit facilities or enthusiasm for multinational manufacture before 1914, and had a modest export record. Vickers, in short, was atypical.

The references by Nicholas to the enterprise of British electrical engineering firms in China and Japan before 1914 equally need qualification.[14] Thomas Ainscough, Shanghai agent of the Bradford Dyers' Association, who cannot be dismissed as a Consular Service dullard, submitted a series of reports in 1915 while acting as the Board of Trade's Special Commissioner in China (see p. 110). These reports, which were endorsed by informed business opinion,[15] include a long section on Szechuan, a western province to which he gave 'premier place' for the 'immense possibilities' which it offered 'the British manufacturing engineer'. The seven Szechuan factories (the mint, arsenal, powder factory, and four light works) using electrical machinery had bought it from German manufacturers, who had recognised the great potential of the province and had put a corresponding effort into its development. But despite their example Ainscough reported that 'British engineering interests have persistently ignored the Province'. The only general British mercantile firm in Szechuan confined itself to exports of produce and general agency business; only one representative of British manufacturing engineers visited the province throughout 1901–14, despite the fact that Chungking could be reached by steamer from Shanghai in eleven travelling days. In contrast German electrical engineers would select a district where foreign machinery was needed, and then send them for a year or so an engineer who 'possesses the *savoir-faire* required in handling Chinese ... until by dint of acquiring the confidence and goodwill of the buyers, and proving the efficiency of his machines, the contracts are secured'.[16] British firms' provision of posters, display racks and translucent window signs, which Nicholas praises as enterprising, hardly seems adequate in comparison (see p. 110). Similarly the British Engineers' Association, formed in 1912 to act as a propaganda and intelligence organisation for British engineering exporters to China, was a fiasco; its bellicose publicity and shady employees harmed British commercial prestige, and its operations indicted British attitudes to export policy in China.[17]

Political considerations of prestige were crucial to the exporting success of British manufacturers for a wide range of products, civilian as well as armaments. The reception accorded to bagmen overseas, as indeed their own attitude to customers, varied not only according to local political conditions, but also according to those of Britain. To an international travelling salesman today it would seem trite to emphasise that an exporting nation's reputation for political stability, monetary strength, social cohesion or industrial efficiency is as important for winning orders as punctual deliveries, productive quality or selling institutions: and yet this question of national prestige has been neglected by historians in assessing Britain's overseas marketing performance. There are some problems in resolving this question of political prestige. Thus Sir Joseph Addison (see pp. 108, 178) reported from the Baltic states in 1929:

> Prestige is a delicate and a fragile thing and it will bear no rough usage ... British prestige in these small countries is up to the top of the thermometer. They ... subconsciously consider (and rightly) that we are the finest nation in the world, and that the British Empire really produces the best of everything, from the gentleman to the aeroplane, with all intermediary articles.[18]

Yet the Report of a Federation of British Industries tour of the USA in 1925, mentioned by Tweedale (p. 70), lamented that:

> in the United States, even in the most friendly disposed quarters, the general impression seems to be that England is definitely 'down and out'. All our difficulties are exaggerated, and the progress we have made towards reconstruction ignored. We are painted as being at the mercy of Communists. One hears that our plants are out-of-date, our methods antiquated, we cannot compete, our spirit of initiative has deserted us, and the British workman neither can nor will work ... Not only is this doing the prestige of Great Britain infinite harm, it is also losing us business, and of that we have definite proof ... This impression of the gradual decline of England is a catastrophe, and that it exists is largely our own fault ... The American is an optimist and he does not understand our national habit of self-deprecation, with the result that he takes all the pessimistic talk he hears as ... probably an understatement of the gravity of the situation.[19]

Both Addison and the Federation of British Industries delegates were shrewd and experienced observers whose opinions deserve respect. The fact that they are directly conflicting does not diminish the value of their observations: it emphasises that in different foreign markets British prestige stood at different levels. For Esthonians, Latvians and Letts in the 1920s the stability, institutional traditions and economic strength of the British Empire seemed a matter of wonder and envy, whereas for citizens of the United States Britain appeared effete, unstable and vulnerable. There is not the slightest doubt that these different views of Britain permeated the reception given in the Baltic and in the USA to bagmen from the United Kingdom. For a clearer appraisal of Britain's experiences as an exporting nation, it is essential to have a more specific global picture of where British national prestige stood high, where it was low, and at what date it started to decline.

Nicholas's view that consular criticism of the sales performance of British agricultural machinery firms was unjust needs to be tempered. Although Germans may not have been superior in method to Ransomes in the Russian market,[20] elsewhere British agricultural machinery firms were unable to mount anything like the co-operative sales effort of their German rivals. In the Ottoman Empire in 1890 the Export Verband deutschen Maschinen Fabriken und Huttenwerke, representing some hundred firms, opened a permanent exhibition at Constantinople displaying ploughs, pumps, tools and traction engines. Subsequently the Export Verband opened agencies at Smyrna, Beirut, Aleppo, Damascus, Haifa and Jaffa.[21] British exports to Asiatic Turkey were worth annually over £3 million in the early 1890s, with Lancashire cotton products, traditionally the chief export, retaining their market hold. But in hardware, cutlery and other metal products Britain's market share was eroded,[22] partly because German manufacturers grouped themselves together in export associations which not only reduced overheads but also provided the means for a wider and more intensive coverage of the local market. In export arrangements British firms were too individualistic to combine in sectoral trading units. As a result they were less competitive in price, less intensely represented locally, and (according to a British observer in Constantinople) unable to imitate German traders who 'study the tastes of the people ... on the spot'.[23] Similar lessons are drawn with equal cogency by Tweedale in explaining the collapse of Sheffield's marketing techniques and business performance in late-nineteenth-century USA (pp. 64–72).

It was to meet this deficiency that in 1916–17 the Board of Trade Advisory Committee on Commercial Intelligence, which almost entirely comprised business-men, adopted a proposal of the British commercial attaché in Argentina and organised an association of manufacturers of jewellery, silverware and electroplate to promote jointly their products in South America (see p. 111). Treasury sanction of a government subsidy of £5000 to the new organisation was obtained: itself evidence that even the most obscurantist officials and businessmen recognised that Britain had lagged behind in organising export associations and combinations.[24]

In the cases of Sheffield cutlery, and hardware too, Tweedale provides little support for Nicholas. He describes how in the US market British manufacturers moved from an apparently unassailable hegemony before 1860 to a position of ignominy by 1930. This was partly the result of the application to the light steel trades of the American System of Manufacture, but more due to organisation and other weaknesses of the British. According to Tweedale success in the American hardware market depended upon production of standardised articles which were not only sufficiently cheap and sturdy to meet the demands of a largely agricultural community, but were also better suited to modern distribution methods. Yet the Sheffield firms continued to produce a vastly variegated range which nevertheless contrived not to satisfy local consumer wishes. Despite explicit advice to the contrary, Sheffield firms kept offering a quality product to be bought only once in a lifetime despite clear evidence that American buyers preferred cheap, easily replaceable products. Tweedale concludes that the small-scale enterprise and individualistic products and selling methods, which created Sheffield's early-nine-teenth-century success in the USA, continued into the twentieth century, although they were the antithesis of what was needed to exploit the rich American market (pp. 73–4). This dismal picture is irreconcilable with Nicholas's roseate general view of merchant houses acting as intermediaries between makers of standardised goods like hardware and cutlery and their foreign markets. In the USA at least the British did not enjoy access to 'a sophisticated distribution system unmatched by other trading nations' with merchant houses which 'reduced uncertainty, provided credit, and assured stable supply by creating a common selling market for British manufacturers'. Nicholas's paean to the 'institutional innovation and major [distributive] adaption' which occurred between 1870 and 1914 in the marketing of standardised goods may be justified in some of the cases which he cites; but so far as Sheffield hardware was concerned, a dirge would be more appropriate than a paean.[25]

Although there were certainly companies not mentioned by Nicholas, like Mather and Platt, with sophisticated and impressive overseas arrangements,[26] historians tempted to reject the traditional picture of British industrialists deploying amateurish marketing techniques and obsolete selling institutions should recall the fate of the British commercial attaché in Berlin who organised a large conference of furniture makers in London in 1913. He provided detailed figures on the market opportunities in Germany where there was a craze for imitation English antiques. Having besought his audience to write to him for introductions and further details, he received only one letter: and that addressed to the Commercial Ambassador, British Embassy, Berlin, France.[27]

Whoever takes up Dr Nicholas's plea for more research in this field cannot discount such evidence of abysmal entrepreneurial failure.

Notes

1. See Richard S. Tedlow, 'Towards a History of Marketing', paper to Business History Seminar at Harvard Business School, 17 April 1985.
2. Philip Kotler, *Marketing Management: analysis, planning and control* (London, 1984 edn); Neil Borden, 'Note on the Concept of the Marketing Mix', in Eugene Kelley and William Lazer, eds, *Managerial Marketing* (Homewood, Ill., 1958).
3. Blair Worden, 'Getting on by Numbers', *New Statesman*, 22 November 1974.
4. Stephen J. Nicholas, 'The Overseas Marketing Performance of British Industry 1870–1914', *Economic History Review*, 2nd ser., 37 (1984), p. 505. Although I contest some passages of this article I should stress that it contains many useful and admirable insights. Another source which supports a favourable appraisal of British marketing is D. C. St M. Platt, *Latin America and British Trade 1806–1914* (London, 1972).
5. Sir Theodore Morison and George T. Hutchinson, *The Life of Sir Edward Fitzgerald Law* (London, 1911), pp. 107–8.
6. R. P. T. Davenport-Hines, *Dudley Docker* (Cambridge, 1984), p. 113.
7. Papers of W. J. Ashley, evidence of 17 March 1916 by Victor Wellesley to Huth Jackson committee on post-war trade relations, Add. Ms. 42245; Davenport-Hines, *Docker*, pp. 68–9, 85–6, 134–5, 194–6, 226.
8. Memorandum of 31 May 1929 by Captain J. K. V. Dible, PRO FO 371/13507.
9. Gerry Rubin, 'From Packmen, Tallymen and "Perambulating Scotchmen" to Credit Drapers' Associations c. 1840–1914', *Business History*, 28 (1986).
10. See 'Livings', in Philip Larkin, *High Windows* (London, 1974), p. 13.

11. On the Master of Elibank (later 2nd Viscount Elibank), see Sir Vincent Caillard and J. P. Davison to Foreign Office, 22 February 1927, Vickers papers 28, Cambridge University Library; on Murray of Elibank, see Arthur Murray (3rd Viscount Elibank), *Master and Brother* (London, 1945); Lady Donaldson of Kingsbridge, *The Marconi Affair* (London, 1962); Desmond Young, *Member for Mexico* (London, 1966).

12. Nicholas, 'Overseas Marketing', p. 504; C. Trebilcock, *The Vickers Brothers* (London, 1977), pp. 127–9, 133.

13. J. D. Scott, *Vickers* (London, 1962), pp. 84–6, 146–9; R. P. T. Davenport-Hines, 'Vickers' Balkan Conscience: aspects of Anglo-Romanian armaments 1918–39', *Business History*, 25 (1983), pp. 287–319; id., 'Vickers as a Multinational before 1945', in G. G. Jones, ed., *British Multinationals: origins, growth and performance* (London, 1986).

14. Nicholas, 'Overseas Marketing', p. 505.

15. Mitchell Library of New South Wales, Sydney, Australia, papers of Dr G. E. Morrison, vols 118 and 196.

16. 'Engineering Prospects in Szechuan', Report by T. M. Ainscough to Board of Trade Advisory Committee on Commercial Intelligence, April 1915, PRO FO 371/2329.

17. *Far Eastern Review* (January 1915), pp. 285–98.

18. Despatch 6, Sir Joseph Addison (Riga), 2 January 1929, PRO FO 371/13982.

19. Vernon Willey (2nd Baron Barnby) and (Sir) Guy Locock, *Report on Visit to the United States of America* (FBI, 1925), pp. 11–12.

20. Nicholas, 'Overseas Marketing', p. 494.

21. Harold S. W. Corrigan, 'British, French and German Interests in Asiatic Turkey 1888–1914' (London Ph.D., 1954), p. 96.

22. Ibid., pp. 21–4.

23. Sir Vincent Caillard, *Report on the Revenues ceded by Turkey to the Bondholders of the Ottoman Public Debt* (London, 1888), p. 29. Caillard was no tendentious friend of the British Embassy at Constantinople of the sort posited by Nicholas: see R. P. T. Davenport-Hines, 'The Ottoman Empire in Decline', in R. V. Turrell and J. J. van Helten, eds, *The City and the Empire* (London, 1985), pp. 118–30.

24. *Report to the Board of Trade by the Advisory Committee on Commercial Intelligence*, Cd. 8815 of 1917, paras 29–33.

25. Nicholas, 'Overseas Marketing', pp. 497, 506.

26. Sir John Wormald, 'The Export Trade of our Engineering and Machinery Business', *Ways and Means* (26 April 1919), pp. 237–8.

27. Sir Francis Oppenheimer, *Stranger Within* (London, 1960), p. 214; Lord Frederic Hamilton, *The Days Before Yesterday* (London, 1920), pp. 174–5.

2 Marketing consumer products before 1914: Rowntrees and Elect Cocoa

Francis Goodall

Introduction

Joseph Rowntree (1836–1925) is justly honoured as a leading social reformer of his time who implemented his Quaker principles in his business as well as his private life. Less is known of Joseph Rowntree the businessman who at the age of thirty-three gave up a successful career in the family grocery firm to help his younger brother Henry Isaac (1838–83) whose cocoa and chocolate business was ailing. At that time there were many other similar businesses: Frys were by far the largest with over 250 employees although Cadburys had begun to expand rapidly. When Joseph became his brother's partner in 1869 there were less than a dozen employees; by 1914 there were 6500. Sales of £7384 were made in 1870; by 1914 these amounted to £1 533 273, a rate of growth of 12.5 per cent compound for forty-five years, in only three of which did total sales fail to increase.

In the mid-1860s British cocoa technology had made considerable progress. Frys had introduced their famous chocolate cream bar in 1866; about the same time first Cadburys and then Frys had adopted a Dutch process for making pure cocoa developed by Van Houten in 1828. By extracting a substantial proportion of the natural cocoa butter from the bean under pressure, a palatable drink could be made without sugar or other additives (see Appendix, p. 49); it also left cocoa butter which could be used to make eating chocolate.

Rowntrees were not great innovators. In 1886–7 they adopted the Van Houten process themselves for their Elect cocoa; their other distinctive product which became a notable success, the fruit gum, was brought to them by a French craftsman confectioner looking for employment in England. They also sold a wide range of other cocoa and chocolates, as did their competitors, at a time when the market for such consumer products was growing sharply. The basis for their ability to outstrip virtually all competition lay in two key factors. The first was a close control of costs achieved through the management accounting systems progressively installed by Joseph Rowntree after his arrival; these returned the firm to modest profitability. The second key factor was a complete turnaround in the marketing strategy of the company in which he played a decisive role. In the early years virtually no advertising was undertaken; when it was decided to adopt a high profile, one product attracted the whole weight of the promotional effort. The success of this policy brought commercial success and made Rowntree a household name.

Elect cocoa, launched in 1887, the premium product of the firm, was, by deliberate decision of the board, the only one to attract sustained promotional investment through advertising. After a decade during which steadily increased advertising brought sharply increased sales, in 1909–10 the premium cocoas such as Elect and Cadbury's Bournville came under severe competition from cheaper cocoas, and sales tumbled year by year until 1914. Rowntrees were faced with the dilemma of cutting price (and profitability) or quality. The Rowntrees strategy of concentrating virtually their whole marketing effort on a single product, Elect cocoa, is questioned and alternative strategies considered. Intensive promotional effort was costly and in consequence Elect was far less profitable than the other Rowntree products. Elect cocoa provides a documented case-study which will be discussed chronologically against the background of competition, not least from the other Quaker chocolate firms of Frys and Cadburys, whose responses to the same business environment showed interesting differences.

Cocoa and other Drinks

When Joseph Rowntree joined his brother in 1869 their ailing local business was in a market on the verge of rapid expansion. Real national income per head was to increase sharply and there was a growing demand for consumer goods of all kinds.[1] Figures 2.1a, 2.1b and 2.1c demonstrate how closely the growing consumption of cocoa as a semi-luxury product related to the economic well-being of the nation, disturbed only by downswings of the trade cycle. Figure 2.1a (GDP) shows 1879, 1886 and 1893 as years of depression. After 1900 there was a slowing-down for a few years until the rapid growth in GDP and real income per head of the previous twenty years were taken up again. Figure 2.1b (cocoa imports) shows a similar contour with only minor leads and lags. Rowntree's sales (Figure 2.1c) achieve a higher rate of growth than total UK cocoa consumption demonstrated by cocoa imports but the same troughs can be identified. The higher growth rate of Rowntrees demonstrates their success as a well-managed company. The high growth rate from 1901 is related to their steadily increasing expenditure on marketing, particularly as competition from imported cocoa and chocolate products was intensifying at that time.

In the late-nineteenth century falling prices for primary commodities were a major factor in raising consumption per capita. Increased consumption of cocoa cannot however be explained in these terms because the drop in wholesale prices of cocoa after 1880 was far less than that of tea or coffee.

As far as other non-alcoholic beverages were concerned, consumption of tea per head grew from 3.8lb per head in 1870 to 6.9lb in 1914. Coffee however showed a steady decline from 1lb per head in 1870 to 0.6lb in 1914. Cocoa had long ceased to be merely a drink for the fashionable rich nor, at 0.2lb per head in 1870, was it yet a popular drink, but by 1914 consumption had risen to 1.7lb per head. In that year 70

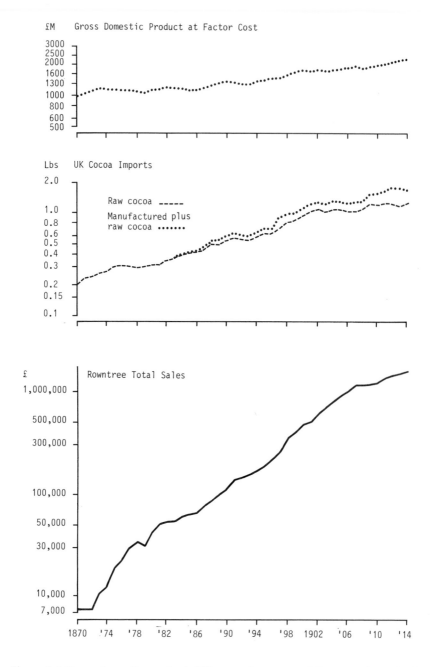

Figure 2.1 Gross domestic product, UK cocoa imports and Rowntree's total sales

Source: a C. H. Feldstein (1972), T12, Table 4(s)
       b Statistical Abstracts
       c Rowntree Archives 692.

Table 2.1 Wholesale prices of cocoa, tea and coffee

	Cocoa	Tea	Coffee
	(1900 = 100)		
1870	72	192	94
1880	116	158	132
1890	100	125	138
1900	100	100	100
1910	102	93	83

Source: Based on A. R. Prest and A. A. Adams, *Consumers' Expenditure in the United Kingdom 1900–1919* (London, 1948).

per cent of cocoa consumed was home-manufactured, imported cocoa products making up the balance; imports far exceeded exports at that time.[2] These figures by 1914 include chocolate products which cannot be separated in the official figures from the cocoa from which they were made. Chocolate even more than cocoa is an indicator of a rising standard of living.[3] (The words cocoa and chocolate were used indiscriminately in common parlance up to the middle of the nineteenth century for a cocoa drink; thereafter chocolate is progressively reserved for cocoa-based confectionery.) By contrast, although consumption per head of spirits, wine and beer increased from the late 1880s to the 1890s, their consumption declined after 1900 or so to a substantially lower level (spirits and wine) or to their previous level (beer).[4]

Technical advances and the rising standard of living were of far more significance to increasing cocoa consumption than the temperance movement of the time. The attempt by philanthropic temperance workers to establish chains of coffee and cocoa houses to rival public houses had some success in a few centres, notably Liverpool, where no less than twenty-five cocoa houses had opened by 1877.[5] These were independent of the cocoa manufacturers and poorly managed. Despite enthusiastic reports to the Select Committee on Intemperance, the movement was short-lived.

At this time the development of multiple shop firms which was to be such a feature of the period up to 1914 had hardly begun: Sainsbury's first shop opened in Drury Lane, London in 1869. Lipton opened his first shop in Glasgow in 1871 and by 1898 he had 242 shops in Britain as well as others overseas.[6] In 1885 there were still fewer than 700 branches of multiple grocers; the number of branches had increased tenfold by 1914 and their sales as a proportion of total business even more impressively. 'Own brands' such as Lipton's tea (and Lipton's cocoa) were offered and if any particular manufacturer wished to distinguish his product, it too had to be branded, for example Mazawattee tea. Some manufacturers were happy to supply goods to be sold by retailers as 'own brands' or unbranded, but this could leave the supplier perilously exposed to competitors. Press advertisements of the period indicate that cocoa brands were promoted far more vigorously than tea or coffee brands. Tea in particular was normally sold on the basis of origin, for example Ceylon or Darjeeling;[7] cocoa being a manufactured and blended product lent itself to branding by type or maker.

Fry's had been promoting their own types of cocoa since the late-eighteenth century, for example Fry's Pearl Cocoa or Fry's Rock Cocoa, to distinguish their products and associate them with the Fry name and reputation for quality, irrespective of the outlet through which they were sold. After the development of 'pure cocoa' in the 1860s and the Adulteration of Food Act 1872 Frys, and especially Cadburys began to promote their products vigorously as did other cocoa manufacturers (but not yet Rowntrees). The emergence of branded lines (Fry's Breakfast Cocoa, Cadbury's Bournville, Rowntree's Elect) was a rather later development. The cocoa manufacturers were among the first food firms to realise the value of advertising, following the lead of Holloway and Beecham who were advertising their pills from the 1850s. In view of the tremendous growth of advertising towards the end of the nineteenth century it is surprising to find as late as 1870 that advertisements for books, sheet music and the theatre took up far more column inches than clothes, furniture or consumer goods.

Consolidation

The business which Joseph Rowntree joined in 1869 had been acquired by his brother seven years earlier when Tuke & Co., another York Quaker family, sold off their subsidiary cocoa interests and then concentrated on their main business of tea merchants.[8] Although Tukes had been selling cocoa and chocolate since the 1780s, production in the 1869s was still not more than 12 cwt (600 kg) a week. In order to move his business from the Tuke premise Henry Isaac Rowntree had purchased an old foundry in 1864, in which he set up cocoa manufacture. On 5 July 1869, when Joseph came into partnership with Henry Isaac, the balance sheet showed stock £1331, book debts £1743, machinery implements and fixtures £1000, hardly a thriving business. The production methods were primitive, though no doubt typical for the small cocoa producers of the period. Much of the work was done by hand, including grinding the cocoa beans and mixing the various grades of cocoa required. Rowntree's main lines of 'Rock' cocoas were sold in block rather than powder form. Orders were brought in by travellers paid on straight commission, who had no incentive to push one product rather than another and the batch method of production made it simple to meet the individual requirements of customers. Nineteen distinct varieties of cocoa were being sold by the firm in 1878; the cost accounts introduced by Joseph Rowntree demonstrate that only four of them, accounting for 70 per cent of cocoa sales, showed a profit.[9] As well as selling their own products, Rowntrees also acted as selling agents for others including local confectioners making speciality chocolates. They also held an agency for Neave's Farinaceous Food for Infants (having 'carefully enquired into its character before consenting to introduce it to our customers').[10]

Like his brother, Joseph Rowntree had strong views on what constituted fair trading and in particular the morality of advertising. In 1870 press advertising was already directed towards two totally different markets; in trade journals, such as the *Grocer*, suppliers and importers sought to place their goods in the hands of retailers, buying in bulk by multiple stores then being virtually unknown.[11] Twenty years later co-operative store managers had considerable freedom in what they stocked and displayed.[12] Advertisements directed at the general public appeared in the *Graphic*, *Illustrated London News* and similar journals. Prominent among the very few consumer goods regularly advertised were Brown & Polson's cornflour, Menier French chocolate and cocoa by Fry, Epps and Taylor. Of the three, only Fry could offer a pure cocoa; the advertisements of Epps and Taylor encouraged the belief that cocoa was good for you ('may save many heavy doctor's bills')[13] possibly because their products were, at best, an acquired taste.

Rowntree's lacked the financial resources to advertise, even if they had wanted to. At this time Frys had annual sales of nearly £150 000 and employed 250 people, making them twenty times larger by numbers employed than Rowntrees and several times larger than Cadburys.[14] Rowntrees had to make a virtue of necessity. A letter in 1870 proclaimed the intention to maintain a high standard of excellence. 'As we do not advertise we are enabled to give greater value for money than firms whose sales depend on advertisements. We prefer to trust to quality ... Steadily increasing sale strengthens our opinion that this is a sound method of doing business.'[15] Twenty-five years later Joseph, addressing the travellers, referred to their determination not to send out defective goods: 'Throw defective goods if you like into the river but never send them out to our customers.' He also referred to the production of top quality goods: 'the price must be fixed to suit the quality and not the quality to fit any low price ... we have not hesitated to sell some important lines at a price higher than that charged by our keenest competitors ... Even small quantities of our best goods will add to the reputation of the firm.'[16]

The emphasis on quality allied with primitive manufacturing facilities meant that the proportion of 'wasters' (saleable but slightly sub-standard goods such as broken chocolate bars) was very high. These were sold at or below cost (49s 3d to 57s per cwt (50kg) against an average cost of 59s),[17] which goes far towards explaining why, in the years 1870–9 while sales increased steadily from £7384 to £30 890, annual profits averaged less than £550. Ten years later sales had almost reached £100 000 but in only two years did profits exceed £2000. Table 2.2 based on Rowntree's cost accounts for the second half of 1878 demonstrates this unhappy picture.[18]

The loss on wasters in that year is by no means untypical; it continued in the following years, and in 1883 reached the staggering figure of £1750. Given the prices charged it is hardly surprising that wasters were much in demand. Even as late as 1900 Rowntrees were having problems in meeting all the orders, which, as they recognised, were unprofitable and reduced their capacity to achieve full-price sales.[19] A determination to give value for money did not mean that only top class goods were sold and much of the cocoa sold in the early days was of inferior quality (see Appendix, p. 49). By 1879 at the latest in the interests of fair trading, loose chocolates were being sold by weight rather than by count.[20]

Table 2.2 Rowntrees' sales and profitability July-December 1878

Cocoas	Weight tons	Profit £	Loss £
Rowntrees Prize Medal Rock (14lb lots)	19	75	
Tuke's Rock A, B, and C quality	5	10	
Tuke's Rock D Quality	6	35	
Pearl	3		11
Diamond	4		11
London Chocolate Powder	4	13	
Homeopathic	4		9
12 other varieties	4		49
Total cocoas (19 varieties)	49	53	
Chocolates and chocolate creams (20 varieties)	30	163	
Jujubes and gums	4	11	
	83	227	
Wasters	133		158
Total	216	69	

Joseph Rowntree's ideas of fair trading also extended to setting fair prices to allow adequate margins not only for the manufacturer but also for his wholesalers and retailers.[21] In a letter to Joseph Storrs Fry, whom he knew well through the Quaker connection, he sought advice on pricing chocolate creams which he intended to make rather than buy in. 'I do not wish to do anything recklessly to injure what ought to be a lucrative branch of our business.' He hoped to elicit Fry's and Cadbury's practice relative to price-cutting firms. 'Of course thou will only answer my questions *just so far* as thou inclines.' He emphasised that 'we are strict with discounts, from a wish not to cut down the profits of the trade'.[22] Right from his earliest days Rowntree was anxious to match the best discounts available, but as a corollary felt able to insist that his goods were not sold at a discount below maker's published list price. Where price-cutting was proved Rowntree cut off supplies until an undertaking was given to abide by published prices.[23] Only three exceptions were noted. Rowntrees never set a minimum price for their most expensive fancy chocolate assortments. Where price-cutting was reported as universal in one town, Rowntree under *force majeure* would have authorised a departure from list price if formally requested by the local

Grocers' Federation. In fact Rowntree had been misled and only a few traders cut prices: Rowntrees therefore reverted to their rule. In the final instance, at a time of intense price-cutting by all manufacturers, Rowntrees offered bulk supplies of cheap cocoa for which no list price was ever set.

The insistence of Rowntree on the maintenance of published prices was typical of a robust Quaker view that vigorous trading in business could be a true vocation of benefit to the community as a whole, while idleness was a sin.[24] Quakers in business would set a fair price and would refuse to engage in bargaining; they were among the very first to mark their goods with fixed selling prices.

While he opposed advertising, Joseph Rowntree recognised that if his business was to enjoy continued growth he had to familiarise his name with the shopkeepers and wholesalers who were his customers. From 1880 he placed occasional small advertisements in the trade press, which ensured that his name appeared in the regular directories of cocoa and chocolate manufacturers.[25] He also spent small sums on point-of-sale promotional material, 600 special Rowntree's cocoa display tins to stand on grocers' counters and a couple of dozen glass showcases marked 'Rowntree's Chocolate'.[26] This was the first step towards a direct appeal to the public. Cadburys and Frys had no inhibitions and their advertising, though still on a very modest scale, was at a far higher level than Rowntrees, who at this time were spending less than £100 a year. Joseph Rowntree was concerned with getting his goods into shops and on display so that their intrinsic worth could be appreciated; evidently his travellers paid on commission did not have time to spend persuading shopkeepers to stock his goods, so he was planning to use 'openers out', young men with some retail experience paid a salary (with only a small element of commission) to call on shopkeepers. This was an idea he had taken from Reckitts, another Quaker firm.[27] Rowntree did advertise to fellow Quakers in the *Friend* magazine, as did Fry and Cadbury, but theirs were the only consumer goods advertised among the classified entries offering schooling and accommodation suitable for Quakers.[28] Joseph's brother edited the *Friend*, which may explain the presence of these incongruous advertisements.

At that time Rowntree was considering how to improve his product range. Pure cocoas were available from Van Houten, Cadbury and Fry, in addition to the normal range of mixtures which were all he was able to manufacture. Despite his desire to produce high quality products, his range, like that of the other couple of dozen small manufacturers, did not include a pure cocoa. With his profit record substantial investment was impossible and he did not want to borrow. He knew the principle of cocoa butter extraction, having visited Cadburys at Birmingham in 1875 and Dutch manufacturers in 1877. In 1880 a better grade cocoa named Elect was introduced but made no impact on the market and was soon withdrawn. This débâcle demonstrates the weakness of Rowntree's marketing stance. His salesmen had no incentive to push the new product rather than the old and without advertising he had no means of influencing either retailers or customers. An occasional entry in a trade journal or directory was no match for the regular advertising of his competitors, directed at the general public.

At the same time a new advertising medium was making its mark. In 1881 George Newnes founded *Tit-Bits*, a weekly magazine full of easily-written features and articles and incorporating advertising sections front and back. *Reader's Digest* is probably the nearest contemporary parallel. *Answers*, from Alfred Harmsworth, followed in 1888.[29] Magazines such as these popularised the use of advertising picture blocks which were far more eye-catching than the repetitive use of letterpress which for a few more years remained the commonest means to create a visual impact on a page of newsprint. Some newspaper editors resented 'that intolerable monstrosity, the picture block' but it became a permanent feature;[30] Liptons were among the early advertisers to develop special newspaper blocks for campaigns and special seasonal advertising. Of the cocoa manufacturers Cadburys were the most aggressive advertiser, followed closely by Epps and Bensdorp.[31]

Struggling to develop a range of top quality goods, Rowntree was clearly stung both by the failure of his Elect brand and by the emphasis placed by his competitors, especially his fellow Quaker Cadbury, on the pure unadulterated quality of their cocoa. Pure food was a very live issue following the Adulteration of Food Acts of 1872 and 1875. Cadbury had lobbied forcibly in favour of the legislation and obviously hoped that cocoa mixtures, such as Rowntree's, would be banned or restricted;[32] Cadbury's cocoa was 'Guaranteed absolutely pure and therefore may be sold with perfect safety under the new Act'.[33] Rowntree's counter-attack in a letter to wholesalers smacks of desperation rather than conviction:

> Because we think it is as much a mistake to take away a portion of the most valuable part of the cocoa as to add any foreign admixture, the whole of this 'butter' is preserved in our manufacturing process. (To skim milk is considered as wicked as to add water to increase the quantity.)[34]

Despite the failure of the first Elect, another premium product introduced by Rowntrees in 1881 was a triumphant success and accounts for the trebling of average profits in the 1880s over the 1870s. At that time the French had a virtual monopoly of gum and pastille manufacture. Rowntrees were visited by a Frenchman, Claude Gaget, who produced samples of fruit gums he had made. Little capital outlay was required to set up in production, so Gaget was engaged by Rowntree and after some months of experimentation crystallised gum pastilles were put on sale early in 1881. These were an immediate success and within a couple of years provided 20 per cent of sales by weight and a much higher percentage of total profit.[35] From the start these equalled the best on the market and the reputation has been maintained. A tremendous range of flavours was developed, some being novelties brought out after an advantageous purchase of fruit in season. Flavours ranged from Honeysuckle, Lavender and Malted Milk to Camphor, Antiseptic, and Menthol and Eucalyptus, as well as the normal fruits, lime, blackcurrant and so on. Gaget continued to work on product development but was not involved in policy matters.

Joseph's failure to break into the premium cocoa market which Cadbury and Fry had been developing steadily for fifteen years must have been a bitter blow. In 1885 the merchants through whom he bought his cocoa beans confirmed his belief that he must develop the best quality product.

> Epps buys strong flavoured beans which will absorb a large proportion of farina. We believe our wisdom lies in keeping to the fine cocoa. People are

getting tired of his thick porridge. The cocoa of the future we believe will be that made of the fine cocoa with the exclusion as much as possible of farina.[36]

This may have been sufficient encouragement. Joseph may well also have considered that after fifteen years' work the business was only modestly profitable. He was approaching the age of fifty-eight at which his father had died, and his own children would soon join the firm. He may well also have been stung by the Cadbury advertising which implied that anything other than pure cocoa was an adulterated foodstuff. If he was to break into the premium cocoa market he would have to make a move soon. Once again he looked overseas for technical expertise. He visited Stollwerck of Cologne who manufactured equipment as well as making chocolate. He also went to the Netherlands and after some negotiation engaged a Dutchman, Cornelius Hollander, at the princely weekly wage of £5, on the basis of Hollander's assurance that he could make a cocoa powder identical to Van Houten's. In view of the fragmentation of the industry and the relative ease with which manufacture could be undertaken, Rowntree was most anxious to keep the details of the process secret even from the other men at his factory. New machinery was installed in 1886 and ingredients were ordered under Hollander's supervision and blended by him behind locked doors before roasting. Production batches failed to reach the standard of the preliminary samples and working arrangements became very strained, not least because of the furtiveness of Hollander. Soon Rowntree's senior people themselves worked out the process to achieve the quality product they required and Hollander was dismissed. Rowntree did not relax his vigilance and for many years the few employees engaged on the final blending were required to bind themselves to secrecy under formal agreement.[37]

After Joseph Rowntree had visited Nestlé's factory at Vevey and seen how Nestlé encouraged visitors, he supported visits to his new Haxby Road works, although visitors were not allowed to enter the workrooms where production processes were conducted. Although periodic discussions were held with Cadbury and Fry on topics of mutual interest, there were always sensitive items, especially recipes and blends, where disclosure could cause severe commercial damage. The Rowntrees board of directors frequently discussed information they had received which might indicate how well or badly their competitors were faring.

Although Elect cocoa, a major technical breakthrough for Rowntrees, was launched in August 1887, the prospects for the new product were not wholly favourable. Production problems had to be resolved and Elect was essaying a market long occupied by Van Houten, Cadburys and Frys. Elect's quality satisfied Joseph Rowntree's criteria and its price closely matched Cadbury's and Fry's but was rather below Van Houten's imported cocoa. Elect was highly profitable – 40 per cent gross profit – on a highly priced article. Excluding Elect, the gross selling value per cwt (50kg) of all Rowntree's other product groups (other cocoa, chocolate, chocolate cream assortments, gums) was in the range of £5.2 to £6.3; Elect was £13.9 per cwt. These prices and their relativity remained unchanged right up to 1914. Elect was expected to be a money spinner, even more than gums and pastilles – but only if it would sell. Eight years after the launch Elect still accounted for only 6 per cent of sales by value, less than 2.5 per cent by weight.[38] During the same eight years total sales had increased two and a half times to £190 000. If Elect, Joseph's prize product, was to become a success in the marketplace its marketing had to be dramatically changed.

Marketing – Bursting Loose from Tradition

Joseph Rowntree's objections in principle to product advertising were not shared by his competitors, and to make a significant impact he had to market his product all the more effectively. This marketing depended on maintaining product quality, adequate discounts to persuade retailers to stock it and a force of travellers on commission to take orders, collect accounts and encourage retailers to promote Rowntree's products. Matters were made more difficult as a substantial proportion of Rowntree's sales were 'own brand' or unbranded, that is, they were sold by the retailer either as his own speciality or completely unnamed. There was a long tradition within Rowntrees of supplying 'own brand' goods; in 1880 Rowntrees supplied 57 000 small sample packets of cocoa (not one of the better blends) which bore not Rowntree's name but that of the retailer.[39] While this might develop the market for cocoa, it did nothing to ensure that customers asked for Rowntree's cocoa or identified the Rowntree name with quality. In the early 1890s Rowntrees were anxious to develop their trade through the co-operative societies, again 'own brand'. Rowntrees arranged for the printing of a standard letter which could be used by co-op buyers in correspondence with their retail shop managers.

> We are sending you a stock of a *first class homeopathic cocoa* which we have taken up with the name of our Society on the label and to which your special attention is invited. This is an article of splendid quality and is designed to sell against Epps' but which having our name on the label becomes thereby *a proprietary article on which we can get a better margin of profit.* I shall be glad if you will therefore instruct your assistants to keep this homeopathic cocoa to the front.[40]

Rowntree's name is not mentioned. Epps was not a quality manufacturer like Cadbury or Fry, but he was a determined advertiser. Epps inserted small advertisements in local papers week after week, just like Beechams, Bengers, Lipton, Neaves, Pears and many purveyors of patent pills, to keep his name to the forefront of public attention.[41]

In the face of these advertising assaults the Rowntree travellers were offered showcards, handbills, billheads and envelopes for cocoa samples printed with the retailers' names for promoting 'own brand' sales. Apart from a few framed showcards, available 'at great expense', for customers who would put them in a prominent position, this represents the sum total of the promotional support offered in 1890 by Rowntrees to their travellers and retail outlets.[42]

There is no documentary evidence to explain what finally produced a change of mind on advertising policy after twenty years. Probably Joseph's purchase of twenty-nine acres at Haxby Road, York in 1890 for a new factory had made him aware of the enhanced opportunities for large-scale production on the new site. Certainly the travellers must have been astonished to learn in a memorandum from York, dated 10 December 1891, that Rowntrees intended to embark for the first time upon national press advertising in 'respectable weeklies of large circulation and wide distribution'. In the first instance they intended to book space of around 10×7 cm and use good lettered advertisements, as 'according to the most experienced advisers, whom we have consulted, picture advertisements just now are rather overdone'. Rowntrees recognised that the 'character of our announcements' would have to be changed 'pretty frequently' and invited their travellers to submit suggestions to improve the effectiveness of the advertising.[43]

This memorandum is revealing on several counts. Rowntrees were very cautious in their choice of papers, as they remained for many years (in 1900 one-third of all their press advertising was split equally between ladies' and religious papers).[44] The stylised signature on the memorandum was adopted as an advertising logo to establish a corporate identity; this was progressive. It was at about this time that logos (notably Beecham's) began to appear in the provincial as well as national press in place of the repetitive use of letterpress to create a visual impact on the printed page.[45] The Rowntree signature logo thereafter appears on Rowntree's advertisements throughout our period, and was registered as a trade mark in 1893.[46] It is also interesting that Rowntree sought suggestions from his travellers; this reflected less the democratic management of the business than the acute awareness that the travellers were far better informed than managers based at York on both competition and customers' preferences.

Although Joseph Rowntree felt that he had imparted a decisive change of direction to the firm he characteristically moved with caution, with considerable justification as at that time he was just bringing into production the first parts of his new model factory at Haxby Road, York to replace the former foundry premises down by the river at Tanners Moat, York. In 1892–3 advertising expenditure doubled but was then allowed to revert to its previous annual levels below £2000 in 1894–5. This general publicity, not linked to a particular product, had questionable efficacy[47]. Sales of Rowntree's goods as a whole were increasing satisfactorily and approaching £200 000, but Elect sales continued to be disappointing.

During 1896 a crucial decision was taken which determined the framework of Rowntree's marketing strategy for the next quarter of a century. Instead of generalised advertising the whole weight of publicity was henceforth directed at a single product, the company's standard-bearer, Elect cocoa.[48] Almost immediately a splendid opportunity presented itself. In 1896 the earliest prototype motor cars had appeared in England creating tremendous public interest. Audaciously Rowntree bought the first motor car to be seen in York, mounted a gigantic replica Elect cocoa tin behind the driver and made a stately progress with the car round the north of England (Plate 2.1), the trip lasting three months in all.[49] The car's itinerary was published, so that wherever it went, it drew large crowds. On one occasion the driver was summonsed for causing an obstruction but released on condition that he did not drive at more than 3 miles an hour, which, as he said, was impossible with that car! It

Plate 2.1 The Rowntree motor car (Rowntree Mackintosh).

seems probable that the purchase of the car owed less to Joseph than to the influence
of the younger Rowntrees, especially Arnold (1872–1951), Joseph's nephew, who
was subsequently board member with prime responsibility for marketing matters.

The sponsored car attracted more interest than the sales message it carried and
Rowntrees therefore decided to seek professional advice. They turned to S. H.
Benson who had set up his own advertising agency in 1893. Many advertising agents
of the time were also engaged in farming advertising space in newspapers and had
divided loyalties. Benson's agency, which from its inception was highly regarded for
its dignity, clarity of purpose and absolute integrity, met Rowntree's requirements

for assistance in advertising at a time when sharp practice was commonplace and fraud by no means unknown.[50]

Benson analysed the problem thus:

> Rowntree's cocoa advertising was an interesting experience in our offices. In the face of colossal advertising by other cocoas, probably then at the aggregate rate of over a quarter of a million sterling per annum, the grocers were, naturally, shy at a new cocoa and the travellers could not get in edgeways. It was, however, imperative to get the article stocked. Willy-nilly the trade must buy. We had to devise a scheme which would stock the trade and at the same time make the public talk about the cocoa. The scheme adopted was called the '*Daily Telegraph* Scheme', and it provided a penny stamp and a sample of cocoa in exchange for a coupon from the paper. Simple as it was, it was extraordinarily effective, a thousand accounts were open in a fortnight and every grocer's shop on the list was besieged.[51]

This scheme was subsequently repeated in Glasgow and elsewhere.[52]

Benson followed this up with an even more dramatic distribution of free samples. He negotiated with two of the leading London bus companies and on 3 December 1897 *Daily Mail* readers were asked, 'Have you had your ride in a Rowntree bus? – Every lady passenger gets a free trial tin of Rowntree's Elect Cocoa'. Buses were decorated and conductors dressed up to cause great excitement. The police, after threatening to stop the whole exhibition as being contrary to the regulations of the City of London, finally allowed it to go on, the Superintendent of Police remarking, 'But, mind, never again!' There was considerable newspaper comment; among others, the *Daily Mail* gave half a column to 'The Cocoa War: A brilliant engagement in London yesterday'.[53]

Benson then moved on to press and poster advertising. Through an agency he bought a design from Beggarstaffs, one of the few of their superb designs that they ever managed to sell. Despite the Beggarstaffs' lack of commercial success their technique used in the Rowntree poster design became world famous, and the Beggarstaffs phenomenon has been described as 'perhaps the shortest and most significant episode in poster history'.[54] The stark design (Plate 2.2) so different from the typical posters of the time intrigued the public but was too much for Rowntrees who soon returned to a conventional design showing mugs of cocoa. Within a few years, dissatisfied with Benson's poster designs, they considered reviving the notable Beggarstaffs design, but decided against it.[55]

As advertising, Benson's campaigns were superb; for Rowntrees they looked at best imprudent and potentially damaging. Sales of Elect had increased fourfold in a year, but advertising costs had risen ten times and took almost two-thirds of the gross sales revenue from Elect. This pattern clearly could not continue; while the board understood that advertising was an investment for the future and would support other Rowntree lines, Joseph took the view that Elect advertising each year would be funded out of Elect's gross profits. The following year (1898) advertising was reduced with little reduction in the rate of growth of Elect sales; the year after that, advertising was cut right back against Benson's advice and Elect sales actually fell for

Plate 2.2 Beggarstaffs' Elect poster (Rowntree Mackintosh).

the first time.[56] Thereafter advertising was resumed and sales recovered their sharp upward trend. Nevertheless it took six years before Elect profits funded this early advertising.[57]

The unprecedented fall in Elect sales may have forced Joseph Rowntree to accept that advertising was a necessary evil, but he was uneasy at the lack of a direct relationship between investment in advertising and increased sales.[58] He regarded its cost as a speculative quantity; for him advertising compelled the taking of a short-term view and militated against adopting a continuous policy for any length of time. As the firm was committed to a rapid building programme at Haxby Road to satisfy increased demand, it was essential to consider long-term business prospects as well as to maintain cash flow to avoid financial embarrassment.

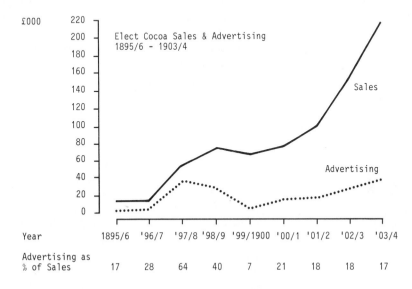

Figure 2.2 Elect cocoa sales and advertising 1895/6–1903/4

Source: Rowntree Archives EC G5/21.

The temporary drop in sales forced Joseph to reinstate advertising on the basis of a budget linked to profits,[59] and finally in March 1902 he produced his own careful tabulations of the financial implications of various advertising policy options at various levels of forecast sales increase and of profitability. Using Joseph's figures, a robust option providing for steadily increasing promotional expenditure was approved subject to profitability and sales remaining within the assumed parameters.

Although Joseph finally accepted the necessity of marketing he realised that the advertising policies of Lever, with Sunlight soap, or Mackintosh the 'Toffee King', were inappropriate to his case.[60] They both had a novel product for a new and expanding market. Elect cocoa was a late entrant into a market crowded not only with direct competitors of almost equivalent quality, but also with heavy competition from cheap cocoas, including Rowntree's own. In these circumstances a direct advertising appeal had brought Elect cocoa to the attention of his customers, but his advertisements could be matched by those of his many competitors unless he was ready and able to dominate the market with his advertisements to swamp and neutralise the competition. Both Cadburys and Frys were larger than Rowntrees; Cadbury, Fry, Epps and Taylor among others had been advertising strongly since the

31

1870s; a marketing policy based on advertising alone would be hazardous. Rowntree also recognised the requirement to maintain the goodwill of the wholesale and retail trade both through point-of-sale promotional material and general discounts. Finally it was necessary to build product awareness by individual customers and to reward brand loyalty.[61]

Joseph Rowntree's strategy for meeting these varying marketing objectives was to divide the task, Benson remaining responsible for general promotions through press and poster advertising, while Rowntrees themselves took responsibility for matters impinging directly on individual customers. Rowntrees managed the delivery of free samples and later canvassing partly with their own staff but sometimes with contract gangs. They organised direct-mail promotions angled at particular occupational groups, such as doctors and teachers. They had their own coupon scheme to encourage regular customers with free gifts, and this created an almost personal relationship between the firm and its customers which proved of inestimable value later. Rowntrees developed such expertise that eventually they recognised that they had built up their own advertising department. They even wondered whether they should take back responsibility for press and poster advertising from their advertising agents, but fortunately realised that the cost of building up the additional expertise to deal with press and printers would outweigh Benson's fees and that they would lose all the benefits of his independent judgement and advice.

The gift scheme was central to Rowntree's direct link with their customers. It was established in 1899 (or possibly slightly earlier) as an alternative to the expensive stunt advertising of the preceding years. Every tin of Elect included a coupon; coupons equivalent to purchases of 6lb entitled the purchaser to a free gift box of Rowntree's chocolates and gums. This was very attractively packaged and was clearly appreciated by customers, thousands of whom wrote to say so. In 1903 100 000 gifts were sent out (a coupon redemption rate of almost 50 per cent), by 1907 the number topped 250 000 (costing £15 000) and reached almost 400 000 in 1913 with an astonishing redemption rate of over 75 per cent. In the face of similar schemes offered by Cadburys and Van Houten the qualifying level was dropped to 5lb. In 1901 there had also been a Coronation special offer reducing the qualifying purchase requirement to 4lb for a short time.[62]

The gift scheme was effective in retaining established customers and carried the additional advantage of a ready-made address list for direct-mail shots, which were used, for example, to offer extra gifts to regular customers who introduced new Elect customers.[63] It perhaps lacked the excitement of the Mackintosh toffee scheme which promised one lucky consumer a free cottage, or the Lever soap promise of a motor car, but was important in consolidating sales at a time of growing competitive pressures. It was not without disadvantages; so long as it ran, Rowntrees had very little control of its cost, which in 1918 exceed £50 000 or about two-thirds of the total advertising budget. The scheme was then discarded. Until then Rowntrees had evidently calculated that they could not risk the potential loss of their regular customers. A few years later the proposed reintroduction of the scheme was rejected as the board recognised that it represented a continuing heavy mortgage on the advertising budget, limited the scope for alternative promotions to combat competitors and was almost certain to provoke retaliation by others.[64] It would be interesting to trace the parallels with the trading-stamp boom of the 1960s and 1970s.

The distribution of samples of Elect cocoa was another promotional activity managed by Rowntree rather than Benson; this had been traditional in the trade and Rowntrees were providing samples for use by retailers at least as early as 1880 when they undertook virtually no other promotional activity. Cadburys also were active samplers and in 1907 made three and even four sample deliveries in some parts of London.[65] Sampling was relatively cheap (around £1000 per million samples delivered) and was directed towards areas in which it was hoped to build trade. Sampling was at first concentrated in middle-class areas but gradually extended to include better working-class areas where Elect might find a sale. The view was taken that the poorest areas, if they used cocoa at all, would prefer the cheapest cocoas, which Rowntrees did not now supply. At the peak Rowntrees were annually distributing well over 20 million samples and this was the largest single component of their total marketing expenditure.[66] Occasionally samples included other goods which the firm wanted to push, chocolate or gums, but for the most part samples were of Elect only. Samples were usually delivered in normal envelopes (14×9 cm) printed with a slogan, but for special occasions something more dramatic was provided.

On the occasion of King Edward VII's Coronation Dinner for the Poor of London, at which 500 000 dinners were provided, every guest received a specially designed tin of Rowntree's chocolates as the gift of the firm. Rowntrees also negotiated to give a special gift of chocolates to the 60 000 stewards 'who will be of greater influence socially than the 500 000 poor'; they hoped to encourage the belief that the gift was from the King rather than themselves, as 'this will be more gratifying to the recipients'.[67] Specimens of the King's gift boxes were sent to the chief illustrated newspapers. Rowntrees also offered other Coronation Committees special packs which the latter could give away: Sheffield, for example, bought 75 000 1d chocolate and 10 000 2d cocoa tins. Rowntrees considered the advertisement value well worth the total cost of £2600 for all the Coronation gift packs. Even so the firm's auditor suggested this should be part of the normal advertising budget rather than an extra and there should be cut-backs; his suggestion was vetoed.[68] In November 1902 Rowntrees received King Edward VII's Royal Warrant as Cocoa and Chocolate Manufacturers. (They had held Queen Victoria's Warrant since 1893; Cadburys received their first Royal Warrant in 1854.)

Sampling reached customers in their own homes. Rowntrees soon realised that they could also get feedback from customers to reinforce the information their travellers (they had eighty to ninety in 1907)[69] brought them through their contacts with retailers; information on customer preference and market share was of especial interest as competition grew more intense. Information gained from customers could also allow selective marketing schemes to be evaluated so that only the most effective would be used. Rowntrees were thus one of the earliest firms to recognise the potential of systematic market research.

Rowntree's sales superintendents in eleven large towns made 4693 calls on customers in March 1909 to get their reactions to Elect samples which had previously been delivered.[70] Of the respondents who had used the sample: 55 per cent said they always used Rowntree's, 17 per cent said they used Rowntree's if any, 8 per cent said they did not like Rowntree's, and 13 per cent said they used Cadbury's. Of the fourteen other brands mentioned by respondents, the top three were Van Houten, Fry and Lipton. One-third of Rowntree's Elect production went to co-operative societies, so it is surprising that the CWS only receives fourteen mentions, although this may refer to cocoa made by the CWS in their own factory rather than Elect purchased through co-ops. It is also surprising that, with Rowntree's sales beginning to sag, over 70 per cent gave Rowntree's as their preferences. Can the sample have been unrepresentative? Perhaps the respondents were showing excessive politeness in providing the answers they believed would be most acceptable to the Rowntree representatives.

This calling on customers in their own homes must be one of the very first examples of this market research technique ever undertaken. Market research was first undertaken in the USA on a significant scale in the 1920s and spread from there to Great Britain.[71] Social surveys had however been undertaken in England in the late 1880s and 1890s, notably by Charles Booth in his monumental study, *Life and Labour of the People in London* (1889–97). Seebohm Rowntree (Joseph's son) was inspired by Booth's work to undertake a similar survey in York in 1899 in the course of which the circumstances of over 11 500 families were recorded. The Rowntrees showed great imagination in carrying over their philanthropic interests into their business activity, the reverse of the usual transfer of business methods to the management of charitable work.

The next step was to move from market survey to direct canvassing of customers. A major house-to-house canvassing campaign was undertaken and over 65 000 calls made and 40 000 interviews obtained; these suggested that one-quarter of the households used no cocoa, but half of the rest used Rowntree's. The proportion reported using Rowntree's was considerably higher where Rowntree inspectors called (hardly a surprise), than where the call was made by the Trade Extension Co. of London, which provided five gangs of canvassers and undertook the vast majority of the calls.

This canvassing had to be undertaken with considerable delicacy. In view of the competition, it was essential that Rowntrees should not upset the retailers who stocked their goods: there was therefore no question of a cash sale on the doorstop which would take business away from local shops. Canvassers instead sought a signed order for Elect which they then passed to the local stockist. In theory this was attractive; the shopkeeper would deliver the cocoa and would have an opportunity to gain a new regular customer. In practice many problems were reported by the Rowntree sales superintendents who made follow-up calls to assess the value of the campaign. Many of the orders were from regular users rather than 'the insigificant number of new customers' (Brighton). Some grocers did not trouble overmuch as 'it is so usual to have orders of this nature repudiated' (Croydon): others would not deliver as orders came from known bad payers (Nottingham). Some orders were left by the canvassers at shops which did not stock Rowntree's cocoa or at general stores which were unlikely to stock Rowntree's goods. 'There are now no less than six gangs selling house-to-house in Nottingham and our customers are sick of being called to their doors.' One superintendent wrote: 'The soap firms have considerably lowered the standard of this form of advertisement and it would be considered "infra-dig" if this was continued' (Hanley). Lever's use of coupons in his promotions had been much brasher than Rowntree's and had earned the active hostility of the grocery trade, as Rowntrees were told by a representative of the Grocers' Federation; but because of their careful groundwork Rowntrees avoided any similar backlash.[72]

In addition to the gift scheme, canvassing and heavy advertising expenditure, the years 1909–14 saw the Rowntree Prize Scheme department promote a couple of dozen smaller schemes aimed at particular markets to build brand loyalty.[73] For instance, '2d off' vouchers were posted from York to 130 000 customers whose names had been sent in by grocers as potential new customers. Each voucher was specific to the grocer who had sent in the name and would be redeemed by Rowntrees travellers from the grocers concerned for 2½d. This coupon scheme was obviously far less attractive than the gift scheme, as less than 10 per cent of the vouchers sent out were ever redeemed. With the vouchers went other promotional material, and all the names were added to the mailing list. Rowntree's mailing list was an early example of sales promotion by post. American stores had been distributing mail-order catalogues since the 1870s but for a different purpose. The preparation of a mailing list targeted to a particular group of customers pre-dates by half a century the extensive use of this technique from the 1960s and 1970s. Other campaigns were angled at school children ('cigarette' cards,[74] painting competitions), doctors, school teachers (blotting book with cocoa sample), and so on.

Rowntree's relations with the grocery trade were punctilious; discounts matched those of competitors and these discounts were defended by Rowntree's insistence that no price-cutting took place with their goods. A special discount was introduced in 1898 to assist the orderly management of the Elect cocoa trade which was highly seasonal. At that time sales had been showing a dramatic increase and it was essential to ensure that manufacturing capacity and factory stocks could meet the demand. The special stocking discount (SSD) allowed wholesalers and retailers an additional 5 per cent discount for orders placed for the two months up to the end of September each year.

Rowntrees not only had an indication of the likely total demand in the coming season but could shift their stockpile to make room for more production. It was also hoped that shopkeepers would use these early stocks to give Rowntrees a prominent display throughout the main selling season. This scheme was popular from its first introduction. In the first year 25 per cent of Elect sales benefited from SSD. By 1903 SSD was given on 33 per cent and from 1910 onwards in highly competitive times over 50 per cent of sales attracted SSD. This suggests SSD had outlived its usefulness; it had shifted the period of peak delivery forward a couple of months but the peak was now higher than ever. There was also the real risk that such large stocks would not be displayed but consigned to a warehouse with some risk of deterioration. (The board worried that the cocoa might be tainted by being in store with, say, paraffin.) Like the gift scheme, SSD was dropped during the 1914–18 war and not reintroduced.

The distinction between in-house promotions and the advertising undertaken by Benson is clear from Figure 2.3a and 2.3b. The steadiest trend is shown by the gift scheme. Shop promotions (point-of-sale showcards, enamel advertisement signs, showcases, window decorations, and so on) also show little variation from year to year. By contrast the value of sampling as a means of developing sales seems to have been taken for granted until the traumatic year of 1909–10 after which sampling dropped away. Figure 2.3b shows clearly how Benson was used to 'top-up' Rowntree's continuing promotional efforts when special campaigns were required. The use of poster campaigns to create a special impact rather than for long-term effect is especially noticeable.[75]

These figures refer specifically to expenditure on Elect cocoa in the development of whose sales advertising had been essential. Neither chocolate nor gums had such a high public profile but they were both very successful. Chocolate sales in particular might have benefited from higher advertising, just as Cadbury's, by promoting their Dairy Milk (introduced in 1905), managed to withstand and ultimately assume market leadership from the very heavily promoted Swiss milk chocolates. Rowntree's attempt to launch an Elect chocolate in 1910 on the back of Elect cocoa, but without specific heavy advertising over several years and without the panache of a Benson campaign, was doomed to failure.[76] Advertising expenditure on chocolate over the five years 1910–14 was less than Benson spent in 1897 alone promoting Elect cocoa. Sales failed to take off, profits were insufficient to cover the low level of advertising and Elect chocolate was cast adrift to sink or swim as best it might. In this case at least, the benefit of the Elect name was non-transferable to another Rowntree Elect product. Figure 2.4 (p. 38) shows sales of Elect cocoa, gums and chocolates in 1907 and 1914 and the amount spent in advertising on each class of goods.

Competition Intensifies

Elect cocoa had a high public profile because of the weight of marketing effort devoted to it as a matter of policy. In terms of gross sales value Elect never provided as much as 35 per cent of Rowntree's total sales. The other major product groups, chocolate, chocolate cream assortments and gums, were all showing steady sales growth. Cocoas other than Elect were something of an embarrassment but were still supplied where ordered even though after 1904 their sales value was less than 5 per cent of Elect sales. With all the products other than Elect there was a continuous adjustment of flavours, prices, assortments and packaging to meet the month-to-month changes in the market.[77] Rowntrees supplied a wide range of chocolates and assortments but Joseph was always determined that they would produce a top range to stand comparison with the best that any other manufacturer could offer. He was confident that the finest goods could be sold profitably, even at a price higher than that of other English makers.[78] Despite efforts over a number of years, and unlike Cadburys, Joseph never managed to his own satisfaction to match the quality of the best Swiss milk chocolate but elsewhere his products made their way in the marketplace with minimal promotional support.

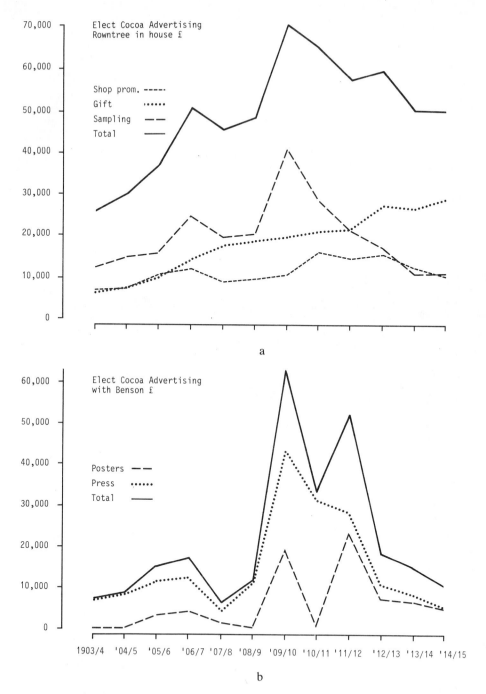

Figure 2.3 Elect cocoa advertising in house and with Benson

Source: Rowntree Archives EC G6/1.

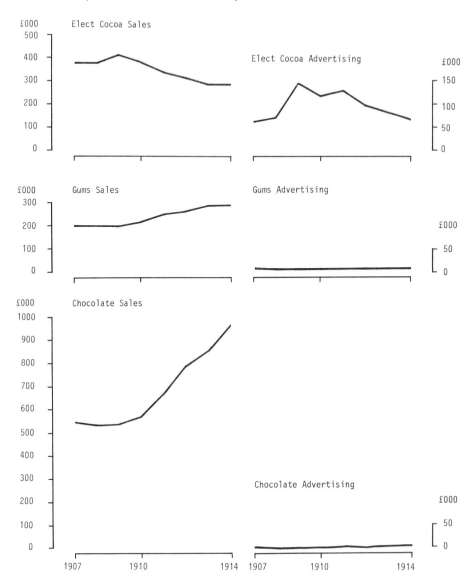

Figure 2.4 Comparison of Rowntree's sales and advertising 1907–14

Source: Rowntree Archives EC G5/21, 2661 G/G7/4, 2661 G1/5.

Elect was a single standardised product which when advertised had rapidly captured a significant part of the best quality cocoa market. When competition became more severe, there was no possibility of adjusting the product as it was so distinctive and heavily promoted. By concentrating all their effort on Elect, Rowntrees had neglected to develop a cheaper grade of cocoa which could have been marketed where Elect quality was not required.

The first hint of impending trouble came in 1904 when Rowntrees heard that Cadburys had reduced the price of their best cocoa from 8½d per ¼lb (the price of Elect) to 7½d.[79] Rowntrees took an immediate decision to maintain quality and price, to introduce SSD earlier and if necessary to embark upon a press advertising campaign. They were a little relieved to discover that Cadbury's price reduction was partly achieved by a small reduction of weight in the pack.[80] Elect sales had been somewhat affected both by the general economic depression and by heavy Cadbury advertising: the increase in sales in 1905 was only 18 per cent over the previous year, compared to 43 per cent the year before. Rowntrees suspected that the growth in Elect sales was actually pushing Cadbury's cocoa sales down and they decided with Benson on a bold advertising campaign with substantial use of posters and repeated sampling.[81] Further evidence of the damage to its competitors caused by Elect and its successful promotion came only a few months later. Cadburys, perhaps with the forthcoming launch of their Bournville cocoa in mind, suggested that Rowntrees should drop their coupon gift scheme. Rowntree's first reaction was to decline, but they discussed the question fully with Benson.[82] The cost of the scheme was increasing year by year and was likely to be more costly still if adjustments became imperative to counter rival schemes. Rowntrees wanted their customers to appreciate the product rather than the gift. They realised however the value of their popular Elect gift scheme in retaining loyal customers, who were unlikely to be tempted away from Elect by another unproven promotional scheme. They decided to retain their existing scheme.

In August 1906 Cadburys introduced Bournville cocoa, a product very similar to Elect, supported by a gift scheme and again at a lower price than Elect.[83] Once again Rowntrees brought forward their SSD to get Elect into the shops and embarked on heavy advertising in shops, the press and with posters. Clearly these measures were successful in defending Elect, as Cadburys made two formal approaches in early 1907 requesting Rowntrees to abandon their gift scheme. Rowntrees courteously declined but, after yet another approach, a working agreement with Cadburys was reached to standardise the weight of purchases required to gain a gift and to set a limit on the value of gifts.[84]

Sales of Elect were now showing signs of faltering, not only because of competition from Cadbury's branded Bournville, but also as the proprietary packs were threatened by the appearance of cheap supplies of loose and 'own brand' cocoas from other makers. The Rowntree board was even discussing the possibility of approaching Cadburys to seek an agreement on a standstill of advertising. Although agreed in principle no action was taken, in deference to Joseph's strong views. Cadburys however advanced a similar proposal shortly afterwards and Rowntrees were glad to accede, together with a related agreement to limit sampling to twice a year.[85] Both Cadburys and Rowntrees were to cut advertising by a third (but excluding the gift schemes) but, because of Fry's weaker trading position, acquiesced in a cut of only 25 per cent by Fry. An approach was also made to the other English and continental manufacturers to seek a general agreeement on a cut in advertising.[86] A decision was taken not to cut back press advertising too severely. The newspapers had been causing Lever great problems as he was trying to rationalise the soap trade through his Soap Trust (and incidentally reduce his advertising expenditure); press hostility had severely damaged his trade.[87] The cocoa manufacturers were anxious that despite their regular discussions there should be no grounds for an accusation that they had formed a Cocoa Trust, and that they should not attract press hostility through an embargo on advertising.[88]

Cadburys had by now raised the price of Bournville to that of Elect and introduced extra bulk discounts. Then yet another approach was made to Rowntrees, this time with a request to abandon the SSD: this elicited the same response as before.[89] However Rowntrees did bring their discount structure more into conformity with Cadburys to give specially favourable terms to large wholesalers, including co-ops, as an optional alternative to SSD.

The co-operative trade in Elect was of great importance to Rowntrees who had appointed special travellers who dealt with co-ops only. Rowntree's own trade tended to be with middle-class customers and the promotional schemes appeared much less successful in working-class areas where price was of more significance than flavour. The co-op trade gave them an opportunity to widen their appeal; in 1910 nearly one family in three was a co-op member. In 1909, the peak year of Elect sales, 31 per cent of Elect sales went to co-op customers despite the fact that the co-ops could if they wished call on cocoa from their own CWS factory. From 1909 to 1914, against the trend of Elect trade elsewhere, co-op sales remained steady at the 1909 level, increasing their share of total Elect sales from 31 per cent to 39 per cent because of the sharp fall elsewhere. This high proportion of sales in potentially 'hostile' hands caused the Rowntree board great concern as its loss could have caused severe damage to Rowntree's financial stability; fortunately the business was retained.

It seems probable that this high proportion of co-op trade was a key factor in enabling Rowntrees to withstand the pressure of price-cutting. Although they did everything in their power to defend resale price maintenance through their normal retail outlets, they had no control over the dividend paid by co-ops to their members. A co-op customer receiving a typical 10 per cent or 12½ per cent dividend on his gross purchases would effectively have been buying Elect not at 8½d but at 7½d or thereabouts.[90] It would be interesting to compare how Bournville sales through co-ops fared during this period.

Cheap cocoas were now coming into the market in force. Epps, Fry, Cadbury and Van Houten among others all introduced cocoas at 4½d per ¼lb.[91] At the cheapest end of the market imported Dutch cocoa was being offered at between 8½d and 1s per lb. Rowntrees, having decided long before to concentrate on Elect, had lost interest in cheap cocoas (annual sales had dropped below £10 000 by 1910) and had been pushed right out of this market. Now they were forced to discuss the possibility of producing a cheap cocoa for sale only in the poorer areas of London and elsewhere where there was no sale for Elect, but decided against it, just as a few years earlier they had declined to make a special low grade cocoa for sale in the temperance cocoa houses.[92] Despite a doubling of advertising in 1909–10 sales peaked and then fell. The possibility of a price reduction was discussed but as this would reduce the cash available for advertising it was dismissed. The possibility of cross-subsidy from the other Rowntree lines does not seem to have been considered, even though Elect was, after deduction of advertising, the least profitable line.[93] Instead it was decided to approach Cadburys in a (successful) attempt to achieve a joint agreement to defend the 8½d price level for top quality cocoas.

The lack of success in defending market-share despite increased advertising led Rowntrees to wonder whether Benson was giving value for money, and whether what he did could be done in-house.[94] Much to Benson's dismay, an approach was made to another advertising agent to look for fresh ideas. Nothing came of this and Rowntrees, although grumbling periodically, stayed with Benson until his death in 1914, unlike Cadburys who made several changes in their advertising agents. Possibly Benson and his staff also found the relationship with such a high-principled firm a difficult one. It is tempting to speculate that Dorothy L. Sayers who worked for Bensons in the 1920s had similar clients in mind when, in *Murder Must Advertise*, a whodunit set in an advertising agency, she wrote: 'A visit was expected from two directors of Brotherhoods Ltd, that extremely old-fashioned and religiously-minded firm who manufacture boiled sweets and non-alcoholic liquors'.

In 1910 the agreement with Cadburys came to an end and Bournville cocoa was reduced to 7½d, the product being supported with heavy advertising. Rowntrees discussed their competitive position with the travellers, who supported the board's preference to hold to the 8½d price level though with extra discounts for bulk and more advertising.[95] A '2d off' token scheme was promoted, but only 30 per cent of the 5 million tokens were redeemed, compared to 60 per cent who were receiving gifts under the Elect coupon scheme at the time, thus justifying Rowntree's judgement in retaining it.

The travellers began to press for a cheap cocoa to compete with Cadbury's 4½d Welfare brand and the board agreed to experiment to achieve something suitable for Rowntrees to sell: 'The 1st thing is to get a really good cocoa.'[96] A relatively cheap cocoa essence was offered at 1s per lb but its sale was minimal, even when the price was cut to 10d per lb. Other ways of reducing price were considered – for cheap cocoas and chocolates only, never for Elect – including the substitution of vegetable oil for cocoa butter and the inclusion of a small proportion of ground cocoa shell. Benson's suggestion that farina should be re-introduced was turned down flat. Joseph felt that sooner or later Rowntrees would have to enter the cheap market and he supported investment in new machinery to ensure any new brand was properly tested on a production scale to achieve a trouble-free launch.[97]

Further pressure was met in 1912. A new high quality cocoa (Sandow) was introduced to the market from Germany with very heavy promotional support, and at the same time the loose cocoas were overtaking the 4½d brands at the other end of the market. Rowntrees decided on a major press campaign to publicise a '2d off' voucher scheme and took the front page of the *Daily Mail*.[98] Unfortunately the campaign hit the papers just at the time of the *Titanic* disaster and so sank without trace.

Immediately conferences were held with the travellers to attempt to assess the likely impact of (a) reducing Elect to 7½d; (b) introducing a cheaper 'Elect' type cocoa at 4½d; (c) improving the prize scheme; (d) improving marketing performance. The conferences produced a clear divergence of views between the southern travellers who were pressing for cheaper cocoas and the northern men who wanted to defend Elect at its existing price.[99] This result is interesting as the converse might have been expected. It was at last decided unanimously to milk the maximum benefit from the Elect name by using it for top quality chocolates, gums and table jellies as well as the original cocoa. The board then calculated the financial implications of these suggestions. Another Rowntree's cocoa would almost certainly reduce Elect sales substantially; margins would be cut and even less advertising could be afforded. If an attempt were to be made to give it a totally new image (such as Red Star rather than No. 2 Elect) the launch costs would be prohibitive. Once again it was decided to continue research on a cheap but good cocoa and persist in defending Elect at 8½d as well as possible.[100]

At last the reports became more cheerful. Despite heavy advertising Sandow's German cocoa was not selling well and the firm was reported to be in financial difficulties. Van Houten's quality had become very variable and staff cuts were being imposed. Frys had lost their premium market completely by concentrating their efforts on cheaper brands. Even Cadburys 4½d Welfare cocoa was reported to be losing ground.[101] Rowntrees had managed to defend Elect quality and price at the expense of some loss of sales volume. For them at least, Lever's aphorism had proved correct: 'Reduce the price and double or treble sales, result loss. Maintain price, sales drop fifty per cent, result profit.'[102]

When war erupted in 1914 the debate on possible reduction of price was still inconclusive. Sales continued to fall, particularly in the south, to the loose low grade cocoas. Elect however was still profitable; a profit had been made every year since 1898 independent of the profit earned by the other Rowntree lines.

The Market Matures

Following the firm establishment of Elect in the home market, Rowntrees started to develop an export business. Agents had been appointed in South Africa, Australia and New Zealand at least by 1900 and for China in 1903. Sales in Europe were disappointing and a possible joint venture in France with Huntley & Palmers, another Quaker firm, was not pursued. Rowntrees appointed a representative to build up the French market in 1904, but this experiment was short-lived.[103] Export sales were £23 000 in 1904, and had risen to £48 000 in 1911, but this represented less than 4 per cent of total sales. By comparison Cadbury's export sales were far higher, possibly approaching a third of total output.[104] Exports by British manufacturers as a whole had been overtaken by imports in the 1890s: by 1914 imports represented around 40 per cent of the total cocoa and chocolate trade.[105]

In export markets Joseph Rowntree was clearly unhappy about security of stocks and delays in payments. Despite pressure from his Australian agents to set up a depot as a basis for building up his trade, as Cadburys had done in 1898, Joseph refused. There was plenty of trade at home without the 'trouble, harass and risk involved' in the export markets. They could not command the trade of the world and must expect to leave some fields not fully worked.[106] He continued instead to operate an indent system of replacing goods as they were sold. He also refused to authorise significant advertising expenditure, taking the view that heavy expenditure would be required to dent Cadbury's dominant position, further development was required at home and that it was dangerous to spread resources too thinly.

Board discussions throughout this period show that the competition offered by Cadburys in particular was a very real concern. Rowntrees from the outset were determined to produce fine quality goods but found themselves threatened by changes in consumer preference. Having achieved a dominant position in the market for top quality cocoa, they found customers moving away to cheaper brands where they had no product with which to compete. As the smallest of Frys, Cadburys and Rowntrees and also influenced by Joseph's innate caution, they tended to follow Cadburys the pacemakers in many cases rather than initiating change. This consistency brought its own benefits in customer loyalty but at a cost.

Of the three firms, Rowntrees invested more in advertising relative to their sales volume than either Cadburys or, particularly, Frys.

Table 2.3 Advertising expenditure and sales

	1910			1913		
	Total sales	Advertising	Advertising % of sales	Total sales	Advertising	Advertising % of sales
	£000	£000	%	£000	£000	%
Rowntree	1201	127	10.6	1470	105	7.1
Cadbury	1670	119	7.1	2211	142	6.4
Fry	1642	58	3.5	1866	78	4.2

Source: Rowntree Archives 441.692 G/G1/4, 2661 G1/5, ECH G1/6; Cadbury Archives Acc. no. 829; D. J. Jeremy, ed., *Dictionary of Business Biography*, entry on J. S. Fry.

(Rowntrees advertising peaked in 1911 when £148 000 was spent, representing just over 11 per cent of sales; Cadburys and Frys peaked in 1913.)

Throughout the period 1909–14 Frys spent an astonishing quarter of their advertising on lettering (putting their name in white or gold lettering on shop windows), rather over half on press and poster advertising, and the balance on shop advertising, enamel plates, showcards and so on. Frys continued lettering long after Rowntrees and Cadburys had adopted more positive marketing strategies and their reluctance to change contributed to their steadily weakening position. Half of Cadbury's expenditure went on sampling and canvassing, about 10 per cent on the gift scheme and the balance on press and poster advertising. Rowntree's gift scheme over this six-year period increased as a proportion of total advertising from 15 per cent to 45 per cent: shop advertising remained steady at around 15 per cent but sampling was cut back from 30 per cent to 15 per cent and press and poster advertising fell from 45 per cent to 20 per cent to accommodate the inexorable rise in cost of the gift scheme within a falling advertising allocation.

Relationships between these three firms were personally intimate. Fry chaired a conference of Quakers at which Joseph spoke. George Cadbury had trained in Joseph's father's shop. Joseph sought Fry's advice on pricing policy, and went on holiday with the Cadburys. These informal links soon developed into regular conferences between the three firms at which matters of mutual concern were aired and agreements were reached on competition. In 1900 they agreed to limit Christmas presents to retailers and Cadbury was to attempt to gain the co-operation of as many confectionery houses as possible.[107] This was later extended to limit loans or other financial support to retail outlets. The general framework of wholesale and retail discount structures was agreed and there was an agreement to notify price changes. Rowntrees were often concerned that Cadburys particularly made price reductions before giving formal notice, wrongfooting Rowntrees and Frys. As competition grew more severe, there was a tendency for special limited discounts to be introduced and, although these put strains on the general agreement, it survived remarkably well. The attempts to limit advertising expenditure mentioned earlier were part of this general accord. Fry took the lead in lobbying Chancellors of the Exchequer Hicks-Beach and Ritchie over the threatened duty on cocoa and sugar in the 1901 budget and again in 1903.[108] Cadbury took the lead in seeking to improve labour conditions in Portuguese St Thomé which amounted to virtual slavery. After privately sponsored fact-finding missions and extensive lobbying of governments over several years had failed to bring an improvement, the firms, with others, finally embargoed any further purchases of St Thomé cocoa until improvements were made. An agreement was reached not to poach staff. There was even agreement to provide mutual help should one of the three suffer catastrophe from fire or other major emergency.[109] Rowntrees, as the smallest of the three, rarely seem to have taken the lead.

Trade associations of rival manufacturers were generally tolerated at this period. Occasionally there was public agitation, as with the self-interested Harmsworth press campaign against Lever's proposed Soap Trust. Cadburys and Rowntrees were anxious to avoid any suggestion of a possible Cocoa Trust; they decided in 1906 when notifying price changes and so on to avoid phrases such as: 'Owing to an agreement with our competitors we are unable...'[110] Details of wage rates were exchanged and the firms discussed labour unrest which at one period was common to both Cadburys and Rowntrees.[111] Agreements could operate across national frontiers. Stollwercks of Cologne attempted to establish an international cocoa-buying ring to control prices and approached Cadburys, Frys and Rowntrees to gain their support in this venture. Although accepting that this was less objectionable than a selling ring, Rowntrees were unhappy with the proposal, which was dropped.[112] No evidence was found to suggest that these regular meetings acted in restraint of competition.

They were restricted at first to the three big Quaker chocolate firms, who were later joined by Caleys of Norwich, also Quakers, and later still by Mackintosh, a Methodist.

The Effectiveness of the Rowntree Strategy

This study demonstrates a marketing synergy containing several elements which taken separately might have produced a different outcome. Rowntree was late entering the market for top quality cocoa where two larger competitors were already well established. His adoption of advertising was slow and hesitant. Even when he was convinced of the necessity only a part of his advertising budget was placed at the disposal of his agent, the larger part being reserved for traditional promotions, sampling, SSD and the gift scheme. SSD after its first few years of successful operation merely brought forward the peak of seasonal orders by a couple of months rather than achieving the promotional effects desired but because of competitive pressure it could not be abandoned. The gift scheme as it was enthusiastically espoused by customers became progressively more costly and latterly inhibited the firm's marketing plans or response to competition. Rowntrees were almost certainly correct in their judgement that the abandonment of the scheme would have produced catastrophic effects on their sales of Elect. The concentration of all marketing effort on a single product in a mature market left that product exposed when it was faced with cut-price competition from other determined advertisers. Any price cut would reduce the scope for promotional expenditure and would appear to be a sign of weakness; the price was not cut and Rowntrees saw Elect sales shrink year by year. The high concentration of sales through co-op outlets had been a cause of concern but proved a source of strength. The board was braced over several years to tackle a new competitive situation, but their nerve held and the onset of the 1914–18 war rendered their contingency plans worthless – the market boomed and Cadburys and Frys quickly brought the price of their premium cocoa up to that of Rowntrees. It is interesting to note the limitations of a marketing strategy based on advertising alone; Rowntrees in the years before 1914 were spending a higher proportion of their sales revenue than Cadburys and Frys, but this expenditure was not sufficient to defend the premium cocoa market from the ravages of price-cutting competition. Rowntree's financial success in these years was based in large part on their non-cocoa products, and also on their ability to retain the loyalty of the Elect customers they had cultivated in the heady years of growth.

No doubt the problems attending its launch and early years gave Elect a special place in the affections of the board and particularly of Joseph Rowntree. By comparison with chocolates and particularly gums, which are hardly ever mentioned, Elect as a mature product was a continuing boardroom preoccupation and also absorbed a disproportionate amount of advertising. Even then the advertising was almost entirely directed at defending Elect's place in the home market at a time when Cadburys especially were building up a dominant position in overseas markets, particularly in the British Empire.

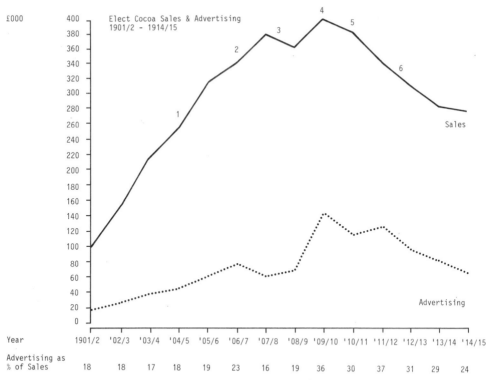

Figure 2.5 Elect cocoa sales and advertising 1901/2–1914/15

Notes: 1 1904–5 Cadbury's reduce price; Rowntree's sales growth is affected.
2 1906–7 Launch of Cadbury's Bournville; Rowntree counter with extra advertising.
3 1907–9 Rowntree, Cadbury, Fry agree to reduce advertising; Van Houten cut prices.
4 1909–10 General introduction of cheap brands; heavy advertising of Elect to defend high price.
5 1910–11 Cadbury, Fry, Van Houten introduce cheap brands; Cadbury cut price of Bournville.
6 1911–13 Heavy promotional activity of all main competitors.

Source: Rowntree Archives EC G5/21.

Rowntrees certainly developed both plain and milk chocolate bars for which they recognised the growing market but were unable to commit themselves to a full-scale launch with continuing promotional support. Possibly Joseph's insistence on excellence, and his view that each product should support its own promotional costs without cross-subsidy, ruled out major promotion of a new line that that was only as good as, but did not have the edge over, competing products. Fruit gums in their markets were never seriously threatened. Elect seriously damaged Cadbury's premium cocoa business, leading to the launch of Bournville which seems to have been as excellent as Elect; Rowntrees reacted instinctively by defending Elect rather than carving out a market for a new product that could benefit from marketing skills

46

which were becoming less and less innovative. It was not until the 1930s that Rowntrees under George Harris (who married one of Joseph's granddaughters) introduced Black Magic, Kit Kat, Aero, Dairy Box and Smarties. Under Harris's leadership, by 1939 Rowntrees were once again poised to challenge for market leadership, just as they had been thirty years before.[113]

The Quaker background gave Joseph a wide range of contacts within the cocoa trade. His own business had developed from that of the Quaker Tukes of York who had been dealing in cocoa and chocolate at least from the 1780s. The Cadbury-Fry-Rowntree conferences may be seen as a natural development of personal contacts within the Quaker community. Such contacts were not without their own tensions where, as the business developed, they came more and more into direct competition. Tensions were also developing within the Quaker community itself between the conservative and more progressive elements. The distinctive patterns of dress and speech were finally abandoned. As the economy flourished so did many Quaker businesses, raising questions of the right use of wealth derived from their profitability as well as questions of what constituted acceptable methods of trading.[114]

Joseph Rowntree as a young man gave a forthright address at a Quaker conference which was somewhat toned down at the request of Joseph Storrs Fry, the conference chairman.[115] The vigour of his early religious views may have persuaded Joseph to persist in his opposition to advertising long after it had been adopted by both Cadbury and Fry. When advertising was finally adopted, it was almost exclusively in Elect cocoa, which at the time was a minor product, on the market for eight years already and producing only 6 per cent of sales by value. Possibly Joseph decided that the quality and value-for-money of his chocolates and gums were self-evident to customers at the point of sale (and demonstrated by their sales growth) whereas strong brand identity cocoas were less easily distinguished. Certainly Joseph's principle of the link of promotional expenditure to value of sales on a year-to-year basis shows commercial prudence but also suggests a conservatism and an inability to understand that the outlay might have been more effectively employed elsewhere.[116] The scope for promoting the whole range of Rowntree's goods or strong support for the launch of new products was severely limited. The gift scheme and SSD neatly matched Joseph's principle, whereas Benson's dramatic promotions did not; only in the critical years of 1909–11 was Benson allowed the resources for major press and poster campaigns, as distinct from the minor allocation he received in the preceding ten years (see Figures 2.3a and 2.3b). Advertising through Benson was a supplement to the careful cultivation of consumer and retailer loyalty rather than the main thrust of marketing. For many of the years under consideration sampling was the largest single item of marketing expenditure.

As Quakers, Rowntrees refused to profit from war. At the time of the South African War (1899–1902) they declined to tender for army contracts.[117] Rowntrees were also the butt of jingoistic prejudice and an attempted boycott, because a Rowntree relation at Scarborough (also a Quaker but unconnected with the firm) called a meeting to discuss the justice of the war; the meeting was broken up and a fracas ensued, with damage to property. Interestingly Cadburys instructed their salesmen not to take advantage of any prejudice by customers against Rowntrees.[118] When the 1914–18 war was imminent Rowntrees decided to establish a trust fund for the relief of suffering, to which any profits attributable to wartime trading conditions should be devoted.

Joseph Rowntree's Quaker beliefs may have influenced his marketing strategy in another way. He was keen to provide model conditions for his employees (his New Elswick estate at York was his response to Cadbury's Bournville); he was also a generous benefactor to outside charities; for these objectives a healthy cash flow from dividends was essential. The necessity for this may possibly have discouraged the board from embarking on heavy advertising of product lines other than Elect, which could have reduced the funds available for Joseph's outside commitments. Rowntrees rarely appear as innovators and this again may reflect Joseph's Quaker background, although very much at odds with the Cadbury approach. The Rowntree caution together with conservative accounting policies enabled the firm to withstand a lengthy assault on Elect cocoa, maintain a consistent record of profitability and to emerge with Cadburys after the 1914–18 war as one of the two giants of the British cocoa and chocolate business.

Frys had joined with Cadburys in 1919, and the Rowntree board, with the exception of Joseph, was also favourably inclined to a merger. Whether Joseph was unhappy about Cadbury's trading practices or feared the business he had built up by his own efforts would be submerged and lose its identity is uncertain; he made his opposition a personal matter and the Rowntree board did not gainsay him.[119]

Hindsight must not blind us to Joseph Rowntree's solid achievement, particularly from the 1890s on. He presided patriarchally over the change from a cottage industry into highly mechanised production (in 1914 only one board member was not a Rowntree). His adoption of positive marketing made Elect one of the best known consumer products at a time of growing prosperity. Patterns of retailing were undergoing rapid change but, despite his active promotional activities which might have worked to his disadvantage with local traders and wholesalers, he maintained his place in the conventional retail trade and with co-operative societies. He kept his nerve and his quality despite intense competition from cheap bulk imported cocoas and a move down-market by Frys. Frys were still the largest cocoa and chocolate firm in England although that position was under threat from both Cadburys and Rowntree himself.

Several factors may be adduced to suggest that Joseph Rowntree's success might have been even more dramatic. By 1914 he was seventy-eight but remained active for several more years. He had introduced his sons into the business to learn by experience, as he himself had learned grocery from his father. Seebohm Rowntree succeeded Joseph in 1923, but his major interests lay elsewhere.[120] There is no evidence of systematic management development; this is hardly surprising given the patriarchal and dominant position of Joseph.

Joseph was unsympathetic towards marketing activity and his attitudes influenced his sons (although not Arnold, his nephew). Having once been persuaded to consult Benson to stimulate Elect sales the experience was so traumatic that Benson never again had a free hand. His advice was regularly sought but his proposals for advertising were often rejected or severely circumscribed. Other products and product ranges, particularly chocolates, were launched by the sales force without a Benson-type direct appeal to the public to make them want to buy; none was memorable, although all must have benefited to some extent from the Rowntrees' Elect advertising. At the same time Rowntrees spent an enormous amount on their gift scheme to buy loyalty to their Elect cocoa. Joseph's principle of linking advertising expenditure to sales may have been appropriate while they were on a sharp upward trend, but as soon as sales started to falter or fall, expenditure should have been cut. As it was, Elect, instead of being a money spinner, was only modestly profitable. Cadburys, spending substantially less as a percentage of sales, had broken the dominance of the Swiss milk chocolate producers in the home market and had developed extensive markets overseas with such success that Joseph Rowntree felt unable to mount a serious marketing challenge.

Joseph's commitment to quality may have aggravated the firm's problems in the cocoa market after 1909 when competition from cheap cocoa was added to the competition from Bournville and similar premium cocoas. Joseph's insistence that any cheap cocoa sold by Rowntrees was to be pure cocoa without farina and was to be of good quality undoubtedly discouraged the board from emulating Frys and Cadburys in quickly adding cheap cocoa to their range.

This case-study demonstrates an atypical but highly successful episode in the early history of the Rowntree company. Against an unsympathetic cultural background a series of marketing techniques were developed before 1914 by Benson and Rowntrees for Elect cocoa, which rapidly brought a sleepy product to market leadership and enabled Rowntrees to benefit from the rapid growth of consumer prosperity and the development of mass markets for branded consumer products. The techniques are seen everywhere today; press and poster advertising, point-of-sale displays, redeemable coupons, special discounts, special gift packs, mailing lists directed at particular groups of customers, canvassing customers in their own homes and the use of canvassing returns for market surveys and to assess consumer preferences. The effectiveness of the marketing of Elect cocoa made Rowntree's a household name and contributed greatly to the commercial success of the firm. Benson played a part, but undoubtedly dominating the firm was the austere figure of Joseph Rowntree, industrial relations pioneer, generous benefactor, conservative innovator and chocolate manufacturer.

Appendix

The cocoa bean kernel contains about 50 per cent cocoa butter; unless this high fatty content is reduced or counteracted any cocoa beverage will be greasy and unpalatable. A Cadbury advertisement in 1849 commended one of their blends 'for all who can appreciate the quality of genuine Cocoa, deprived of its strong and often rank oily flavour'. Manufacturers used various additives to counter the fat; sugar alone in the best grades but also treacle, arrowroot (for homeopathic cocoa), sago, flour, potato, and to provide colour red earth (and even peroxide of iron or red lead).

Various flavourings such as vanilla could be added. Possibly the worst 'cocoa' ever sold in England contained only 20 per cent cocoa – it was described as a comforting gruel.[121] The cocoa bean shell could be stewed into a beverage colloquially known as 'miserable'; some shell was exported to Ireland and some went to workhouses as an occasional change to the diet. Later a process was developed to grind it so finely that when a proportion was added to cocoa powder it was indistinguishable. In the early years of cocoa-butter extraction the surplus was exported to the Continent for pomades and so on. When cocoa butter's qualities as a very high grade vegetable fat were better understood a higher proportion was extracted and other cheaper vegetable fats were substituted in lower quality products. The cocoa butter not required for chocolate manufacture could be sold.

Following the passing of the Adulteration of Food Act 1872 there was a considerable confusion as to whether cocoas with additives could be sold as 'cocoa'. A parliamentary select committee reviewing the operation of the Act heard that a trader had been charged with selling adulterated cocoa; the case was dismissed on the specious technical grounds that the product was 'chocolate', not 'cocoa'. Even as late as 1891 the Food and Drugs Inspector brought a test prosecution in relation to Rowntree's lowest grade of rock cocoa which contained 40 per cent cocoa, 16 per cent sugar and 44 per cent starch. The magistrates dismissed the case, accepting that rock cocoa was a well-understood trade description for a cocoa admixture and there was no possibility of confusion with pure cocoa. The inspector also said his family liked it![122] Another prosecution in 1904 (not involving Rowntrees) also failed on the same grounds although the product only contained 30 per cent cocoa to 70 per cent sugar and sago.[123]

Acknowledgements

The author gratefully acknowledges the imaginative support and guidance of Dr D. J. Jeremy, without which this chapter would not have been written; and the help of the staff of Rowntree Mackintosh plc at York, particularly Mr Colin Murray who opened the archives and answered all his queries most willingly. Dr Stefanie Diaper and Professor T. C. Barker made helpful suggestions on an early draft.

This essay refers to the period before metrication of weights and decimalisation of currency. The ton was divided into twenty hundredweights (cwt) of approx 50 kg; each hundredweight had 112 pounds. The pound weight (lb) equals 0.454 kg.

The pound sterling was divided into twenty shillings (s) each of twelve pence (d), 2.4 old pence being equal to one new penny.

A price of 8½d per ¼lb equals 31.2 new pence per kg.

Notes

1. See (i) A. R. Prest, 'National Income of the UK 1870–1946', *Economic Journal*, lviii, 229 (March 1948); (ii) A. R. Prest and A. A. Adams,

Consumers' Expenditure in the United Kingdom 1900–1919 (1948); (iii) W. W. Rostow, *The Great Depression, 1873–1896* (1948); (iv) T. C. Barker, 'History, Economic and Social', in C. B. Cox and A. E. Dyson, *The Twentieth Century Mind*, I, 1900–1918 (London 1972).

2. *Statistical Abstracts* (HMSO).
3. See J. Othick, 'The Cocoa and Chocolate Industry in the Nineteenth Century', in Derek J. Oddy and D. S. Miller, eds, *The Making of the Modern British Diet* (London, 1976).
4. Derek J. Oddy, 'The Working Class Diet 1886–1914' (London Ph.D.), p. 65.
5. Parliamentary Papers 1877, XI, Select Committee on Intemperance, pp. 171, 271, 418.
6. James B. Jefferys, *Retail Trading in Britain 1850–1950* (Cambridge, 1954), p. 23; see also D. J. Jeremy, ed., *Dictionary of Business Biography*, 5 vols (London, 1984–86), entries on Lipton, Sainsbury.
7. See, for example, the Civil Service Supply Association catalogues for the period.
8. G. H. Mennell, *The Romance of a Great Industry 1725–1921* (Darlington, 1922).
9. Rowntree Mackintosh plc, Archives, ref. Arch 1833; and see Table 2.2.
10. Arch: letter to customers, 3 January 1870.
11. *The Grocer*, passim.
12. Arch, printed specimen letter of 189.. for use by co-op buyers to store managers.
13. Othick, op. cit., and *Illustrated London News*, 7 May 1870.
14. Jeremy, op. cit. entries on Cadbury and Fry.
15. Arch, letter to customers, 3 January 1870.
16. Arch 949, 1 March 1907.
17. Arch 441, 692.
18. Arch 440.
19. Private Minutes of Directors' Conferences (Board), 24 July 1900.
20. Arch 1082.
21. Arch 3301, Note of 13 March 1879.
22. Arch 1833, letter of 23 March 1872; see also Anne Vernon, *A Quaker Business Man, Joseph Rowntree 1836–1925* (London, 1958), pp. 62–3.
23. Board, e.g. 27 June 1905.
24. Paul H. Emden, *Quakers in Commerce* (London, 1940), p. 17.
25. e.g. *Grocer*, 4 September 1880; *Grocers' Chronicle*, June 1883.
26. Arch 351.
27. Arch 2901, Note of discussion, 6 February 1885.
28. *Friend*, August 1880–February 1881.
29. T. R. Nevett, *Advertising in Britain: a history* (London, 1982), p. 104.
30. e.g. *Halifax Courier*, passim; Nevett, op. cit.
31. e.g. *Tit-Bits* (1891), passim.
32. Parliamentary Papers HC 1874, VI, Select Committee on the Adulteration of Food Act 1872.

33. *Grocer*, 5 December 1885; and see Appendix.
34. Arch, letter dated 27 June 1887.
35. Arch 2901.
36. Letter, J. P. Thol to Joseph Rowntree, 3 December 1885; Arch 2901.
37. Board, 22 May 1900.
38. Arch 441.
39. Arch 351.
40. Arch, printed specimen letter of 189.. for use by co-op buyers to store managers.
41. e.g. *Halifax Courier* (1890–5), passim. One of the panaceas offered was Peppers Quinine and Iron Tonic — for great bodily strength
  — for great nerve strength
  — for great mental strength
  — overcomes weakness
    fatigue
    irritability
    depression
  — cures indigestion
    neuralgia & atica
    nervous head pains
    melancholia
  — promotes appetite
    healthy pulse
  — restores vitality
    health, strength and energy
42. Arch, Memorandum to Travellers, 30 January 1891.
43. ibid. 10 December 1891; the papers mentioned by name in the memorandum were: *Tit-Bits, Answers, Great Thoughts, Pearson's Weekly, Cassell's Saturday Journal, Illustrated London News, Graphic, Christian World, British Weekly, Christian Herald, Methodist Time, Enquire Within, The Queen, The Lady*, Weldon's Journals.
44. Board, 10 July 1900; Rowntree's approach to religious papers was completely ecumenical; the Quaker *Friend* has already been mentioned; Others used in 1897–98 include *Church Times, Christian Herald, Catholic Fireside, Sunday Companion, Methodist Recorder, Baptist Times, Sword and Trowel, Wesleyan Methodist Sunday School Magazine, Free Methodist, The Rock, Church Bells*, and many more.
45. e.g. *Halifax Courier*, passim.
46. Arch 2901.
47. Nevett, op. cit. p. 71. He quotes Turner Morton, an experienced commentator writing in 1905 in *Pearson's Magazine*. Anything less than a 'reasonable' figure of £2000–£3000 was likely to be a waste of time and £20 000–£30 000 would be needed for anything like a sensation.

The contrast of the cautious Joseph Rowntree with the dynamic John

Mackintosh is compelling. Mackintosh started making and selling toffee in 1890, was advertising extensively within five years, notably in the trade press and at exhibitions, and started national consumer advertising in the *Strand Magazine* in 1898. When he decided to break into the American market, on his first day in New York he signed a contract with J. Walter Thompson, the advertising agent, 'to spend £100 000 in the first two years of business in America'. Jeremy, op. cit. entry on John Mackintosh.

48. At about this time, Frys also switched from generalised advertising and placed all their emphasis on one product, Fry's Pure Concentrated Cocoa. Whether Frys followed Rowntrees or vice versa is unclear.
49. Arch, *Cocoa Works Magazine*, November 1913.
50. Nevett, op. cit.; Jeremy, op. cit. entry on Benson.
51. Geo. Edgar, in *Modern Business* (1908): Business Builders, XVI, S. H. Benson.
52. Board, 11 October 1898.
53. S. H. Benson, *Wisdom in Advertising* (1901), *Daily Mail*, 4 December 1897.
54. Maurice Rickards, *The Rise and Fall of the Poster* (Newton Abbot, 1971), p. 19; see also *Poster* magazine, 4 vols (1898–1900).
55. Board, 24 February 1903.
56. Board, 6 June 1900.
57. Arch 2661, G 3/5–9.
58. Board, 26 February 1901; 25 June 1901.
59. Board, 7 October 1901; 18 March 1902.
60. Charles Wilson, *The History of Unilever* (London, 1954); George W. Crutchley, *John Mackintosh* (London, 1921); Jeremy, op. cit. entries on Lever, Mackintosh.
61. Board, 4 May 1906.
62. Arch, EC G1/8, G1/19, G1/26; Board 7, 21 May 1901.
63. Board, 5 May 1903. The first offer of a cottage as a competition prize came from George Newnes; his short story competition in November 1883 offered Tit-Bits Villa as the prize.
64. Arch, EC G1/23. It is interesting to note that Lever's experience paralleled Rowntree's; his Sunlight soap gift scheme proved a serious drain on his resources.
65. Board, 14 June 1907.
66. Board, 3 June 1908, 20 September 1910; Arch EC G6/1.
67. Board, 15 April 1902, 7 May 1902.
68. Board, 16 September 1902.
69. Board, 1 January 1907.
70. Board, 27 March 1906; Arch, G7/5.
71. See, for example, Max K. Ader, *Lectures in Market Research* (London 1965); G Schwartz, ed., *Science in Marketing* (New York, 1965). The first social survey with systematic sampling was undertaken in 1911; see 'Working-Class Households in Reading' by Prof. A. L. Bowlby, *J. Royal Statistical Soc.*

(1913). See Donald A. MacKenzie, *Statistics in Britain 1865–1930* (Edinburgh, 1981), for a discussion of early use of statistical methods for social studies which developed from an interest in eugenics.

72. Board, 28 February 1907.
73. Arch EC F3, F5 etc.
74. Board, 11 March 1902; in a series featuring famous people, pictures of soldiers and actresses were to be 'rigorously excluded'.
75. Arch 441, 692, ECG6/1, SG2/1, G/G1/4, G1/5–6.
76. Arch ECH G1/6. In 1911 £7500 was spent in promoting Elect chocolate, £12 000 in 1912 but only £5250 in 1913 and less still in 1914. Sales rose from £15 000 in 1911 to £22 500 in 1912 but fell back slightly as soon as the pressure of advertising was slackened, just as Elect cocoa sales slipped in 1899 from a similar cause.
77. Board, passim.
78. Arch 949, speech to travellers, 1907.
79. Board, 15 August 1904.
80. Board, 14 March, 4 April, 1905.
81. Board, 19 December 1905.
82. Board, 25 April 1906; 4, 9 May 1905.
83. Board, 10 August 1906.
84. Board, 18 February, 6, 19 March, 3 April 1907.
85. Board, 14 June, 10, 25 July 1907.
86. Board, 17, 22 October, 6, 13 November 1907.
87. Wilson, op. cit. pp. 74ff.
88. Board, 6 November 1906.
89. Board, 12 February, 4 March 1908.
90. Arch EC G3/5, 39/4, 39/10.
91. Board, 9 February 1909.
92. Board, 14 April 1909.
93. Board, 13 July 1909; 13 April 1910.
94. Board, 18 May 1909; 13 November 1911.
95. Board, 15, 22 February, 4 April, 1910; Arch 441.
96. Board, 18 April, 25 May 1910; 11 January 1911.
97. Board, 22 January 1912.
98. Board, 30 January, 22 February, 22 April, 1912. Rowntree's first use of a full page advertisement in the *Daily Mail* was on 7 November 1903.
99. Board, 6 May, 12 June 1912.
100. Board, 17 October, 11 November 1912.
101. Board, 24 December 1912; 31 March, 7 July 1913.
102. Quoted in Wilson, op. cit. p. 118.
103. Board, 21 November 1899; 6 June, 6 November 1900; 20 January 1903; 16 August 1904.
104. Board, 22 September 1914; see also, G. G. Jones, 'Multinational Chocolate: Cadbury overseas 1918–1939', *Business History*, 27 (1985).
105. *Statistical Abstracts* (HMSO).

106. Board, 6 November 1900; 13 December 1901. Joseph was still standing out in 1914 (Board, 25 August 1914).
107. Arch, 3001 (1895); Board, 8 February, 13, 20 June 1900.
108. Board, 9 April 1901; 24 February 1903; 1 November 1904.
109. Board, 19 January 1914. The Fry archives include a full set of minutes of these meetings and the agreements reached. For an outline of the Cadbury presentation of the St Thomé affair, see Iolo A. Williams, *The Firm of Cadbury 1831–1931* (London, 1931).
110. Board, 6 November 1906.
111. Board, 17 March, 15 December 1913.
112. Board, 9, 22 October 1907.
113. Jeremy, op. cit. entry on Harris.
114. For further consideration of Quakers in business see, for example, Vernon, op. cit.; Elizabeth Isichei, *Victorian Quakers* (London, 1970); T. A. B. Corley, *Quaker Enterprise in Biscuits: Huntley and Palmers of Reading 1822–1972* (London, 1972); id. *How Quakers Coped with Business Success: Quaker industrialists 1860–1914* (1982); M. W. Kirby, *Men of Business and Politics: the rise and fall of the Quaker Pease dynasty of North East England 1700–1943* (London, 1984); Sir Adrian Cadbury, *Quaker Values in Business* (London, 1985); Gillian Wagner, *The Chocolate Conscience* (London, 1986).
115. Vernon, op. cit.
116. Modern marketing theory suggests the need to concentrate on the potential 'star' products rather than the mature 'cash cows' or products in terminal decline, the 'old dogs'.
117. Board, 7 November 1899.
118. Board, 20, 27 March 1900.
119. In 1930 Rowntrees approached Cadburys to propose a merger (without success). Notes prepared by Seebohm Rowntree include this reference: 'You will recall that you approached us in 1918. At that time the whole board, except Joseph Rowntree, were favourably inclined to accept your proposals. He made it a personal matter (not at all I need hardly say out of any feeling against you, but because of certain ideas and principles with which he had grown up) and out of affection for him we accepted his view, though it was against our own business judgement.' (From Cadbury archives, quoted in Jeremy, op. cit. entry on Joseph Rowntree.)
120. Seebohm Rowntree was brought up to play a key role in the family business, particularly following the premature retirement through ill-health (1899) and early death (1905) of his elder brother John Wilhelm. Seebohm read chemistry for two years at Owen's College, Manchester but soon his interest in social questions took more and more of his time. He became a director when the firm was converted into a limited company in 1897, with responsibility for labour matters at the Haxby Road works. In a talk in 1921 Seebohm makes it clear that he is not a marketing man at heart: 'We must recognise the growing tendency in the trade since the war to ask for something new – something with

colour. Against our natural inclinations and perhaps our own artistic standards we shall if we are to maintain our turnover have to meet this demand.' (Arch.) See Asa Briggs, *Social Thought and Social Action: a study of the work of Seebohm Rowntree 1871–1954* (London, 1961). 'His interest in business was real but seldom completely absorbing' (ibid. p. 3).

121. Williams, op. cit. pp. 13, 19, 37; *Cocoa: all about it*, 'Historicus' (R. Cadbury) (London, 1896), p. 71.
122. Select Committee on the Adulteration of Food Act 1872, Parliamentary Papers, 1874, *VI*, p. 262; *Kentish Independent*, 22 December 1891.
123. Board, 29 November 1904.

3 English versus American hardware: British marketing techniques and business performance in the USA in the nineteenth and early-twentieth centuries

Geoffrey Tweedale

Introduction

In 1876 at the Centennial Exhibition in Philadelphia English hardware[1] manufacturers were presented with dramatic evidence of America's developing skills in the steel and toolmaking arts. High grade steel ingots and sections by the leading Pittsburgh makers, such as Park Bro & Co., were judged to be equal in every respect to those of English competitors. Magnificent and imaginative displays of axes, saws and files by Collins, Disston and Nicholson gave notice that the USA was now the world leader in the production of those articles upon which England had previously had a stranglehold.

The performance of the Americans can be traced statistically in the US State trade accounts.[2] Shortly after the Civil War the USA imported $1 105 419 of English cutlery, as well as $928 011 of penknives, pocket-knives, and jack-knives; by 1872 total English cutlery imports had fallen to $1 729 154; and five years later the figure was only $654 973. In other hardware products such as saws the decline in English imports was even more pronounced. In 1866 17 057 hand saws, 429 dozen back saws, and substantial quantities of cross-cut and mill saws were imported by the USA from England. The value of imported saws and other tools slumped heavily thereafter to only $8160 in 1877 (the 1866 figure was $108 478) and ten years later no saws were tabulated in the US import accounts; indeed by then America was exporting over $2 million of saws and tools herself, many of them to England. Soon afterwards, though the USA before 1860 had been almost entirely dependent upon English files, it had also become largely self-sufficient in their manufacture by the 1890s and was only importing a few of the more specialised hand-cut files which had not succumbed to the American drive for mechanisation.

This brilliant American success story, which Duncan Burn first highlighted many years ago in a discussion of the 'genesis' of American engineering competition, was partly a reflection of America's superior mass-production techniques – the so-called 'American System of Manufactures'.[3] It was the mechanisation and consequent cheapening of traditional European products that gave the USA its advantage in hardware manufacture. However, so far-reaching and so rapid were American strides in world hardware markets that, as contemporary English manufacturers recognised, it was obvious that other factors were at work.[4] Mass-production technologies also required mass-distribution techniques, a field in which, we are told, the Americans also excelled. This aspect of entrepreneurship though, as regards the English hardware trades, has received little detailed attention from historians. The Manchester and Birmingham industries have been studied[5] but Sheffield which produced some of the major lines of hardware – particularly cutlery and edge tools – has been neglected. This essay, drawing on a wide range of business records and contemporary trade journals, looks at the performance of English manufacturers in the American market during the late-nineteenth and early-twentieth centuries and attempts to answer the following question: was it the case, as some historians have asserted, that English manufacturers were pushed aside in world markets because of their inability to sell and advertise their products as successfully as their competitors?[6]

The American Market: Opportunities, Obstacles and Early Successes in the Selling of English Hardware before the Civil War

In the late-eighteenth and throughout the nineteenth centuries America exerted an irresistible fascination for Sheffield manufacturers. The opportunities that the US market offered before 1860 are self-evident: across the country thousands of miles of railroad tracks were being laid; immigrants were filling the country; urban centres were expanding rapidly; and above all there were demands for producer and consumer goods, especially cutlery and hardware. In the words of one Sheffield worthy: 'The [American] settler needed his axe to fell the primeval forest, his spade to break the hitherto untilled ground, his saw, and chisel, and file, and scythe, and shears for constant use in building and agriculture, as well as the necessary domestic utensils in setting up a new home.'[7] Thus by the 1800s Sheffield's hardware trade with the USA was quickening in readiness for the remarkable expansion which occurred after 1820.

The marketing of Sheffield hardware was a product of eighteenth-century conditions.

> It is a tale oft-told by every historian of Sheffield...how primitive, far into the eighteenth century, were the trading relations between Sheffield and all outside its borders. Aforetime, there were no merchants to undertake the useful task of distribution and to place manufacturers in direct communication with distant or foreign markets; and no bankers.[8]

From the 1770s however largely due to the stimulus of the American trade a more sophisticated network of distribution was set up with the emergence of hardware factors and merchants. By the beginning of the nineteenth century it was said that eighteen Sheffield 'export houses' dealt with the US market (compared with nine to other foreign countries). After 1815 about ten Sheffield firms began to trade directly with America, establishing their own offices on the American east coast.[9] During the 1820s the names of the most prominent Sheffield steel and hardware firms – Marsh Bros, Sandersons, Cammells, Jessops, Butchers, and Vickers – appeared in the New York, Boston and Philadelphia city directories. The main American office of each Sheffield firm held a stock of the company's product and gave the resident agent – often himself a family member or partner of the English parent – a chance to keep a close eye on US conditions, sending in orders and information on local demand. Sanderson Bros, a front-ranking crucible steelmaking concern, relied on Edward F. Sanderson, who by the 1840s had become one of New York's richest citizens. His office in Manhattan was the channel for American orders for tool steel for New York sawmakers such as Richard Hoe, besides files, machine parts and even skilled operatives for American industries.[10] Marsh Bros, a typical Sheffield family enterprise which traded mainly in cutlery, also had a New York office which was a major factor in the English firm's expansion. Like other enterprises, it had 'travellers' armed with illustrated catalogues (the so-called Sheffield 'Lists'), who toured the main sales areas – in Marsh Bros' case the American south (Plate 3.1) – drumming up business.[11] It also relied to a certain extent on American agents who, though they reduced profit margins, had an indispensable knowledge of local conditions and could supply a firm with detailed knowledge as to what was required. The number of Sheffield agencies in America, staffed either by Englishmen or often by Americans, grew rapidly before the Civil War; by 1860, for example, Jessops had offices in New York, Boston, Philadelphia, St Louis, Cincinatti and Rhode Island.

Sheffield merchants were helped by an American market that in the early nineteenth century was still (relatively) a small one, with customers mostly located in New England and other major clusters of settlement. English merchants and their agents in the seaboard cities were able to dominate the commerce in the interior, dependent as it was on small local storekeepers. The preference of Americans, as chance survivals in American tool boxes and workshops show, was still largely for English-style tools, made by the traditional labour-intensive Sheffield methods. Products sold on 'name' and a Butcher plane iron, a Wostenholm knife or a Spear saw, was the main assurance of quality. This reflected both the unsophisticated nature of the American market and the character of the Sheffield hardware industry itself, which was small-scale, often pursued in a rural setting, dominated by the guilds and unions and dependent upon the work of hundreds of craftsmen producing an immense variety of patterns and type.[12] The need for wholesale merchants to offer a comprehensive 'range' was thus to the advantage of Sheffield's numerous small and weakly-financed family concerns.

On the other hand some formidable difficulties had to be overcome in trading with the USA. In terms of travelling time in the nineteenth century America was a great distance from Sheffield. In the early part of the century letters took a minimum of two weeks to cross the Atlantic, while goods could take several months to reach their destination. The advent of steamer services improved matters but shipped goods still had to survive the hazards of the transatlantic

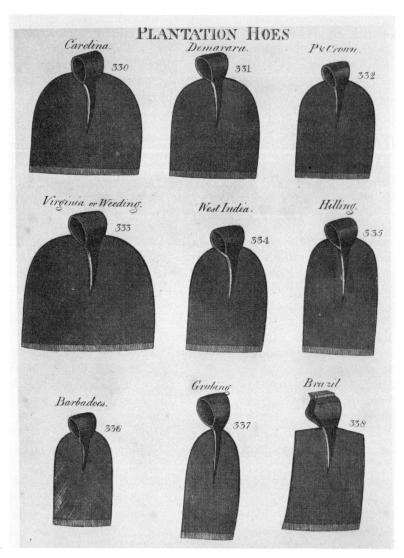

Plate 3.1 A page from Marsh Bros trade catalogue, c.1818, showing American-style plantation hoes (Sheffield City Library).

journey. Products could be damaged, misdirected, returned by Customs or lost in shipwreck.[13] Concerning problems over one shipment of steel in 1865 Marsh Bros wrote to their New York agents:

> We advised you of the trouble in getting goods to Liverpool; from what we hear it appears we have been quite fortunate; it seems Naylor Vickers Co. lost a large parcel for six weeks when the lot turned up in Dublin and J. H. Andrew lost 20 tons of wire rods...during ten days.[14]

What this meant for American customers can be seen from the correspondence of the sawmaker Richard Hoe, which is dominated by continual requests for faster service. A typical letter in 1843 to Sanderson Bros of Sheffield began by asking for the utmost speed and then repeated the point at the foot of the page.[15] Hoe frequently had the task of writing to disappointed customers explaining that orders could not be completed because of a lack of steel.[16] When American saw plates and tools did arrive on the scene Hoe, though happy with the Sheffield product, seized on them with alacrity.

Mistakes when they did happen were not so easily rectified when those concerned were separated by the Atlantic. In 1864 a consignment of steel from Marsh Bros was found to be unacceptable by one of its customers in Syracuse, New York. An extended wrangle took place over the shipment which was only settled by the personal intervention of a representative from the Sheffield firm.[17]

It may be true that other traders faced similar problems over long distances but in some ways Sheffield was a special case. The communications lag had a particularly important relevance for the tool steel trade, since existing specifications often needed to be modified to suit the needs of individual customers, necessitating a close liaison between the steelmakers and the engineer.[18] In Sheffield it was common practice for a steel merchant to hold quantities of a customer's favourite brand until it was required. Where possible the same policy appears to have been adopted in America, where Sheffield subsidiaries were able to lavish on buyers what Firths called the 'personal element' that Sheffield makers thought so important. However these services could not be offered by every Sheffield steelmaker in America, and so eventually when American steelmakers appeared in the 1850s and 1860s it was soon reported that US consumers were favouring the domestic product because they could, if necessary, maintain daily contact with the makers.[19]

Nor did circumstances usually allow Sheffield agencies in the USA to carry a very heavy stock. This was a difficult problem for exporters and the stock position is the one subject common to all extant correspondence of Sheffield's US trade. How much stock dare a manufacturer hold in America without incurring losses? The Marsh Bros correspondence shows that there was no easy answer to this question. The most careful calculations could easily be upset by tariffs, exchange fluctuations, technical developments in the foreign market, or by war. All these factors played a part in influencing Marsh Bros' attitude towards its New York stock in the period 1863–6. The violent fluctuations that resulted have been too well documented by Professor Pollard to need repetition here, but his conclusion may be repeated: 'In less than three and a half years...the policy of the American branch had been changed no fewer than ten times, chiefly on account of external influences on the American market for steel and cutlery goods.'[20] The implication, probably a correct one, was that Marsh Bros could do little to influence events short of entering the American market itself, something which the firm felt was 'entirely out of the question' since it had no capital to spare apart from its current business.[21] The lack of capital was exacerbated by the accumulation of stocks in New York and deficiencies on remittances from the USA; in 1857 the deficiency amounted to £12 000 and had increased to over £18 000 by 1864.[22]

Before 1860 however English traders appear to have done quite well. The evidence, based on fragmentary sources, is not conclusive but even allowing for the fact that American competition could largely be ignored by Sheffield makers before about 1840 the English performance is impressive. Until the mid-1830s Sheffield virtually monopolised the US hardware market: about half of the total exports of the British manufactured steel industry went to America. After the 'glorious' year of prosperity in 1835 the trade declined: however the USA remained the best foreign market until 1860, taking about a quarter of English hardware exports.[23] On the eve of the American Civil War, for example, Sheffield still accounted for about 90 per cent of total American cutlery imports.

Sales to America seem to have been backed by some aggressive and imaginative marketing tactics. In Sheffield itself Rodgers, who alongside Wostenholms were the leading cutlery manufacturers, caused a sensation in 1821 by opening the world's first cutlery showroom. Awed Americans recorded their impressions when they saw displayed giant scissors large enough to walk beneath and knives with over two thousand blades, 'like the horrid quills on a porcupine's back'.[24] Rodgers, alongside over ninety Sheffield exhibitors, also figured prominently at the Great Exhibition of 1851 where Sheffield's triumph was almost complete: 'almost every country is a tributary to its works', reported a Royal Commission.[25]

To press this superiority home leading Sheffield manufacturers set out across the Atlantic in search of orders. George Wostenholm the cutler, beginning in 1836, undertook thirty visits to the USA during his lifetime and pursued orders as far west as San Francisco.[26] Such a commitment to the distant American market was by no means unusual and eventually some of the town's manufacturers became 'a stranger in their own land and infinitely better known in Broadway [than in Sheffield]'.[27] On foreign soil the Sheffielders soon impressed upon Americans the advantages of doing business with the world's leading hardware centre. The world-famous Collins Axe Co. in Connecticut was visited by a representative from the Sheffield steelmakers Firths, who in the 1840s 'made such representations and named terms that induced [the Americans] to give them [their] business...exclusively for about 20 years'.[28] Vickers, whose chief business in the mid-nineteenth century was the export of Swedish bar iron and sheets of steel to the USA, made arrangements in the 1840 with a young German by the name of Ernst Leopold Schlesinger Benzon to act as their agent in New York and Boston. Observed Benzon: 'The business we can do in the way of direct orders without outlay of Capital is without end, but it requires much personal effort to obtain it.'[29] So successful were Benzon's own personal efforts at promoting the sales of Vickers' products in the USA that he eventually became a partner and then chairman of the Sheffield firm, even though he cultivated so much wealth and prestige in America that occasionally there was some friction between him and the Sheffield family members.

Sheffielders were also willing to cater for American tastes from a very early date. By the 1820s American-style plantation hoes (Plate 3.1) and woodworking tools were displayed in the town's trade catalogues. In 1836 responding to a demand on the frontier for scalping knives one Sheffielder, Hiram Cutler, wrote to the American Fur Co. in Michigan concerning a knife 'that would probably suit Indians'.[30] By the mid-nineteenth century such adaptation had become quite widespread. 'Drabble [of Sheffield] has aimed at competing in American styles with domestic

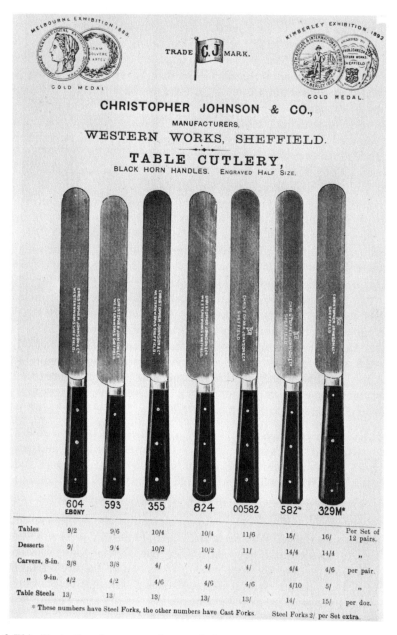

TRADE **C.J** MARK.

CHRISTOPHER JOHNSON & CO.,
MANUFACTURERS,

WESTERN WORKS, SHEFFIELD.

TABLE CUTLERY,
BLACK HORN HANDLES. ENGRAVED HALF SIZE.

	604 EBONY	593	355	824	00582	582*	329M*	
Tables	9/2	9/6	10/4	10/4	11/6	15/	16/	Per Set of 12 pairs.
Desserts	9/	9/4	10/2	10/2	11/	14/4	14/4	,,
Carvers, 8-in.	3/8	3/8	4/	4/	4/	4/4	4/6	per pair.
,, 9-in.	4/2	4/2	4/6	4/6	4/6	4/10	5/	,,
Table Steels	13/	13/	13/	13/	13/	14/	15/	per doz.

* These numbers have Steel Forks, the other numbers have Cast Forks. Steel Forks 2/ per Set extra.

Plate 3.2 This illustration from an early twentieth-century trade catalogue shows a major marketing weakness of the Sheffield industry – the huge number of patterns produced by individual cutlery makers. This is only one of a number of pages showing scores of knives which hardly differed in size or style. (Courtesy Sheffield City Library)

63

[cutlery] manufacturers for some years', wrote Marsh Bros in 1867.[31] Marsh Bros themselves were attentive to the needs of Americans, asking the firm's New York agent to obtain 'leading styles' of American table-knives.[32]

One of the most notable instances of Sheffield adapting itself to the American market was in the Bowie knife trade, which was established in the 1830s, expanded during the 1840s and reached its peak in the 1850s. Sheffield firms, especially Butchers and Wostenholms, monopolised the Bowie knife trade before the Civil War. Trade was particularly heavy in the American south and west, where knives engraved with such delightful inscriptions as 'Death to Abolition', 'I Can Dig Gold from Quartz', 'For Stags and Buffaloes', and 'Celebrated Arkansas Toothpick', were marketed with great skill and enjoyed a ready sale.[33]

However other signs were less encouraging for Sheffield manufacturers. By 1850 the US hardware industry aided by a tariff which had risen to 35 per cent *ad valorem* in 1862 was securely established with over 400 manufacturers producing $3.8 million of cutlery and tools. Particularly impressive strides had been made in the manufacture of US saws and axes, with makers such as Disston and Collins soon winning an international reputation as early as the 1840s. English visitors to America at about this time and witnesses at the Great Exhibition noted the increasing US proficiency in hardware manufacture, frequently commenting on the strength, lightness and elegance of American woodworking and edge tools.

Despite Sheffield's attempts at adaptation, some long-established English products did not always find favour with the Americans. In scythe manufacture, for example, the USA had already captured a large share of the market before 1850 with a product that was cheaper and better designed than its English competitor. Sheffield makes were judged too broad and heavy:

> In fact [commented one Sheffield newspaper] it is next to impossible to find a man [in America] who will wield the broad, useful, and effective [Sheffield] scythe among the heavy and extensive fields of grain and grass which this country in some portions produces, and that too under an almost tropical climate.[34]

By mid-century Americans were also complaining about the presentation of Sheffield goods. In the 1850s a Marsh Bros agent in the mid-west was informed by one American retailer that since American makers were now packaging their products Sheffield's methods were 'twenty years behind the age'. Examining the respective displays the agent was obliged to agree: 'On the shelves our goods in bundles beside those of other people in boxes (making neat square bales) with handsome black, gold & green labels, do certainly look...very "old fogyish".'[35] These comments hint at the more efficient marketing techniques with which Sheffield had to deal after the American Civil War.

English Marketing Performance and the Transformation of the American Distribution System, 1865–1914

In the early-nineteenth century the Sheffield industries had to cope with rapid

American advances in technology; after the Civil War technology, at least in the USA, became less crucial than the problem of marketing. The vast expansion of the American market, the emergence of wholesale hardware trade assocations and department stores, the practice of selling under-advertised brand names, often through controlled retail outlets and fierce price competition, all contributed to the erosion of the traditional selling methods on which Sheffield had depended so heavily.[36] After the Civil War standardised American hardware products swept the market attracting the consumer by price, fitness for the purpose and skilful advertising and distribution. In all of these areas Sheffield proved deficient.

The 1870s and 1880s proved to be pivotal decades, especially since in this period American mechanisation drove domestic prices of cutlery and hardware downwards, while the tariff raised the prices of imports. In cutlery production this meant that by the end of the century Sheffield competition was no longer a serious threat to the American manufacturer; US imports of English cutlery falling from $1 146 272 in 1889 (about 10 per cent of US output), to only $285 002 in 1894.

Wostenholms' American agent noted in the early 1890s that the susceptibility of cutlery products to price changes was a major sales factor. Covering a territory that was evidently his firm's main hunting ground – the south and mid-west – the agent Edward Beckett found that it was an uphill struggle to place Wostenholms' goods on the shelves of American stores. Cheaper American knives had given domestic purchasers an attractive alternative. The policy of one of Wostenholms' customers in New Orleans was fairly typical. Wrote Beckett: 'Since joining a syndicate in purchasing cheap cutlery in large quantities they appear to have sold less of our goods...It is evidently a question of profit entirely with them and they are selling Cutlery on price alone, quality not being considered.'[37] Concerning another retailer, he informed Sheffield:

> I am quite sure it is not that they cannot sell [Wostenholm] IXL but [their reluctance to buy] is mainly owing to the fact that they are making a good profit on American goods. They have certainly increased their line of Ulster [US] knives...50%. To illustrate to you the difference as to their prices & ours take our knife 16144 as made by the Ulster Knife Co. [Ellenville, New York]. [They] buy the Ulster knife for $4.50 per doz & sell it for $6.75, making a profit of $2.25 per doz...16144 costs them to import $7.83 and for them to make the same amount of profit they would have to sell them for $10.00 per doz, so you can readily see where our goods are at a disadvantage.[38]

In Sheffield at this time, largely due to the dominance of the trade unions and the nature of the domestic market which favoured a multiplicity of patterns and type, the introduction of machinery made slow headway so that even at the end of the nineteenth century no hardware factory was fully mechanised along the American lines. Thus there were few opportunities for achieving any great economies of scale or for standardising output (Plate 3.2). Viewed through the eyes of a present-day consumer, when stainlessness, standardisation and presentation are taken for granted, the productions of Sheffield's small workshops would appear rather motley. Nineteenth-century observers thought so too. In the 1880s the *Ironmonger* frequently commented on the unfavourable appearance of Sheffield cutlery when compared to American articles, especially from 'the inequality in lengths and breadths of knives, and also in making, grinding, and hafting', whereas the Americans 'always attached the utmost importance to such matters'.[39] The *Sheffield Independent*'s American correspondent, in a detailed review in 1875 of the decline of the town's US trade, went even further, complaining of the 'third-rate quality' of Sheffield exports, and arguing that: 'No country in the world took, for so long a time, anything like the quantity of poor goods...than the United States did.'[40]

The Americans were also unhappy with the design of English woodworking tools, especially Sheffield's inability to adapt to the US's innovative saw patterns, which had been stimulated by America's vast resources of wood. Sheffield makes designed for the European market were found unsuitable for American timber. As one Sheffield newspaper put it:

> the extraordinary cheapness and abundance of all kinds of woods here will account for a portion of the advantages which American manufacturers have gained over the English, especially when the immense protective tariffs are borne in mind; but still absence of adaptability has done a great deal to decrease purchasers...The portion of timber sawn up [in America] is soft and needs a wide-toothed, peculiarly ground saw, to work easily and free itself rapidly; far different from those most suitable at home. Now, for a long time, Sheffield makers either could not or would not understand and supply this alteration.[41]

The repercussions of this failure to adapt were felt not only in the US market but also closer to home. By the 1870s American hardware products such as Disston saws and Jennings augers sold readily even in Sheffield, largely because of their superior design which overcame cost considerations. By 1880 one Sheffield hardware manufacturer and retailer, William Marples & Sons, was specialising in the British sale of American hardware and 'ironmonger novelties'. By 1896 saws and tools exported from the USA totalled $2 197 450, and $229 489 of that amount was destined for the UK; only Australasia was a more important American market.

It was in Australasia that Sheffield manufacturers felt the full force of American competition. The US invasion of these neutral markets generated an enormous amount of comment in the leading English hardware journal, the *Ironmonger*, in the late 1870s.[42] Though many of the articles and editorials expressed confidence in the ability of English makers to compete with their rivals there was also the underlying suspicion that American tools were superior in design and adaptation.[43] One Auckland dealer, emphasising the superiority of American saws, argued that 'unless the English manufacturers bestir themselves I believe the time is not far distant when [the Americans] will monopolize [the trade]. Do you ask how is this, when we can undersell them? It is simply because their goods are better and more adapted to our requirements.'[44] English makers however proved slow to heed such warnings, so that by the early-twentieth century even the leading brands of Sheffield saws in Australia had 'gone right out of the market'.[45]

Sheffield seems also to have been slow to make the most of more sophisticated methods of marketing and distribution by fully advertising its famous name. At the trade exhibitions Sheffield soon appears to have fallen away from the high standards it had set in 1851. At the Great Exhibition of 1862 Sheffield products were less in evidence and the town's traders complained that the event followed too closely upon those of 1851 and in Paris to warrant the trouble and expense of exhibiting.[46] At the Paris Exhibition of 1867 a Royal Commission remarked:

> it can hardly escape notice that Sheffield is very badly represented...It is very much regretted that this should be the case, and that the English manufacturers of cast steel, hammered iron, and hardware should have declined to take this opportunity of inviting a comparison of which they could not be afraid.[47]

It was reported that the Sheffield cutlers were 'tired of exhibitions, and profess to see no advantage in appearing at them'.[48] At the Philadelphia Exhibition in 1876 several Sheffield businesses did make the effort to contribute, including Wostenholms, whose cutlery 'was unsurpassed in quality, finish, and beauty of style'.[49] However in saws English observers noted that: 'Great Britain has not a single representative, although for years Sheffield supplied not only our own country but nearly all the world'. And the general conclusion of a Parliamentary Report was as follows: 'in table cutlery, tools, and safes, America was before Great Britain' and 'A strenuous effort will be required from Sheffield to hold its own in the race of progress.'[50] The Sheffield showing at Philadelphia however was to be typical of a general reluctance to exhibit which became increasingly manifest in the later-nineteenth century.

Sheffield attempts to advertise itself in other ways were also not very impressive in the period 1865–1914. In the 1870s Sheffield had taken up a good deal of advertising space in American trade journals such as the *Iron Age*. The issue of 2 January 1873 may be taken as a typical example. In it Sheffield advertisements for cast steel (Jessops, Sandersons, Wardlows, and Cockers), cutlery (Rodgers, Wostenholms, Dickinsons, and Wards), and saws, files, and edge tools (Spear & Jacksons, Butchers, Wilkinsons, and Fishers) dominated the pages, with only one or two American firms such as Singer, Nimick & Co. offering any display. But with the growth of American competition by the end of that decade Sheffield advertisements declined abruptly. After the 1880s in fact Sheffield advertisements in the *Iron Age* became increasingly rare. Moreover when Sheffielders did make the effort their advertisements were typically unimaginative – usually simply stating the name of the manufacturer, the product, and the address of an agent, with no attempt at illustration. This can be contrasted with those of the American sawmaker Henry Disston, who began placing advertisements in the *Iron Age* in the 1870s, consisting of eight full pages illustrated with over a hundred wood engravings.

Such products were also superbly packaged, a point highlighted by the *Ironmonger* in 1879.[51] By then some Sheffield firms had begun to copy American methods; Spear & Jackson had discarded paper wrappings for its products and was packing them in neat cardboard boxes.[52] But the lessons seemed to have been imperfectly learned. When a Spear & Jackson director visiting Australia in 1905 was asked by a storekeeper for some advertising matter he was unable to provide it. 'Could we not get up some such thing, either calendar or large show-card?' he wrote to Sheffield.[53]

Some attempt was made to cater for the mass market. Sheffield cutlery and razors were well to the fore in the early Sears Roebuck catalogues. In the 1908 publication, for example, Wostenholms' products were described as 'the standard the world over'. For $1.80 a customer could order a Wostenholm de-luxe carving knife and fork. However US makers displayed an attractively boxed sixteen-piece knife set for $4.65 – a sign of things to come.[54] Gradually Sheffield products became too expensive and they were significantly beginning to be overshadowed by German products by the early-twentieth century.

Sheffield's failings can be directly contrasted with the success of their hated rivals, the Germans, particularly in cutlery manufacture. The German industry had a greater variety of goods to sell in the US market and its factories and workshops produced both high grade goods and those at the cheaper end of the scale. Though Sheffielders had nothing but contempt for 'cheap German trash', as a Wostenholm agent put it succinctly, Germany's percentage share of American cutlery imports rose in the period 1884–1914 as the English share steadily fell.[55] With their greater willingness to adapt to the American market the German manufacturers were better able to cope as the American marketing trends already apparent before 1914 accelerated after the First World War.

English Hardware in the USA in the Era of Mass Marketing, 1914–1930

The transition from the small shopkeeper toward the large-scale retailing enterprise in America commenced before 1900 but it was after that date, particularly after the First World War, that the most important developments occurred. The changes were due largely to a great increase in the intensity of competition, a more rapid rate of technological change and greater freedom of choice, the latter the result of the changing pattern of income and the higher standard of living. Marketing conditions were transformed above all as the mass retailers came into their own. The first decade of the twentieth century in the USA saw the department stores make their greatest impact; the second, mail-order houses; and the third, chain stores.

In the face of these immense changes however Sheffield's approach to the American market remained largely uncoordinated and poorly organised, hindered by an absence of official intelligence and the lack of a centralised marketing organisation. Even in the 1920s commercial intelligence through the British Consular Service in the USA was weak. Consuls lamented the failure to provide a commercial reference library with up-to-date business files in any of the consulates.[56] In 1920 the British government toyed with the idea of increasing the number of consuls and of giving them a wide discretion in visiting their district, but it was abandoned because of the cost. Instead a more informal system of commercial correspondents composed of men willing to act either formally or informally as intelligence scouts was to be employed.[57] The net effect, it was felt, was undermanning. The San Francisco consul (whose area included California, Nevada, Utah and Arizona), despite the help of two subordinates in San Diego and Douglas, had no regular official throughout the whole of Nevada and Utah.[58] Nor did the problem occur only in the West. A consul travelling through Cincinnati, Ohio was surprised to find that there was no official at such an important centre, despite the openings for the sale of Sheffield tool steel.[59]

This probably did not bother Sheffield traders over-much. In evidence submitted to the Committee on Industry and Trade 1926–7, the Sheffield Chamber of Commerce paid tribute to the useful work done by the Department of Overseas Trade, knowing full well that for the most part they relied upon their own individual and permanent representatives in foreign markets.[60] This was as true in the 1920s as it was in the mid-nineteenth century. Yet as one official report pointed out,[61] many products of the iron and steel industry had by then attained such uniformity that little or no variation was to be found from a standard common to all manufacturers. Price therefore and not individual quality had become the dominant commercial factor. Thus the report recommended the setting up of an Export Sales Association. The point was stressed again by the National Federation of Iron and Steel Manufacturers in 1919 and by the Iron and Steel Trades Confederation before the Committee on Industry and Trade.[62] Clearly what was envisaged was an organisation on the lines of the United States Products Co. Ltd, which was one of the main selling agencies for American producers in the UK. The main obstacle was how to achieve it, especially in Sheffield where the problems appeared in their extreme form.

The Company of Cutlers might have provided a lead but after it had been stripped in the early-nineteenth century of its wide-ranging powers to control the industry it had largely contented itself with the domestic regulation (and occasional international defence) of trade marks and purely ceremonial functions. When questioned by the Committee on Industry and Trade the Sheffield steelmakers had to admit that little had been done to set up an alternative organisation. As one of them testified:

It seems to me it is emphatically an individualist trade, in the sense of being a trade which must be managed by individual enterprise and personal knowledge. I do not suppose there is any city in the country where there are so many small manufacturers as there are in Sheffield...and that has been in the past the strength of the Sheffield industry. How these things can all be co-ordinated and managed from any headquarters, I cannot imagine.[63]

Yet the attempt may have been worth making. Though a concerted selling effort may not have helped the producers of tool steel after 1918 (the technological and cost advantages of the Americans seem to have been too great), in hardware products, particularly cutlery, there is a suspicion that some kind of organisation, perhaps headed by leading Sheffield makers such as Wostenholms or Rodgers, would have benefited exports to the USA. It would, for example, have enabled resources to be pooled to pay for advertising and promotion.

As the Department of Overseas Trade emphasised, by the 1920s advertising had become an almost indispensable factor in selling goods in America. Yet because of the tariff and American competition British exporters were unable to compete individually in the exceedingly expensive business of advertising their products.[64] Furthermore buyers in America had become so used to attractive offers of 'service', to quick deliveries to conform with the existing 'hand-to-mouth' buying policy, to merchandising under the instalment plan, that the trouble involved in importing foreign goods was often considered scarcely worthwhile. In these conditions collective advertising may have helped. The Commercial Counseller in Washington remarked in his 1926 Report that the merits of Sheffield cutlery were not widely known in the USA, adding in 1927 that group advertising of Sheffield goods could scarcely fail to improve matters.[65]

The criticisms of Sheffield manufacturers were well-founded. In America's only cutlery journal, the *American Cutler*, Sheffield steel was in evidence in the early-twentieth century, with firms such as Firths and Wardlows trying to tempt the American cutlery manufacturers with their stainless and high quality steels; but significantly there were almost no advertisements by Wostenholms and Rodgers (who curiously never followed up the great success of their cutlery showroom). And this was not because the cutlers were devoting their attentions to publications with a wider circulation; a perusal of the more popular American periodicals in the 1920s, when it might be thought that the prospects for selling high quality English goods in the USA were so good, failed to reveal a single advertisement for Sheffield cutlery.[66] High quality Sheffield cutlery and plate were absent even from such journals as *Vogue*, although other British manufacturers such as Wedgwood were buying space. Instead advertisements from the American Oneida Community dominated the pages, frequently catering for the 'quality' silver-plate and cutlery market that in the past Sheffield had regarded as its own. Hardly surprising that one man told a Sheffield newspaper in 1922: 'Of one thing I am absolutely certain — our British manufacturers fail miserably to advertise the quality of their products.'[67]

Sheffield agents and travellers in the USA were certainly aware of American skill in advertising in this period. A representative of Wostenholms found out that what was selling best was:

> a range of rather novel polished stainless steel tang knives for kitchen use…The knives have a specially shaped wooden handle and are being put up in attractive boxes…There are about a dozen patterns in the line…Housewives are being persuaded by advertising to gradually collect the whole set.[68]

Sheffielders also paid tribute to American methods: 'The American retailer certainly knows how to display his goods to the best advantage, and it is a pity that their methods in this particular department cannot be taken up more extensively by the English retailer,' commented another member of Wostenholms.[69] But plans for adopting such techniques were only slowly formulated in Sheffield itself towards the end of the 1920s.[70]

Sheffield's reputation also meant nothing, as two Federation of British Industries' observers made clear in 1925, without a close study of the US market.[71] This involved not only studying the American market but also adapting products to the needs of the foreign consumer. Despite their uneven performance in the nineteenth century Sheffield manufacturers continued to modify their products into the 1920s. Wostenholms asked its American representative to find out about Remington's methods of manufacture: 'The Remington Bakelite knives…are a line we ought to very carefully consider going in for.'[72] In some cases it was only by imitating the

70

Americans that success could be achieved at all. This was even true in Canada. A Spear & Jackson director in Vancouver remarked: 'I suppose Rodgers know how well-known and popular their American namesake's brand is out here. The Am'n patterns are wanted.'[73] Spear & Jackson itself could only compete with the US sawmakers Simonds by carefully copying its designs. After talks with the lumbermen around Vancouver, Spear & Jackson secured a share of the trade but only on the understanding that it could deliver the desired article. The development of saw technology meant that there was a new man to please at the lumber camps – the filer. The Sheffield firm was warned: 'these men do nothing but file these saws and if there is anything at all they think is not quite right that ends the matter'.[74] Hence the Spear & Jackson man's reminder to the Sheffield factory (after a shipment of saws had departed from the regular patterns): 'SIMONDS SAWS MUST BE IMITATED EXACTLY, TO THE SMALLEST DETAIL.'[75]

For Sheffield to succeed in America it would also have to adapt to newer methods of distribution. As one of Wostenholms' New York agents remarked: 'Our national methods of distribution today through mail order houses and chain stores, with department stores, hardware, cutlery and other outlets for our lines, must be considered carefully.'[76] The policies and practices of these distributors had much in common with and often were directly derived from the wholesale jobber. Like the jobber their basic objective was to assure a high velocity of stock turn. Perhaps the most important of these in the twentieth century was the chain store which was becoming the standard instrument of mass retailing in the USA.

The Sheffield manufacturers cast worried glances at the low prices and high sales of the chains. To show what the Americans could do, in 1934 Spear & Jacksons' itinerant director sent home a set of Woolworths' hacksaws which sold at only 20 cents each, along with a complete hand saw which sold at the same price. 'I never saw a better made Handsaw H'dle or a better polished blade', he commented. Woolworths anticipated selling 200 000 dozen of the saws throughout its 2000 stores.[77]

The American chain stores and mail-order houses were better suited to tapping the demand from rural communities and an increasingly mobile and suburban population. Sheffield appears to have missed out on this. Personalised selling methods meant little in these conditions, and the fact that buyers were usually responsible for private branding and advertising of a product was also essentially alien to Sheffield practice.[78] Sheffield cutlery was also too costly to compete in traditional retail outlets. 'Only stores of the very highest class seem at all interested in our goods', complained a Wostenholm man and even then demand was limited. He noted after a visit to Wanamakers – 'the finest store I have even been in' – that although the store was well disposed to Wostenholms, 'our goods have a very slow sale'.[79]

'Both [in the US] and in Canada people seem to be calling for cheap goods', Wostenholms were informed.[80] But Sheffield hardware manufacturers steadfastly refused to listen and remained largely wedded to the production of an article which (they believed) was only bought once in a lifetime. Nowhere was this attitude more costly than in the development of the safety razor. Aided by one of the most successful advertising campaigns in history, which taught consumers that blades were expendable, the Americans led by King C. Gillette had established a world lead in razor manufacture by 1930.[81] US safety-razor production rose from virtually nothing in 1900 to over $24 million in 1920, with Gillette accounting for a major share of the output. By the 1920s the Boston firm had set up a world-wide marketing organisation with several European subsidiaries. Sheffield's role was reduced to that of mere supplier of razor steel and the Sheffield straight razor was henceforth consigned to the museum.

Generally Sheffield makers disdained to cater for this cheaper end of the market. The Germans continued to be more obliging. Wrote one of Wostenholms' agents in New York:

> There are very few people who are interested in English made cutlery, because of the developments that have taken place in this country during the last few years, which have resulted in the production of a better article and also because there is a cheap German product being imported which supplies another class of trade.[82]

The latter were the kind of blades flooding the market which were noticed by a British consul in Chicago in 1920, where sales were effected mainly by means of excellent samples and prompt deliveries.[83] The German reputation was enhanced by Boker's successful cutlery plant at Newark, New Jersey, which allowed them to avoid the tariff and avail themselves of the latest American technologies.[84] Though relative to the English proportion of US imports in cutlery, the amount of German cutlery was diminishing slightly after the high point before the First World War, the German product still predominated and was ostensibly the main target of the Fordney McCumber Tariff which in 1921 once more raised the duty on hardware products.

Since in the 1920s in the USA there was still 'an outlet for an attractive quantity of the higher-grade merchandize',[85] faced with the tariff and cheap medium quality American hardware the English city should perhaps have concentrated on the luxury market, drawing upon its reputation by advertising. Even in the 1930s the Sheffield trade mark still meant something to Americans. In 1934 a Spear & Jackson director referred to 'the magic name "Sheffield" which still has a good reputation amongst the American people'.[86] This led American manufacturers to adopt some shady practices by illegal branding, which provoked sardonic comments from Sheffield businessmen. A Sheffield cutler noticed in Montreal stainless steel table knives being retailed at 21 cents each by 'Glen Plate & Cutlery Co., Sheffield'. 'I wonder who they are?' he asked.[87] Others came across the same methods in saw retailing. 'The card has just the word "Sheffield" in big letters on the top above the saw; below the saw is "E. C. Atkins & Co., Sheffield Works, Indianapolis", as usual.'[88] Sheffield's indifference to advertising however was matched by the doggedness (which continues to this day) with which it defended itself against the fraudulent marking of goods. The Company of Cutlers in Hallamshire pursued expensive litigation with the US authorities in the 1920s when it attempted to prevent an 'unscrupulous' American firm from registering the word 'Sheffield' world-wide.[89] A special fund was instituted to deal with similar cases. Though such a policy is understandable it seems a pity that similar attention was not paid to more positive advertising. Widespread illegal branding, then as now, proved extremely difficult to combat; it continued in the USA into the 1930s and beyond, though by this time it was more a minor irritant than a major factor in the declining English trade.

By the 1920s, even though on occasions it was fondly believed otherwise,[90] Sheffield hardware manufacturers were floundering in the American market: indifferent advertising techniques coupled with an inability to provide Americans with the style of goods they demanded, and tariffs which forced Sheffield prices beyond the pocket of the average consumer, produced the logical result when trading conditions began to worsen. By 1930 Wostenholms had closed its New York agency after trading at a loss throughout the previous decade. Spear & Jackson hung on for a time in the 1930s, competing against the 'slaughtered prices' of American sawmakers, but the firm's directors admitted after reviewing the firm's New York agency's prospect in the early 1930s that the position was hopeless. These experiences were symptomatic of the almost total eclipse of Sheffield hardware in the US market during the 1930s.

Conclusion

The production of hardware was one of the great successes of the nineteenth-century American economy, which exemplified the much-discussed 'American System of Manufactures'. In sawmaking and file manufacture America moved from a position of almost total dependence to one of virtual self-sufficiency during the course of the nineteenth century. In cutlery progress was equally dramatic: by the 1930s *total foreign* exports of cutlery to the USA amounted to a mere 2 per cent of the American output. Sheffield products had been almost totally excluded from the American market by 1930, creating a spirit of defeatism amongst the city's leading manufacturers, one of whom believed:

> It is quite useless for us to travel in America today. I remember the time when we used to stream over there a dozen at a time, and there was plenty of business for us all, but today it is a waste of time to go to America to sell Sheffield goods.[91]

A number of social and economic factors contributed to America's astonishing achievements in these light steel trades. Of major importance was the distinctive character of the US market which gave American manufacturers great advantages. The susceptibility of the American market to standardised goods, the absence of craft traditions which facilitated the introduction of machinery, and the country's enormous resources which acted as a stimulus to innovation, provided the ideal conditions for American manufacturers to alter completely the design of many of Sheffield's traditional products. Underpinning the 'American System' was a marketing and distribution network which, within a generation, had transformed the older factoring system by all the instruments of modern mass retailing – department stores, chain stores, mail-order houses and advertising.

As early as 1850 the writing was already on the wall for Sheffield. The town's newspapers regularly commented on the need for mechanisation and the dire consequences that would result if Sheffield makers failed to adapt. 'Whatever [Sheffield's] customers *want* she must *make*, or towns *will* be found in Germany that will', predicted one correspondent in reference to the declining American trade.[92] But the obstacles that prevented England from following the American example were well known, too. Another commentator, having correctly identified Sheffield's competitive weaknesses and the need for far-reaching changes, ended with the words: *'With regret it must be confessed…that the jealous constitutions of trade unions make any approach to such a versatility of energies highly problematical.'*[93]

Once due allowance has been made for the less favourable English conditions how are we to assess Sheffield's performance in the USA? The nature of the American market increasingly presented the Sheffield cutlery and edge toolmakers with major sales problems. Despite the evidence that some firms were ready to adapt to American styles and advertising techniques this essay has shown that Sheffielders were all too often out of their depth in America in this period. Small-scale enterprise and individualist products and selling methods, which had proved so useful in opening up the US trade in the early-nineteenth century, were exactly the opposite of what was required later. Here there does seem to have been a failure on the part of the Sheffield makers, especially in comparison with their more amenable Swiss and German rivals, not only to modify the design of traditional products but also to tap the wealthier sections of the US community. Certainly the continued sale of German and Swiss cutlery in America shows that there was still a place, albeit a small one, for foreign products. In the 1920s, when one would have expected Sheffield makers to make the most of rising US prosperity, the city's cutlery and hardware manufacturers were either in retreat or dissipating their resources in attacking fraudulent trade mark use rather than in making the Sheffield name more widely known through advertising.[94] The American market was potentially one of the richest export markets for Sheffield tool manufacturers and the failure to exploit it fully – a failure which was to be repeated in the so-called 'neutral' colonial markets – was a major landmark in the subsequent decline of the Sheffield hardware industry.[95]

Notes

1. In the nineteenth century the term 'hardware' (as it still is) was extremely wide-ranging and could denote anything from buttons to agricultural implements. Here it refers to high grade steel and particularly its allied products, cutlery and edge tools.
2. The following figures have been culled from the US State Papers. To save space separate citations are not given here; the published figures are in the respective vols of the Treasury/Bureau of Statistics Commerce and Naviga-

tion Accounts. Full references can also be found in G. Tweedale, *Sheffield Steel and America: a century of commercial and technological interdependence* (Cambridge, 1987).

3. D. L. Burn, 'The Genesis of American Engineering Competition, 1850–1870', *Economic History*, 2 (1931), pp. 292–311. For the most recent discussions of the 'American System', see: O. Mayr and R. C. Post, eds, *Yankee Enterprise: the rise of the American System of Manufactures* (Washington, DC, 1981); D. Hounshell, *From the American System to Mass Production, 1800–1932: the development of manufacturing technology in the United States* (Baltimore, 1984).

4. In March 1877 the *British Trade Journal* published an article, 'Sheffield Industry and the American Trade' (repr. in *Bulletin of the American Iron and Steel Association*, 11 (21 and 28 March 1877), p. 82), in which several of the town's leading makers – Frederick Brittain, Mark Firth, George Wilson, William K. Peace, John Hobson and Samuel Osborn – many of whom had recently returned from the USA, summarised the causes of the decline of Sheffield's American trade, blaming: first and chiefly a prohibitive tariff; second the depression of trade; third the folly of manufacturers and workmen in not adapting themselves to the requirements of their customers; fourth the aversion of Sheffield workmen to the use of machinery; fifth the higher wages paid in Sheffield for labour; and sixth the presence of Sheffield skilled workmen in the States.

5. See E. Surrey Dane, *Peter Stubs and the Lancashire Hand Tool Industry* (Altrincham, 1973), pp. 132–57; S. R. H. Jones, 'The Country Trade and the Marketing and Distribution of Birmingham Hardware, 1750–1870', *Business History*, 16 (March 1984), pp. 24–42; E. Robinson, 'Boulton and Fothergill, 1762–1782, and the Birmingham Export of Hardware', *Univ. Birmingham Historical Journal*, 7 (1959–60), pp. 60–79; id., 'Eighteenth Century Commerce and Fashion: Matthew Boulton's Marketing Techniques', *Economic History Review*, 2nd ser., 16 (1963), pp. 39–60.

6. The debate over the alleged failings of English businessmen is explored in P. L. Payne, *British Entrepreneurship in the Nineteenth Century* (London, 1974).

7. A. Gatty, *Sheffield: past and present* (Sheffield, 1873), p. 197.

8. R. E. Leader, *Sheffield in the Eighteenth Century*, 2nd edn (Sheffield, 1905), p. 89. For a discussion of the activities of an early Sheffield merchant house, see B. A. Holderness, 'A Sheffield Commercial House in the mid-Eighteenth Century: Messrs Oborne and Gunning around 1760', *Business History*, 15 (1973), pp. 32–44.

9. For information on the growth and organisation of marketing in the Sheffield hardware trades, see J. Hunter, *Hallamshire*, rev. A. Gatty (Sheffield, 1869), p. 174; *Parliamentary Papers* (hereafter *PP*), 1812, III, Reports from Committees: Orders in Council, pp. 132, 145–52, 155. General background can also be found in N. S. Buck, *The Development of the Organisation of Anglo-American Trade, 1800–1850* (New Haven, 1925).

10. Hoe Papers, Butler Library, Columbia University, New York City. F. E.

Comparato deals with the Sanderson-Hoe connection in some detail in *Chronicles of Genius and Folly: R. Hoe and Company and the printing press as a service to democracy* (Culver City, Ca., 1979), pp. 111–29.

11. Marsh Bros correspondence in Sheffield City Library (SCL), especially in this instance SCL Marsh 14, 'Extracts of Letters from the United States 1833–40'. Some idea of the kind of goods Sheffield was offering at this time can be seen from a surviving trade catalogue. See J. Smith, *Explanation or Key, to the Various Manufactories of Sheffield, with Engravings of Each Article*, ed. J. S. Kebabien (Vermont, 1975).

12. The best general study of the Sheffield hardware trades remains G. I. H. Lloyd, *The Cutlery Trades* (London, 1913).

13. Apparently one of the factors which influenced the US ploughmaker John Deere in his decision to patronise Pittsburgh suppliers was that steel from Sheffield became heavily rusted during the Atlantic crossing. See N. M. Clark, *John Deere: he gave to the world the steel plow* (Moline, Ill., 1937), p. 42. Spear & Jackson mention a large consignment of garden tools returned to England by US Customs because they were not marked with the place of manufacture. Another store received the firm's goods by mistake. See SCL SJC 83, Coombe to S. & J., Pittsburgh, 4 July 1925. On goods damaged in a steamship collision, see SCL Wos R3, 'Letters to America, 1895–1896', letter to F. B. Gurney, New York, 14 February 1896.

14. SCL MD 1485, letter to Woodcock, New York, 18 November 1865.

15. Hoe Papers, 'Letter Book 15 December 1842–15 April 1846', Hoe to Sanderson, 13 November 1843 (Box 21).

16. See esp. Hoe Papers, 'Letter Book 25 February – 19 September 1850', letter to E. Pratt & Bros, Baltimore, 11 March 1850; letter to [?] 18 March 1850; letter to Albany customer, [?] March 1850.

17. MD 1485, Letters October/November 1864.

18. 'Tool Steel from a Salesman's Point of View', *Iron Age*, 91 (20 March 1913), pp. 706–8.

19. *Bulletin of the American Iron and Steel Association*, 12 (30 October 1878), p. 251.

20. S. Pollard, *Three Centuries of Sheffield Steel: the story of a family business* (Sheffield, 1954), p. 40; see also pp. 22–7, 35–40.

21. MD 1485, letter to New York, 11 December 1865.

22. Pollard, op. cit. p. 38. One cause of deficiencies in remittances was the extended credit that firms such as Marsh Bros felt obliged to give to Americans who sold the company's goods. To compete with other Sheffield houses in St Louis, one Marsh Bros agent noted that credit arrangements that extended up to a year were necessary. See SCL Marsh 248, letter J. Mollison to Marsh Bros, 4 June 1858.

23. J. Potter, 'Atlantic Economy, 1815–1860: the USA and the Industrial Revolution in Britain', in *Studies in the Industrial Revolution: essays presented to T. S. Ashton*, ed. L. S. Pressnell (London, 1960), pp. 236–80.

24. Z. Allen, *The Practical Tourist* (Providence, RI, 1832), I, pp. 288–9.

25. *RC Report of the Juries, Exhibition of 1851*, p. 10. Over ninety Sheffield firms exhibited at the Crystal Palace. For descriptions of the various displays, see *Illustrated Exhibitor*, No. 12 (23 August 1851); *Sheffield Independent* (5 April 1851), p. 8; (19 April 1851), pp. 2, 5; (10 May 1851), p. 2.
26. See G. Tweedale's Wostenholm entry, in D. J. Jeremy, ed., *Dictionary of Business Biography* (London, 1984–5), V. Wostenholm's perambulations were surpassed by Albert Vickers, who apparently undertook thirty-four journeys to America. But both of them were dwarfed by the seventy-three sea voyages of Arthur Balfour (Lord Riverdale) (ibid. I, pp. 121–4).
27. *Ironmonger*, 28 (2 September 1882), pp. 326–9, commenting on Albert A. Jowitt.
28. Connecticut Historical Society, Ms. 72190, 'The Collins Company Historical Memoranda, 1826–1871', compiled by Samuel W. Collins, 14 February 1868, fo. 195. The representative was probably Mark Firth, another frequent visitor to the USA.
29. Cambridge University Library, Vickers Papers, Lehmann Letters (602), Benzon to Frederick Lehmann, Boston, 14 September 1853. See also J. D. Scott, *Vickers: a history* (London, 1962), pp. 7–13.
30. C. P. Russell, *Firearms, Traps, and Tools of the Mountain Men* (New York, 1967), p. 191.
31. MD 1485, letter to New York, 19 April 1967.
32. ibid. 13 May 1867.
33. R. Abels, *Classic Bowie Knives* (New York, 1967); W. R. Williamson, *I*XL Means I Excel: A Short History of the Bowie Knife* (1974).
34. *Sheffield Times* (7 April 1849), p. 3. According to this source Sheffield scythe exports to the USA declined from $73 081 in 1835 to $29 823 in 1848. For an insight into American progress in hardware manufacture at this time, see N. Rosenberg, ed., *The American System of Manufactures* (Edinburgh, 1969).
35. Marsh 248, J. Mollison to Marsh Bros, New York, 22 January 1858.
36. See G. Porter and H. C. Livesay, *Merchants and Manufacturers: studies in the changing structure of nineteenth-century marketing* (Baltimore, 1971). See also W. H. Becker, 'American Wholesale Hardware Trade Associations, 1870–1900', *Business History Review* 45 (1971), pp. 179–200.
37. SCL Wos R 12, letter to Wostenholms, 1 June 1893.
38. ibid., letter 18 July 1893. The prices of American saws also fell swiftly after 1865. At Disston's Philadelphia works, probably the largest in the world by 1870, back saws fell in price from $11.54 per dozen in 1870, to $8.08 per dozen in 1888; over the same period 60 inch circular saws were reduced from $147.00 to $64.60 each. Information from a typescript history of the Disston works at the Eleutherian Mills Historical Library, Wilmington, Delaware.
39. *Ironmonger*, 37 (15 January 1887), pp. 88–9.
40. *Sheffield Independent* (17 June 1875), p. 5.
41. *Sheffield Times* (7 April 1849), p. 3; (21 April 1849), p. 6. See generally, B. Hindle, ed., *America's Wooden Age: aspects of early technology* (New York, 1975).

42. See, for example, *Ironmonger*, 17 (1 October 1875), p. 1214; 25 (21 May 1881), pp. 693–4.

43. American hardware products such as the axe were generally agreed to have been more scientifically designed with a greater regard for strength and lightness, compared to their clumsy European counterparts. See 'The Axe Trade in Australia. Position of Sheffield manufacturers', *Implement and Machinery Review*, 23 (2 February 1898), pp. 22443–4.

44. *Iron Age*, 14 (20 November 1879), p. 20.

45. SJC 79, Spear & Jackson director's business diary, 9 March 1905. Examining an American handsaw in Australia, the Spear & Jackson man admitted on 21 February 1905: 'the great thing about it is its finish which certainly beats anything I have yet seen'.

46. *Ironmonger*, 3 (31 May 1861), p. 148.

47. *PP*, 1867–8, XXX, Reports on the Paris Universal Exhibition, 1867. Pt 2, IV, p. 258.

48. *Sheffield Independent* (9 February 1867), p. 6. On the poor Sheffield presence at Paris, especially in the light trades, see *Sheffield Independent* (29 December 1866), p. 6; (14 January 1867), p. 3; (22 February 1867), p. 4.

49. *PP*, 1877, XXXVI, Reports on the Philadelphia International Exhibition, p. 120. Sheffield participation is also described in *Sheffield Independent*, 14 March 1876, p. 3; 17 March 1876, p. 4; 11 April 1876, p. 6.

50. *PP*, 1877, XXXIV, Reports, op. cit., 'Edge Tools, – etc.', pp. 153, 133.

51. 'We know very well, and all British manufacturers and merchants must also be aware of the fact, that the headway made by the American exporters is largely owing to the superior way in which their wares are sent out.' See *Ironmonger,* 22 (2 August 1879), pp. 173–4.

52. ibid 22 (6 September 1879), pp. 338–41.

53. SJC 79, letter, 30 June 1905.

54. J. J. Schroeder, Jr., ed., *1908 Sears Catalogue* (repr., Ill. 1971), p. 767. See also 1887 edition (New York, 1968), with an introduction by S. J. Perelman and R. Rovere.

55. Wos R3, letter from San Francisco agents, 21 January 1896. Total American cutlery imports were £296 000 in 1884–5, with the UK and Germany both accounting for 49 per cent of the total. By 1913–14, the figures were 19 and 67 per cent respectively, from a total of £282 000. See Committee on Industry and Trade, *Survey of Metal Industries* (1928), p. 271.

56. Public Record Office, FO 115/2578, Dispatch 8 January 1920.

57. FO 115/2581, Foreign Office Circular, Washington, 16 April 1920.

58. ibid., Reply to above, 9 June 1920.

59. ibid., Report from W. S. Paul, 23 July 1920.

60. Memo submitted to J. H. Doncaster, Committee on Industry and Trade, *Minutes of Evidence Taken before the Committee on Industry and Trade*, I, p. 315.

61. *PP*, 1918, XIII, Report of the Departmental Committee Appointed by the Board of Trade to Consider the Position of the Iron and Steel Trades After the

War. Cd. 9071, pp. 16–17. The same point is made by T. H. Burnham and G. O. Hoskins, *Iron and Steel in Britain, 1870–1930* (London, 1943), pp. 210–12.

62. See evidence of Arthur Pugh, Committee on Industry and Trade, *Minutes*, op. cit. I, p. 277.

63. ibid. p. 323.

64. Dept. of Overseas Trade, J. J. Broderick and A. J. Pack, *Report on Economic Conditions in the United States of America, 1927*, pp. 87–94.

65. Dept. of Overseas Trade, J. J. Broderick, *Report on the Finance, Industry and Commerce of the United States of America, 1926*, p. 26; 1927 Report, op. cit., p. 91.

66. Periodicals sampled included: *Colliers; Forbes; House and Garden; Independent; Ladies Home Journal; McCall's Magazine; Saturday Evening Post; Vogue; Woman's World.*

67. *Sheffield Daily Telegraph* (28 August 1922), p. 4 (letter). The leading British hardware journal had once written: 'advertising on a bold scale is looked upon as a *necessity* in the States, whereas not a few British firms believe they confer a favour on the journals if they advertise at all'. See *Ironmonger*, 29 (28 April 1883), pp. 587–8.

68. Wos 13a, letter to B. W. Nixon, Wostenholms, 27 March 1931.

69. ibid., letter to Colver from H. Bexfield, 17 March 1931.

70. 'Advertising Sheffield, the Chamber's Scheme', *Sheffield Chamber of Commerce Journal* (August 1927), pp. 6–7.

71. F. V. Willey and G. Locock, *Report on a Visit to the USA* (FBI, 1925).

72. Wos R13a, letter, 9 March 1931. Wostenholms was also interested in copying Remington's display case, Wos R12, letter F. Holroyd to A. S. Keeton, 13 April 1930.

73. SJC 86, 17 August 1934.

74. ibid., undated letter 1934.

75. ibid., letter, 24 May 1934.

76. Wos R12, letter from G. Walter Davis, 4 December 1931. The revolution in American distribution methods is well summarised in A. D. Chandler, 'The Visible Hand: the managerial revolution in American business' (Cambridge M.A., 1977).

77. SJC 88, letter, 4 October 1934. For comments on cheap cutlery sold through the chains, see F. B. Colver, Wos R13, letter, 31 March 1931.

78. The stores devoted particular attention to the promotion and display of hardware. See R. R. Williams, *The American Hardware Store: a manual of approved methods of arranging and displaying hardware* (New York, 1897).

79. Wos R13, Colver to Wostenholms, 3 March 1931. Added the Sheffielder: 'In 1930 Wanamaker's, Philadelphia, and New Y[ork] stores only had $500 worth of goods from us (£50 at Sheffield prices).'

80. Wos R13a, Colver to Boswell Son & Naylor, 26 February 1931.

81. See R. B. Adams, *King C. Gillette: the man and his wonderful shaving device* (Boston, 1978); ibid. (p. 85) quotes Gillette's memo to his board in 1912: '*The whole success of this business depends on advertising.*'

82. Wos R12, letter from Swedish Steel Mills, New York, to J. B. Thomas, 10 December 1931.
83. FO 115/2580, A. H. King, Chicago, 11 September 1920.
84. No Sheffield hardware manufacturer began production in the USA until 1935, when Spear & Jackson established a factory in Oregon. Wostenholms did however contemplate partnering an American firm in 1919, though nothing came of the negotiations (in Wos R8, R12). This contrasts with the Sheffield specialty steelmakers, who established several American subsidiaries in this period. See G. Tweedale, 'Transatlantic Specialty Steels: Sheffield high-grade steel firms and the USA, 1860-ca.1940', in G. Jones, ed., *British Multinationals: origins, management and performance* (London, 1986).
85. Letter (n. 82, above).
86. SJC 88, letter, 4 October 1934, Philadelphia.
87. SCL Wos R13a, letter to Boswell Naylor & Co., Sheffield, 26 February 1931.
88. SJC 86, letter, 4 October 1934. Ironically Sheffield cutlers themselves had once been adept at illegal branding, frequently copying London marks in the seventeenth century. See J. F. Hayward, *English Cutlery* (HMSO, 1957), pp. 9–11.
89. L. du Garde Peach, *The Company of Cutlers in Hallamshire in the County of York 1906–1956* (Sheffield, 1960), pp. 61–2. See *Extracts from the Records of the Company of Cutlers in Hallamshire in the Country of York* (Sheffield, 1972) where plate 55 reproduces a label used by a non-existent American firm (the Sheffield Cutlery Co.) in 1889 on boxes of cutlery offered for sale in Denmark.
90. Sheffield complacency was typified by the following statement in one of the city's promotional leaflets: 'When these American cutlers require the highest class pen-knives, hunting-knives and hand-forged table knives they send to Sheffield. They willingly pay heavy freight and import duties in order to obtain goods which they themselves cannot equal.' See *Sheffield Development Department, Town Hall, 1922, The Metal Industries of Sheffield* (1922), pp. 8–9.
91. Lord Riverdale, address to Sheffield Junior Chamber of Commerce, *Quality* (February 1935), p. 165.
92. *Sheffield Times* (30 June 1849), p. 2.
93. ibid. (7 April 1849), p. 3.
94. The same criticisms could be levelled at the Sheffield industry after the Second World War. For numerous references, see S. Pybus *et al.*, *Cutlery: a bibliography* (Sheffield, 1982).
95. The view presented here therefore differs from a recent interpretation, which suggests that 'the traditional picture of the British industrialist employing amateurish marketing techniques and outdated selling institutions is misleading'. See S. J. Nicholas, 'The Overseas Marketing Performance of British Industry, 1870–1914', *Economic History Review*, 37 (November 1984), pp. 489–506, 505.

On recent visits to America the author noticed that Swiss pocket-knives and German table cutlery are still on prominent display on the east coast. Some French cutlers, with the help of clever marketing, have also been doing well in the

USA recently. See 'Opinel: un success a double tranchant', *L'Enterprise*, 5 (October 1985), pp. 84–5. Meanwhile Sheffield goods have completely disappeared in America – the end result, it would appear, of the neglect of marketing.

4 Marketing high technology: educating physicians to use innovative medicines

Jonathan Liebenau

The peculiarities of marketing in the pharmaceutical industry have frequently been noted. The distanced relationship between producer and final consumer, the role of the physician as mediator and the actions of the State as price fixer or limit setter, complicate the relationship. The desire for quality at the expense of marginal costs and the willingness to take the advice of experts during times of illness have all been seen as constituting the unusual criteria for marketing medicines.[1] Historically this characteristic of drug marketing developed slowly, taking on its recent form only in the late-nineteenth century. Previously medicines had been marketed to the general public based on the understanding that common knowledge, or a 'commonplace book', would provide any necessary knowledge.[2] By the interwar years physicians found themselves reliant upon manufacturers for information about the products they were responsible for, and patients came to accept the increased distance from understanding.[3]

Introduction

The drug industry has been credited with two major innovations in marketing. One was the extensive use of newspaper advertisements to achieve national brand recognition.[4] The other was the use of 'detail men': company representatives with substantial technical knowledge who visited physicians in their offices to explain the contents, use and value of new products.[5] These two innovations developed into one of the most elaborate and expensive forms of marketing of any industry.[6]

The key to this growth in sophistication and parallel rise in costs was the increasingly technical character of new therapeutics and the consequent distance between the knowledge held by the company and necessary for the use of the drug, and the knowledge which every practitioner could be expected to have. As drug companies required increasingly technically advanced people for research and development, and as medical scientists were increasingly available for industrial employment during the interwar period, the use of new science became the central element of competition.[7]

The crucial period for drug companies in this respect was around the First World War. It was then that large numbers of new products emerged which required greater medical or chemical knowledge than physicians generally possessed. The development of such sophisticated products forced a role reversal within the medical community. Pharmaceutical suppliers moved from a position in which they had been the servants of physicians, supplying whatever materials the doctors might need, to one in which they were the leaders, guiding medics towards new products and pioneering the development of therapeutics. The evolution of this educative function within the industry and the market's consequent reliance upon producers are the main themes of this chapter.

The pharmaceutical industry has produced the majority of new medicines as well as imaginative science and considerable profits since the nineteenth century. As drug companies grew from apothecary shops to family firms and then to large corporations their relationship with the medical community also changed. Apothecaries held a tenuous place in the early-nineteenth-century medical world, despite providing important services to those members of the public who did not use physicians, and supplying those who did with medicines. Towards the end of the century drug makers distanced themselves from pharmacists and their informal practice of medicine. Reputable manufacturers who sought the professional market – 'ethical' pharmaceutical producers – also distinguished themselves from popular 'patent medicine' makers, although they hoped to reap profits from patent or proprietary medicines. The manner in which they distinguished themselves was by developing a reputation for quality. Adapting to developments in scientific medicine, by the 1890s many of the leading companies were projecting a new and avowedly scientific image: they began to employ medical men and to maintain laboratories for quality control, standardisation, and in some cases product development. These small laboratories gradually evolved into significant research and development facilities which by the First World War were supplying products to a medical world newly insistent on novel scientific therapies. (Plate 4.1)

The market for medicines has long been distinguished from other consumer goods. With physicians acting as intermediaries between producer and ultimate consumer the responsibility was spread widely between those making, selling, prescribing and buying drugs. Occasionally there were demands for a remedy for a particular disease but more generally manufactures offered what they had on hand. This allowed for a substantial amount of initiative on the part of the companies. They took it upon themselves not only to promote their products, but also to ensure that their market recognised and understood the significance of a new medicine. Drugs sellers turned to ingenious advertising before other manufacturers out of necessity. Operating in conditions of almost unlimited potential demand with products easy to produce on a large scale, the pressures to pioneer in marketing were strong.

The Basis: Changing Therapeutics

Drug companies began scientific research for a variety of reasons. A few proprietors

Plate 4.1 Burroughs Wellcome Co. home representatives at the 1896 British Medical Association meeting, Carlisle (Wellcome Institute Library).

showed some interest in providing the public with new cures. Most companies saw a need for standardisation, or in the United States and Germany were forced to standardise by government regulation, and therefore to employ a scientific and medical staff for the purpose. Many were primarily concerned with the spin-offs from having technically trained personnel, and pursued the advertising advantages that an association with a scientific image provided. In other cases the need for liaison with the medical and academic communities was particularly important, especially for those companies at the forefront of development and marketing.

The set of new approaches, techniques, teachings and interpretations embodied in scientific medicine promised to transform not only the pharmaceutical industry but also medical practice. That promise manifested itself in revised prescribing patterns. Since drugs provided the most effective means for physicians to exercise their new therapeutic function as scientifically advanced practitioners, the pharmaceutical companies became increasingly central to the medical community.

Drug use has always been associated to some extent with therapeutic theory. Up to recent times medicines were compounded and administered both by doctors and by pharmacists. Both patients and medical practitioners identified the immediate and dramatic reactions caused by most drugs as part of the cure. Competing in a crowded marketplace for patients, doctors needed to demonstrate the efficacy of their treatments, and the remedies they prescribed were designed to cause easily perceptible changes in the physical state of the patient. Coupled with the mutual faith which physicians and patients had in these treatments, drastic remedies served to satisfy the demands of patients for effective cures.

The basis of this faith was a coherent system of therapeutic theory.[8] Beneath it lay the notion that the body was in a constant dynamic relationship with its environment. Equilibrium was associated with health, imbalance with disease, and the purpose of therapeutics was to restore order. The body was seen as a system of intake and outgo, each part inextricably related to every other. Physicians and patients could see and judge excretions or appetite: these therefore seemed an obvious monitor of health. Therapy, as a result, concentrated on diet, excretion and perspiration as the aspects which could be controlled to produce a stable system.

If a person had a wound, for example, he or she might be treated with a salve locally, but the holistic implications for the body might well necessitate the administration of a stimulant in addition. Special medicines were also administered in periods of flux such as teething, puberty, marriage, accident or familial misfortune, or at changes of season, when a patient's body was thought to be more liable to lose its healthy equilibrium. Cathartics, for example, were given in the spring and autumn to help the body adjust to these cyclical changes.

Therapeutic practices changed markedly in the decades after the mid-nineteenth century. Former practices were not abandoned but they were used less routinely, and smaller, less powerful doses were administered. There was a shift in attitude from dispensing massive doses of basic medicines to the careful prescription of small quantities of specifically targeted commercial preparations. By the 1880s physicians were exercising increased precision in the use of drugs. The pharmacopoeia became an explicit standard-setter, drawing on information newly disseminated in the pharmaceutical associations, schools and journals.[9]

The Changing Industry

The 1890s were watershed years for the pharmaceutical industry because of changes in company structure and the availability of new science. In the United States corporate reorganisation was fostered by expanded opportunities for the exploitation of national markets. These were encouraged by the dynamic national economic between the 1880s and the First World War. Fundamental shifts in processes of production and distribution made possible by the availability of new sources of energy and by the increasing application of scientific knowledge to industrial technology, brought about the modern business enterprise.[10] In Britain the pressures of change took on a different form. The industry was characterised by a large number of small firms based on traditional business practices of importing and refining basic raw materials and packaging them for distribution to apothecaries. Family control persisted well into the middle of the twentieth century and arrangements were made to market novel German products through distribution contracts.[11]

In contrast the American drug industry expanded greatly in the decade from 1890. New forms of finance fuelled this growth, while large-scale manufacturing technologies and co-ordinating business networks made it practicable. The typical structure of pharmaceutical companies, as with other manufacturing firms, had consisted of direct family control over all aspects of production, marketing and sales. In the course of the decade this changed radically with the development of physical departmentalisation and managerial hierarchies.[12]

The H. K. Mulford Company, established in the early 1890s, was one firm organised from the beginning with an eye to efficient large-scale production. Henry Mulford, an imaginative pharmacist with a knack for advanced manufacturing techniques, invited a pharmacy college acquaintance, Milton Campbell, to organise the business aspects of the firm. Campbell co-ordinated the rate of production with distribution by controlling the purchasing, manufacturing, sales and shipping sections. Even while small, Mulford was structured to allow the addition of new components to its system. One of the first of these new components was the laboratory.[13]

The changes in company structure at places like Mulford were conveniently timed in the history of the industry. In the 1890s bacteriology was emerging from a long debate over the validity of the germ theory of disease. Though by 1890 over sixteen disease-causing agents of a bacterial type had been identified the therapeutic impact of these discoveries was minimal. Despite this bacteriology had considerable allure and came to be associated with the best of medical science. Medical schools which taught it were seen as progressive and enlightened, and practitioners began to look to the bacteriological laboratory for explanations of the cause and spread of disease and for new means of treatment.

For many companies in America and elsewhere adaptation to the new ideals of science meant in practice a greater standardisation of drugs. Then, as today, the best-selling medicines were for the relief of dyspepsia, headache, sore throat, constipation, cough and anaemia. Most large firms also sold popular tonics, antipyretics, antiseptics and even aphrodisiacs. Mulford offered a remedy for colds which contained small quantities of some of the most common harsh agents: strychnine, morphine, quinine and arsenous acid.[14] The touchstone for the producers of such products was the latest pharmacopoeia. During this period the challenge was to set standards above those of the most recent edition and thereby to appear all the more scientific. Assaying, standardising and 'advanced' nomenclature were the main areas of interest and the easiest ways for these companies to compete along scientific lines. Statements like the following, issued by Parke, Davis, were echoed by many firms.

> The United States Pharmacopoeia has omitted to provide for a scientific standard in the determination of the strength of the official fluid extracts... Indeed, as an extra precaution over and above the requirements of the USP, we test all crude drugs by assaying wherever practicable.[15]

A new form of competition, then, was developed, based on one-upmanship in offering a greater number of routine laboratory procedures. These were explicitly compared with the pharmacopoeia standards, as with the advertisement quoted above, or implicitly directed at major competitors.

The British firm most like Mulford in ambitions was the Burroughs Wellcome Co. Wellcome had been formed by two Americans who combined a formal pharmacy training and interest in pharmaceutical science of the German style with novel marketing ideas which they believed would be successful in Britain.[16] (Plate 4.2)

Selling Science

The character of this effort to develop new products while addressing the now scientifically self-conscious practitioner changed with the invention of a cure for diphtheria. Diphtheria antitoxin was based on novel notions about the ability of healthy blood to produce serums which counter specific organisms. In 1894, after five years of painstaking work in Berlin, Frankfurt and Paris, a clinically effective antitoxin was announced. The antitoxins and related biologically-produced medicines (in contrast to traditional extracted or compounded drugs) forced the transformation of the medical industry.[17]

The procedure for making antitoxin was to inject a horse with progressively greater amounts of toxin cultured from the Klebs-Loeffler bacillus, the diphtheria bacterium, and allow the immune bodies within the horse's blood to produce antitoxins. How exactly this process worked was not well understood, but it was seen to be effective. The horse was then bled, the serum separated out and prepared, through a series of refining steps, for clinical use. A trained scientific staff was henceforth needed to supervise and adjust the careful bacteriological and immunological processes involved in producing serums. Mulford hired a staff whose experiences had been in bacteriology, pathology, public health and veterinary medicine. The stature of this laboratory staff was emphasised in advertising: 'The Biological Laboratory... is thoroughly equipped for original research and the preparation of the various biological products.' Workers and consultants to the laboratory were listed, complete with degrees and academic and hospital affiliations.[18]

Tetanus antitoxin, which had been developed in Germany along with diphtheria antitoxin, was the second biological medicine produced. The feeling at Mulford was that 'all disease would soon be conquered by anti-toxins':

It seemed so easy. All that need be done was to grow the germs in quantities, filter off the toxin, inject it into horses in increasing quantities until the antitoxin was good and strong, draw off some of the horse's blood, let it clot, inject the serum into a human patient and he was safe.[19]

The laboratory staff tried this straightforward technique on almost all known diseases. During the first year Mulford sold around 40 000 doses of antitoxin and was building a major advertising campaign around favourable reports from physicians and public health departments.[20] But there remained widespread resistance to using it. The most significant problem was that created by the difference between serum

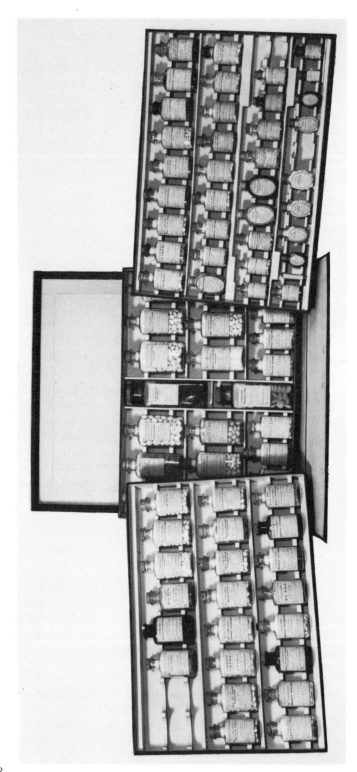

Plate 4.2 Drugs sample case c.1911 (Wellcome Institute Library).

therapy and all other known therapeutic methods.[21] For most practitioners the conceptual change seemed impossible to grasp.

The crucial step in popularising diphtheria antitoxin and other biologicals was the education of potential users. Antitoxin had not only to be portrayed as an effective cure statistically and epidemiologically but also had to be seen as a benevolent therapy, easy to use and comprehensible to the average physician. At Mulford great effort was made to 'place in the hands of physicians and pharmacists ...scientific information concerning [new drugs] just as soon as sufficient data were published by medical scientists'.[22] This was part of 'an educational propaganda in which booklets, pamphlets, stock-lectures, lantern slides and moving pictures were employed, all of such a scientific character that universities and boards of health freely used them for educational purposes'.[23] In other companies too this new notion of an educational propaganda held sway. Somewhat later in Britain at the Wellcome Co. similar pamphlets were produced, and staff from the newly formed Wellcome Physiological Research Laboratories were encouraged to prepare appropriately worded research papers.[24]

Although direct contact with persuasive salesmen was the best means of imparting such information pamphlets were the most common method. The style of publications changed over the years, remaining 'serious' and 'scientific' in appearance but variously taking the form of sales leaflets, general information pamphlets, scientific reports (either reprinted from a journal or mimicking scholarly form), or even the style of review articles, summarising the literature and debate over a therapy. Their content varied far less. Generally the drug would be introduced first, rather than the company, which was sometimes identified on the title page only as the pamphlet's publisher. A discussion of the therapy would follow. Explicit instructions would be given for dosage, administration and follow-through, with careful distinctions made for differing forms of the illness. Early pamphlets placed these instructions within the context of basic bacteriology and immunology, explaining the relationship between bacteria and toxin and the neutralising effect of antitoxin. For diphtheria antitoxin, Mulford and Parke, Davis presented their new selection by means of a description, with photographs of how the product was made.[25]

A favourite selling device was to advertise the epidemiology of diphtheria with the statistical effect of antitoxin. This was presented in one early pamphlet by quoting the mortality rates from some unspecified place: deaths ranged from 34.8 per cent to 62.5 per cent without antitoxin, but from 4.6 per cent to 17.64 per cent with the drug. Later pamphlets showed full epidemiological charts. An American advertisement from 1905, for example, showed the mortality rate for diphtheria from 1893 to 1904 for Baltimore, Newark, New York, Phialdelphia and Rochester (NY) with impressive reductions following the use of antitoxin after 1895.[26]

Another advertising technique was to provide the reader with reusable information. Some price lists contained 'A Condensed Glossary of Biological Terms' or a guide to common diseases and frequently-used remedies. One pamphlet offered eight colour plates of bacilli charts, as an aid to identification. Others had extensive scholarly bibliographies, diagnostic charts or summaries which might be useful in preparing lectures.[27] In 1916, for example, Mulford offered a wall chart showing the official changes in the ninth revision of the *US Pharmacopoeia*. The message was not left to the dispenser's imagination:

NOTE: Mulford Pharmaceutical and Biological Products conform to the Standards of the New Pharmacopoeia and in many cases Conform to Standards which are Considerably More Stringent than those of the USP IX. The Mulford Label is a Guarantee of Purity, Accuracy and Reliability.[28]

Mulford salesmen were trained to present scientific information in great detail. This they were able to do at a variety of venues including trade shows and exhibitions. For more specially targeted audiences they were aided in their presentations by collections of photographs and a series of lantern slides illustrating the diagnosis of diphtheria and tetanus, Mulford's method of producing antitoxin, and the different packages available. This method of direct education reached a peak after the war with the opening of the Mulford School of Bacteriology and Immunology. Intended primarily for company employees, the lectures were open to local physicians who wished to attend at no cost. Twenty-five Mulford workers were paid full salaries while attending classes. A former Professor of Bacteriology at Cornell University offered three consecutive courses in 1919. The first, on general bacteriology, included instruction in sterilisation, culture techniques, and microscopy. This was followed by an advanced course covering pathogenic organisms, prophylactic action, and therapeutic use of biological products. The course was attended primarily by the sales staff of the company, the material being too elementary for trained scientific workers.[29]

In 1918 a new service was discussed at Mulford's executive meeting concerning the 'desirability of our quietly interesting our leading distributors in making arrangements to do laboratory work for physicians, such as making diagnostic tests, differentiating types of infection etc.'. This service had two business purposes, the first was to make better use of the staff and extensive laboratories possessed by the company. In addition, 'any druggist who shows the proper activity and knowledge in this direction will naturally secure the bulk of the biological business in his entire community'. Diagnostic services opened a large area for the company with little extra effort. Samples were collected in pharmacies and sent through the mail or by company representatives. At the firm experimental laboratories could easily be used for routine testing and within a few years this inexpensive service was available for the diagnosis of a dozen infectious diseases, along with general services such as urinalysis. A 'complete hay fever service' was offered to complement Mulford's extensive line of pollen extracts. It was then hoped that therapies could be supplied to the physicians who sent specimens to be tested. Such services benefited the medical community as well as the company, and strengthened the ties between them.[30]

One of the most conspicuous means companies used to enhance their connections with the medical community was through the publication of promotional journals. Parke, Davis launched a variety of occasional magazines aimed at their different markets: the *Druggist's Bulletin* for pharmacists, *Therapeutic Notes* for physicians, and 'Working Bulletins' for those interested in technical details.[31] Mulford and others began publishing their journals shortly before the First World War. Mulford expanded from occasional publications and their own scholarly 'Bulletins', and produced a quarterly, the *Mulford Digest*. Edited in a separate town office by a physician, the *Digest* assumed the style of a mainstream medical journal. It had a board of editors, all respectable medical scientists, and its layout, print and binding was much like the *Medical Record*, a journal of impeccable standing. With a sub-title announcing that it was 'Devoted Particularly to Serum-Therapy, Bacterin-Therapy, Vaccine-Therapy, Immunization, and Drug Standardization' it published a pot-pourri of laboratory and clinical reports, reprints from textbooks and other journals and long explanatory product advertisements.[32]

In Britain the Evans Co. similarly established their journal, simply titled the *Evans' Journal: medicine, pharmacy, therapy, bacteriology*, and ran technical articles about recent developments, and background on matters such as 'The principles of vaccine therapy', and on standardisation. Beginning in 1912, well after Parke, Davis's innovation, the journal continued through the war irregularly but maintained its high quality, ensuring that attention would be given to the advertising it contained.[33]

British Developments

In Britain the character of marketing followed a somewhat different pattern. The 'detail man' was introduced by Henry Wellcome, an American who had gone to Britain as the representative of the Philadelphia-based Wyeth Bros before establishing his London-based company with an American partner, Silas Burroughs. Both had been trained as pharmacists in Philadelphia and went to Britain first in 1875. Impressed by the market opportunities, Wellcome gave up the Wyeth agency and concentrated on building his own business.[34] The use of trained pharmacists and occasionally physicians as travelling representatives was an early innovation he used. Wellcome's achievements in changing the practice of drug marketing were preceded by patent medicine sellers such as Beecham and Holloway.

Thomas Holloway accumulated great wealth from his patent medicines and exemplified the successful drug seller. As a popular model in his own age, his story shows much about the transition from huxtering 'medicine men' to the more sedate and profitable, even if not more honourable drugs merchant. His tactic was to sell simple remedies, ploughing back the largest part of his income into newspaper advertising. Holloway's entry into the patent medicine field was well timed because it was a period of increasing interest in self-medication, using preparations less harsh than those prescribed by physicians, but still available in shops.[35] By exploiting an advertising style already widespread among patent medicine makers, and by employing a network of foreign agents, Holloway was able to expand his efforts to colonial and native overseas markets. He spent all he could on placard advertisements and to gain a wider market he is said to have visited the docks daily to offer samples to the captains of vessels and passengers sailing to all parts of the world.[36]

His success grew as he increased his investment in printed advertisements which rose from £5000 in 1842 to £10 000 in 1845, £20 000 in 1851 and £50 000 in 1883.[37] This increased expenditure, along with his strategy for international marketing, was boosted by a policy of using foreign language package labels and directions in Chinese, Turkish, Armenian, Arabic, and many of the dialects of India, among other languages. Advertisements were also placed by agents in newspapers in all parts of the world.[38]

Holloway represented his medicine as both solidly British – and thereby reliable – and exotic, with occult healing powers gleaned from both far reaches of the British Empire and distant frontiers of medical knowledge. His mastery of what was already a well-established genre of advertising among patent medicine sellers was always a keystone of his success. He adroitly played upon the fears, hopes, vanity, and sense of social place of the middle and working classes by conveying the message that users of Holloway's pills were enlightened people. His advertisements emphasised the imperial and international character of his clientele and the mysterious origins of his uniquely efficacious concoctions. One advertisement combined the images of Britannia, Queen Victoria, a sailor and a guardsman, surrounded by a Red Indian, a Zulu, a turbaned Oriental, and veiled Muslim ladies along with traditionally-dressed Chinese women.[39] Holloway did not use detail men, relying on his personal charisma and advertising, but he did appeal to the general sense that medical science of occult character would help.

The difference in attitude between American detail men and those British pioneers which the Wellcome Co. used is explicit in the proceedings of the 'Convention of Home Representatives, 1907'.[40] Numerous light talks were presented on topics as concrete as 'Obstacles met with in medical propagatory work and the best means of overcoming them', and as abstract as a technical review of the leading work in medical therapy. Candid discussions revealed salesmen's attitudes, and their awareness of shortcomings. On the need for quality printed material to leave with physicians there was general agreement. Their failing was contrasted with 'continental and American firms [who] are able to publish as advertisements signed medical reports, sometimes from well-known men'.[41] These were regarded by the Wellcome sales staff as of first-class quality, unlike their own leaflets which were acknowledged to be 'extremely meagre and mean in appearance'.[42]

Other problems were recited, often in contrast to American practices. The telephone was under-used as a tool for selling and marketing.[43] Delayed orders, sometimes accompanied by tactless letters, were embarrassing to detail men, especially as they usually had sympathies with the ordering physicians or pharmacists against the packaging department.[44] Problems of packaging resulting in broken shipments and of Wellcome's unusual policy of refusing to exchange outdated medicines were much commented upon.[45] Price sensitivity, while playing a minor role generally, was commented upon for some products, and general financial terms of trade were more often mentioned.[46] Standardisation was recognised as a concern for the future, especially considering the importance of German and American law, and the apparent imminence of British legal standards.[47]

The problems associated with new products about which physicians and chemists might be unfamiliar arose continually. Two reasons were cited: the general ignorance of physicians ('the average medical man does not know sufficient pharmacy even of the crudest kind')[48] and the problem that 'chemists are not educated [about new serums, vaccines and so on] and want to know all we can tell them on the subject'.[49] Generally there was some disdain for physicians who as a rule:

> think a very great deal of their knowledge, and generally the less they know the more they think of it... it is not always policy to let him know that you know more than he knows. It annoys him: it must be put in such a way as to make it appear that he knows a great deal.[50]

The need for salesmen to sound expert was frequently repeated. These characteristics of the drug trade were of most interest to convention participants, but more universal aspects of marketing continued to play a role.[51] The value of promoting special push lists was particularly emphasised.[52] Familiarity and sincerity were stressed in one proposed credo:

> know your product
> study your man
> speak with the power of conviction.[53]

Wellcome's self-consciousness about marketing is apparent also in their willingness to establish foreign selling agencies. Already before the First World War there were offices in South Africa (1902), Italy (1905), Canada and the USA (1906), China (1908), Argentina (1910) and India (1912). In this way as much as their attitude toward preparing representatives, Wellcome contrasts dramatically with most domestic competitors.

The Whiffen Co. was typical of many British producers, concentrating on simple refining and repackaging. Thomas Whiffen established his manufacturing pharmacy in Battersea, south London in 1854. After acquiring some older drug businesses, his company gained a reputation for quality standard products such as medicinal oils, alkaloids and minerals. Their domestic markets were largely based on supplying chemist's shops and on acting as agent for various German manufacturers who sold them exclusive rights to large territories.[54] The ascendancy of the German fine chemicals industry changed the character of business substantially. Based on the strength of the dye industry and the expansion of Germany's economic sphere of influence, German companies began to compete on a variety of fronts.[55] To organise that competition German chemical makers began to use marketing agreements among themselves and soon to include foreign concerns. Whiffen was at the centre of many such arrangements. By 1910 these included agreements in iodine (1887), camphor and salicine (1894), bormine (1897), strychnine (1907), caffeine (1908) and codeine (1909).[56]

One example of the balance between Whiffen's typical marketing practice and their dependence upon German sources is evident in the case of the disinfectant Lysoform. A relatively simple combination of alcohol and essential oils, Lysoform was easily reproduced in their London plant. Following the formula published in Germany, the business began in 1906 under the British Lysoform Company Ltd, formed initially in Berlin and London.[57] The intention was to work in close co-operation with Whiffen and other British fine chemical merchants, but this plan soon ran into trouble. Of the initial capital offered of £36 000, only £29 000 was issued by the end of the first year. Most of the capital assets, £24 770 worth, was attributed to patents and trade marks, very little was invested initially in machinery and plant (£186 minus £121 in depreciation = £65).[58] By 1907 the Lysoform Company had limited its operation to that of licensing agent and engaged another small chemicals firm to manufacture crude Lysoform. With Whiffen acting as principal distributor this arrangement worked reasonably well in business terms. It did after all fit in with the other lines of products that they dealt in. Technical problems continued to plague the operation however. While the legal and commerical relations from Berlin through the Lysoform Co. and the London agents worked well, there were persistent problems in maintaining product standards.[59]

In addition to acting as British agent for German products Whiffen controlled a number of foreign selling agents, but continued in the main to manufacture and process raw materials in London. Whiffen in other ways exemplified the marketing behaviour of a number of the mainstay British fine chemicals firms during the fifty years after 1880. Successful as they were in maintaining their small businesses and a turnover of basic products, and given few incentives to grow, firms such as Howards, Evans, Morsons, Bells, even Allan & Hanbury's, did relatively little to extend their markets.[60] All were small companies depending on family management and traditional distribution networks through pharmacies. None expanded dramatically until late in the interwar period.

The trend towards more international trade accelerated after the First World War. Wellcome consolidated their foreign agencies in 1924 and Whiffen established selling agencies in Belgium and Spain (1919), and Egypt (1923). These agencies did not encourage the use of detail men, and selling in general was haphazard for Whiffen, where it deviated from the routine of domestic distribution and supplying foreign agents. Detail men were only first employed in 1930 when they found a man 'competent to interview doctors, hospital authorities'.[61]

Taking advantage of the temporary weakness of German companies, British and American manufacturers successfully encroached on new markets. At the same time there was a rise in the specialisation of product areas both domestically and internationally. Perhaps the experience of F. C. Merrington exemplifies the ambitions of drugs salesmen of that period. Previously a detail man for Burroughs, Wellcome & Co., he approached several lesser firms and put together a portfolio to include the Netherlands agencies of May & Baker, Shouthall Bros & Barclay, The Distillers Co. (malt extract only), The Washington Chemical Co., Smith & Co., Leslie's Plasters, and a few others. This experience turned out badly. Unused to British products and unwilling to help Merrington to construct a marketing network, the Dutch business made him little money.[62] One of the few activities which did occupy the marketing people was shows and exhibitions. Self-justifying and forming a closed sort of competition among regular exhibitors, such shows occupied the energies and drained the marketing budget of many firms. Their impact, especially on retailers not to mention final consumers, must have been small, and they were of doubtful value for increasing actual sales. Merrington, in his *Reminiscences of an Agent* for May & Baker, described the dubious value of such shows:

> In 1928, much to my surprise, I received advice from Battersea that space had been booked at a so-called British Trade Exhibition to be held in Melbourne. This was contrary to my wishes but space having been booked I had no alternative but to go ahead and make the necessary arrangements. Incorrectly described as a trade exhibition it was, in fact, an ordinary exhibition open to the public. In spite of the fact that I succeeded in making quite an attractive display in blue and gold, this exhibition, costing as it did well over £300 excluding the booking fee, was quite worthless from a business point of view. Apart from the expense, it wasted quite a lot of my time which could have been utilised to far better advantage. Pharmaceutical chemicals, packed in bottles and cartons are not calculated to interest members of the public. Except for an order... from a local chemist who put up a proprietary line, no business whatsoever resulted from this exhibition.[63]

Even by the late twenties, then, there was still significant confusion about how to reach the best markets most efficiently. With the increasing complexity of the business in both Britain and America, new ways of conceptualising the market needed to be institutionalised.

By the first decades of the twentieth century many pharmaceutical firms had become science-based, not merely associated in a superficial way with science. Many of their products emerged from the laboratory, and they conducted their advertising campaigns in scientific terms. Their disputes were necessarily waged on a new level, carried on in a language that laymen could not ordinarily follow. They would, for example, call into question the laboratory facilities or the method of production of a competitor's wares.

Growing Sophistication

During the interwar period in both the United States and Britain a wide range of scientific qualities, such as specific effect and level of toxicity, came to be associated with new drugs and were used in their promotion by the leading companies. A range of acceptable terminology was implicitly established. Drugs could be described, for example, as having been 'tested' or 'standardised'. Advertisements placed in the medical press and on pamphlets directed at physicians more often cited technical literature, a practice extended to include a wide range of English, French and German works. While the producers of biologicals were the first routinely to use extensive technical citations in advertisements for their medicines, the practice soon spread to other sectors.

This period saw also new involvement by governments in the pharmaceutical industry, in America in the form of the 1902 and 1906 Acts regulating drug production and in Germany with similar regulation.[64] There was a lack of concern in Britain for anything other than narcotics until the international trade conventions governing the export of biological products required standardisation supervised by the government.[65] American companies had fought State intervention in the shape of the public health boards' production of antitoxins, but many approved other kinds of government involvement.[66] In particular the larger, more scientifically advanced companies welcomed regulation because it gave legal definition to the substance of their commercial disputes: it defined the level of scientific equipment and expertise that any manufacturer must have.[67] The staffs of government regulatory bodies in Washington came to know the leading companies well. Standards were often set by assessing the abilities of the leading producers to maintain a certain level of purity or concentration or follow a particular laboratory procedure. The head of the United States Public Health Service laboratory visited the Mulford Co. frequently and used its laboratory methods both to check other producers' antitoxins and vaccines and to help set guidelines for concentration and toxicity for the industry as a whole. He worked for the Public Health Service until he was induced to join Mulford as head of their new plant and director of biologicals productions.[68]

The effects on marketing of regulation were widespread. Leading manufacturers saw their incentives to set criteria which could not easily be met by competitors. The companies insisted on a high standard of purity that could not be met by small operations. They could also rely upon the support of the medical community to testify to the efficacy of their scientifically advanced medicines. Even though Mulford and other manufacturers could not hope to take over from patent medicine makers completely, they did gain in prestige as champions of scientific therapeutics by vilifying the so-called quacks.[69]

With drug makers expanding into ever more highly theoretical areas like chemotherapeutics, physicians increasingly relied on them to provide information. The educational function which a growing number of companies assumed before and during the First World War became the acceptable and expected function of drug makers during the 1920s. Although physicians began to look more critically at the information they were receiving, they were also resigned to the fact that only scientists within companies and physicians who had conducted clinical trials for manufacturers had full information about a new product. Within a few months after the introduction of a drug medical journals might begin to have independent results to publish, but this was not always the case and the results were often far less complete or conclusive than company-provided information.

Whatever the bewildering range of functions early company scientists actually performed, in every case their presence was recognised to be a distinction for the firm. It was a sign that they were manufacturing new and unusual products, medicines which required scientists for their manufacture and, presumably, comprehension. It was not far from this company role to the development of a broader image which leaders in the pharmaceutical industry adopted: the image of high technology companies. And what this self-styled élite among manufacturers produced and sold was not simply a range of pharmacy products, but the very image of advanced medical science itself.

Conclusion

We have seen the evolution of an established manufacturing sector into a high technology industry, and its adaptation of a scientific image which was most useful for marketing its products. The question of the control of information about drugs continues to plague the medical world and its regulators. Recent studies in Britain and the United States have shed some light on the continuing role of manufacturers as sources of information. Company representatives still supply most information about the existence and cost of drugs, and whereas scholarly periodicals may be of greater influence and regarded as more reliable sources about the efficacy of new medicines, they are clearly less accessible. (Tables 4.1, 4.2)

Through the systematic use of trained representatives, the detail men, drug companies continue to maintain close personal contact with physicians. They frequently give doctors gifts and 'reminder items'. In the US they gave away almost two hundred small gifts per doctor in 1973, just to establish a relationship and solidify the contact.[70] Marketing and sociological studies have shown that doctors seeing detail men tend to prescribe drugs from the detail men's companies after the visits. There seems to be a direct relationship between the number of visits from a particular company and the propensity to prescribe a particular drug, and this closely matches the company's advertising expenses.[71] Peter Temin concludes from this that:

> The prescribing habits of doctors are characterized by diversity. Doctors use many different drugs in the course of the year, including similar drugs from many different manufacturers and different drugs for the same diseases. They use far too many drugs to have accurate information on their comparative costs and benefits even if this information existed.[72]

Table 4.1 To show the sources of drug information for British general practioners, 1967

Source	%
Drug firm representatives	78
Articles in medical journals	76
Recommendations from consultants	71
MIMS	67
Refresher courses	61
Professional contacts with other doctors	59
Advertisements in medical journals	53
Drug firm literature	52
Local clinical meetings	51
Medindex	47
Drug firm meetings	37

Source: *Report of the Committee of Enquiry into the Relationship of the Pharmaceutical Industry with the National Health Service, 1965–1967* (Sainsbury Report, 1967), p. 131.

Table 4.2 Percentage of US doctors seeking drug cost information from various sources, 1973

Source	%
Detail men	54
Pharmacists	53
Peer colleagues	22
Periodical newsletters	17
Consultants	14
Other professional meetings	11
Compendia or formularies	10
Hospital staff meetings	10
Medical journal articles	9
FDA *Drug Bulletin*	7
Journal advertisements	6
Direct mail advertisements	6
Package inserts	5
Textbooks	5
Drug information centers	4

Source: P. Temin, *Taking Your Medicine* (Cambridge, Mass., 1980), p. 104, from a 1973 US Food and Drug Administration survey.

In both Britain and America, then, drug marketing has evolved from small-scale selling in competition with patent medicine makers to expensive and intensive marketing which reflects the sophistication of their products. While British manufacturers grew more slowly than the American during the interwar years, and in particular relied on traditional markets and more conservative production methods, with the increasing internationalisation of the industry, techniques for controlling information continued to concentrate in the industry.

Notes

1. There is no standard literature analysing the economics of the drug industry but among recent books, Peter Temin, *Taking Your Medicine; drug regulation in the United States* (Cambridge, Mass., 1980), is the most balanced account for America. Analyses from the political right can be found in W. D. Reekie and M. H. Weber, *Profits, Politics and Drugs* (London, 1979), pp. 120ff., and W. D. Reekie, *The Economics of the Pharmaceutical Industry* (London, 1975). A more realistic account of the marketing behaviour of drug manufacturers is to be found in M. Silverman and P. R. Lee, *Pills, Profits and Politics* (Berkeley, 1974), pp. 48ff., and M. Silverman, *The Drugging of the Americas* (Berkeley, 1976).

2. The colourful history of patent medicines and self medication is covered in such books as J. H. Young, *The Toadstool Millionaires: a social history of patent medicine in America before Federal Regulation* (Princeton, 1961), and

id., *The Medical Messiahs: a social history of health quackery in twentieth-century America* (Princeton, 1967); G. B. Risse, R. L. Numbers, and J. W. Leavitt, eds, *Medicine Without Doctors: home health care in American history* (New York, 1977). For Britain see S. Chapman, *Jessie Boot of Boots the Chemists* (London, 1973); and on Beechams see A. Francis, *A Guinea a Box: a biography*; and H. G. Lazell, *From Pills to Penicillin; the Beecham Story* (London, 1975).

3. J. M. Liebenau, *Medical Science and Medical Industry; the formation of the American Pharmaceutial Industry* (London, 1986).

4. See J. H. Young, *Toadstool Millionaires*, op. cit., and J. M. Liebenau, 'Thomas Holloway (1800–1883), Patent Medicine Manufacturer', in D. J. Jeremy and C. Shaw, eds, *Dictionary of Business Biography*, 3 (London, 1985), pp. 323–5.

5. W. H. Becker, 'The Wholesalers of Hardware and Drugs' (Johns Hopkins Ph.D., 1969); and P. Temin, op. cit. pp. 84ff.

6. See M. C. Smith, *Principles of Pharmaceutical Marketing* (Philadelphia, 1968).

7. J. Liebenau, 'Industrial R & D in Pharmaceutical Firms in the Early Twentieth Century', *Business History*, 26 (1984), pp. 329–46.

8. C. E. Rosenberg, 'The Therapeutic Revolution: medicine, meaning and social change in nineteenth-century America', in M. J. Vogel and C. E. Rosenberg, eds, *The Therapeutic Revolution: essays in the social history of American medicine* (Philadelphia, 1979), pp. 7–9. See also E. A. Ackerknecht, *Therapeutics from the Primitives to the Twentieth Century* (New York, 1973), pp. 99ff.

9. G. Sonnedecker, 'The Pharmacopeia and America — 150 Years in Service', *Pharmacy in History*, 12 (1970), pp. 156–69; and E. Kremers and G. Urdang, *The History of Pharmacy* (Madison, Wis., 1974).

10. A. D. Chandler, Jr., *The Visible Hand: the managerial revolution in American business* (Cambridge, Mass., 1977), p. 376.

11. Liebenau, 'Industrial R & D', op. cit.

12. ibid.

13. J. M. Liebenau, 'Medical Science and Medical Industry, 1890–1929' (Pennsylvania Ph.D., 1981), pp. 183–236; this section is based entirely on Mulford Co. records, Merck & Co. archives, West Point, Pa. 'Mulford Records'.

14. Mulford, *Price Lists*, 1893, 1900 (Mulford Records).

15. Parke, Davis & Co., *Organic Materia Medica* (Detroit, 1890), p. iv.

16. H. Turner, *Henry Wellcome: the man, his collection, and his legacy* (London, 1980); Wellcome Foundation, *One Hundred Years 1880–1980* (London, 1980).

17. H. J. Parish, *A History of Immunization* (Edinburgh, 1965), pp. 118–40; F. W. Andrews *et al.*, *Diphtheria, its Bacteriology, Pathology and Immunology* (London, 1923), pp. 126–9; H. Zeiss and R. Bieling, *Behring, Gestalt und Werk* (Berlin, 1941), pp. 54ff., 106, 248; E. Behring and S. Kitasato, 'Ueber das Zustandenkommen der Diphtherie-Immunitaet und der Tetanus-Immunitaet bei Thieren', *Deutsche medicinische Wochenschrift*, 16 (1890), p. 1113; E.

Roux, 'Sur les serums antitoxiques', *Congr. Internatl. d'hyg. et de Demog. c.r., 1894 Budapesth*, 2 (1896), p. 27.

18. *Keystone* (Mulford company newsletter), 1 (1 January 1919), p. 1.
19. ibid.
20. F. E. Stewart, 'Twenty Years, 1891–1911' (unpublished Ms., 1911, Mulford Records); id., 'Mulford growth shows great achievement', *Northwest Druggist*, 30 (1922), p. 14.
21. See the 1898 issue of the *Journal of the American Medical Association*, vol. 30, which published numerous articles debating the utility of antitoxins.
22. H. Mulford personal file, Mulford Records.
23. ibid.
24. W. Dowson, 'The Wellcome Physiological Research Laboratories Exhibit at the St Louis Exhibition, 1904' (London, 1904).
25. Parke, Davis & Co., *Price List*, 1895; Parke, Davis, 'A Souvenir of Parke, Davis and Company', circa 1915; Mulford, 'Diphtheria Antitoxic Serum' 'pamphlet', 1902.
26. Mulford, 'Diphtheria Antitoxic Serum' 'pamphlets', 1896, 1905.
27. Advertisements collection, Mulford records.
28. Mulford, Wall Chart, 1 September 1916, Mulford Records.
29. *Keystone*, 2 (8 September 1919), p. 3.
30. Mulford, 'The complete hay fever service' (advertisement), Mulford records.
31. *The Druggist's Bulletin*, 1 (Detroit, 1887). See also T. Mahoney, *The Merchants of Life: an account of the American pharmaceutical industry* (New York 1959), p. 71.
32. *Mulford Digest*, 1 (Philadelphia, 1912).
33. *Evans' Journal: medicine, pharmacy, therapy, bacteriology* (Liverpool, 1912).
34. Turner, *Wellcome*, op. cit.; Dowson, 'The Wellcome Physiological Research Laboratories', op. cit.; W. Haynes, *The American Chemical Industry*, VI (New York, 1954), pp. 60ff.; F. A. Coe, Jr., *Burroughs Wellcome Co., 1880–1980, Pioneer of Research* (New York, 1980).
35. J. M. Liebenau, 'Thomas Holloway (1800–1883), Patent Medicine Manufacturer', op. cit.; see also 'Patent Medicines', *Medical Circular* (1853).
36. D. E. Owen, *English Philanthropy 1660–1960* (Cambridge, Mass., 1964).
37. *Illustrated London News*, 5 January 1884; 20 June 1885; 3, 10 July 1886; *Pall Mall Gazette*, 28, 29 December 1883; 16, 19, 25 January 1884; Holloway Sanatorium, *The Story of Thomas Holloway (1800–1883)* (Glasgow, 1933).
38. Holloway Sanatorium, *Holloway*, op. cit.
39. ibid.
40. 'Convention of Home Representatives, 1907', typescript, Wellcome Archive.
41. ibid. pp. 6, 42.
42. ibid. p. 6.
43. ibid. p. 17.
44. ibid. p. 20.
45. ibid. pp. 27, 29ff.

46. ibid. p. 36; see also letters of 7, 8, 9, 10 March 1906, WF 'Business Correspondence 1895–1910' E2DW, Wellcome Archive.
47. 'Convention of Home Representatives, 1907', p. 98.
48. ibid. p. 9.
49. ibid. p. 42.
50. 'Convention of Home Representatives, 1908', p. 29.
51. ibid. pp. 15ff., 29; see also '1907', op. cit. p. 42.
52. ibid. pp. 13–35.
53. ibid. p. 23.
54. J. M. Liebenau, 'Thomas Whiffen (1819–1904) Fine Chemicals Manufacturer', in Jeremy and Shaw, op. cit., vol. 5.
55. Whiffen Records, B/WHF/25, 154, 157, 161, 162. Greater London Record Office; see also 'The Story of a visit to Whiffen's Fine Chemical Works', *Chemist and Druggist* (January 1948); and R. S. Low, *The End of a Chapter; the story of Whiffen & Sons Limited, fine chemical manufacturers* (London, 1973).
56. Whiffen Records, B/WHF/161, 162.
57. ibid. B/WHF/163.
58. ibid.; see letter of 13 November 1906.
59. ibid.
60. Liebenau, 'Industrial R & D', op. cit.
61. Whiffen Records, B/WHF.
62. F. C. Merrington, *Reminiscences of an Agent* (Dagenham, 1967).
63. ibid. pp. 24–5.
64. Temin, op. cit.
65. Liebenau, 'Industrial R & D', op. cit.
66. B. G. Rosenkrantz, *Public Health and the State* (Cambridge, Mass., 1972), pp. 123–6.
67. Liebenau, 'Medical Science', op. cit. pp. 352ff.
68. ibid. p. 396.
69. ibid. pp. 258ff.
70. Temin, op. cit. p. 115.
71. ibid. pp. 111ff.
72. ibid. pp. 118.

5 The British Engineers' Association and markets in China 1900–1930

R. P. T. Davenport-Hines

The purpose of this paper is threefold: to explore the origins of British manufacturers' export associations seeking to develop foreign markets; to evaluate the quality of both British institutional facilities available to exporters and of British business representatives abroad; and to place these factors within recent discussion of British entrepreneurial performance in overseas marketing.[1] For almost a century it has been customary to decry the arrangements made by industrialists and government to market British products in overseas markets. On one side the complaint has been that the Board of Trade was insular and antiquated in organisation, publishing reports on foreign markets which were too obscure and indigestible to be useful to busy practical men of business; that the Foreign Office's diplomats *en poste* were too idle, snobbish or ill-trained to help English businessmen seeking orders; and that generally Whitehall disdained helping exporters with the energy, ruthlessness, co-ordination and institutional sophistication that character-ised, say, the French or Germans. Alternatively it has been lamented that British industrialists seldom sent representatives to investigate foreign markets, or push products in them, relying instead on appointing local merchant houses to agencies in which little initiative was encouraged or shown. Such representatives that were despatched, moreover, are often said to have been personally unreliable, ignorant of the languages and customs of the countries they visited, equipped with literature in the English language alone, accepting quotations only in avoirdupois, and generally condescending and offensive to the foreigners with whom they dealt. Above all the British arrangements were faulted for their excessive individualism. Whereas other nationalities combined in collaborative manufacturers' export bodies, the British dissipated their efforts in an irritable, unseemly and self-negating scramble against one another.[2]

Armaments manufacturers, followed by members of the British Electrical and Allied Manufacturers' Association, both in capital-intensive sectors, were probably the first industrialists to recognise the necessity of co-operating if they were to compete with Schneider-Creusot or Krupp, General Electric, Westinghouse, AEG or Siemens, for big foreign orders before 1914. But apparently the first British manufacturers' export association for the general engineering trades was the British

Engineers' Association set up in 1912 to attack the Chinese market. The context in which this body was formed, its personnel and methods during its foundation phase, and the reasons for its failure, form the crux of this chapter.

Trade was historically the chief interest of westerners in China. Until 1757 the Manchu dynasty placed few restrictions on foreign traders, but thereafter they were confined to Canton, a port as far from Peking as possible, and were subjected to numerous inhibitions. Merchants were forbidden to settle or to introduce their women, were prevented from learning Chinese and were kept outside city walls in 'factories' which combined warehouse, office and residence. These restrictions were a measure of the contempt and apprehension with which the Manchus regarded the non-Chinese world: to them, China was the Middle Kingdom and centre of the universe, its emperor was Son of Heaven, and foreigners who wished to treat with them in the Forbidden City were consigned to the Hall for the Governance of Barbarians. Indeed until 1898 China had no Foreign Ministry because relations with barbarian foreigners were neither wanted nor deemed necessary. Initially westerners paid for their tea and chinoiserie with silver and then, increasingly after 1773, in opium. The latter trade not only occasioned the Opium Wars of 1839–42, which broke the hitherto inexpugnable prestige of the Manchus, but heightened the venality of the Chinese Empire as officials and middlemen were bribed by dealers and smugglers. If the Opium Wars were a just cause of Chinese resentment, the opium trade was a serviceable pretext for western traders to regard Chinese officialdom as despicable and corrupt.[3]

Under the treaty which ended the first Opium War in 1841 Britain received Hong Kong and concessions in five coastal towns, later known as Treaty Ports, where British traders could own homes and businesses in areas ruled by British officials and laws. The treaty terminating the second Opium War extended this principle of 'extra-territoriality' to ten more Treaty Ports, which as autonomous fortifications in the strategic centres of China were reviled by many Chinese. British influence was paramount at Shanghai, the Treaty Port at the mouth of the Yangtse river, the valley of which was the most rich and populous area of China. Great trading houses, such as Jardine Matheson, Butterfield & Swire, and Dents opened up Chinese trade in co-operation with the Chartered Bank of India, Australia and China, or the Hong Kong and Shanghai Banking Corporation. The Treaty Port atmosphere is conveyed by a description of 1898 by Patrick Chance, concession-hunter and former Irish Nationalist MP: 'The English gentries of Shanghai are cocktailing, kicking coolies, riding ponies (and American ladies), deploring exile from a mother country which does not really miss them, and generally living on the fat of the land, with a new crisis or bogey every morning all fresh and hot'. The mining engineer Algernon Moreing described Shanghai in 1898 as 'that wonderful emporium of foreign trade and microcosm of Western civilisation, dumped down inside the entrance gate of the most conservative people in the world'.[4]

Britain knocked more persistently than any other nation at the hermetically sealed door of China. In 1841 the British forced that door ajar and wedged it open with the Treaty Ports and the ceding of Hong Kong; later Ulstermen like Sir Robert Hart created the Chinese Imperial Customs, which taught China the rudiments of international finance. A Briton, Gabriel Morrison, built the first Chinese railway from Shanghai to Woosung in 1874, only for it to be torn up after twelve months through the reactionary prejudice of those who realised that if the railway system was extended, it would ruin Chinese exclusiveness. Another Briton, Claude Kinder, in the 1890s converted the horse tramway of the Kaiping Collieries into the Imperial Railways of North China. Other British engineers 'first taught the Chinaman how to make big guns and carry on steel works, build modern ships, develop their harbours, and erect and run engineering works, cotton factories, sugar refineries, flour mills and cement works'.[5]

Table 5.1 To show British trade with China (including Hong Kong) 1854–1900 (millions of pounds at current value)

Year	Exports	Imports
1854	1.0	9.1
1860	5.4	9.3
1865	5.3	11.4
1870	10.0	9.9
1875	6.2	18.0
1880	9.5	13.0
1885	9.6	9.6
1890	9.5	6.0
1895	7.5	4.1
1898	7.4	3.4
1900	8.5	3.5

Source: D. K. Fieldhouse, *Economics and Empire 1830–1914* (London, 1973), pp. 222, 428.

As shown in Table 5.1, British trade dominated until the 1880s but then suffered a decline in both value and proportion. Already by 1885–6 German officials were pushing commercial interests so hard in China and Japan that the Foreign Office felt obliged to review its own diplomatic and consular assistance to British trade. In July 1886 re-fortified instructions were issued by the Foreign Office to its overseas representatives on assistance to traders, and these quickened Anglo-German trade rivalry and political antagonism globally.[6] The Chinese hegemony of the Chartered Bank, and of the Hong Kong & Shanghai Corporation, was broken by the formation of the Deutsche-Asiatische Bank (1889), the Yokohama Specie Bank (1892) and the Russo-Chinese Bank (1895). By 1898 Moreing could write of:

the threatened gradual elimination of the British merchant. The old order of 'hongs' is plainly changing, when merchants used to conduct a lucrative British trade with China, and when their spacious houses of business were both offices and residents (of the old-fashioned English type) for the managers and clerks. The first modification of this *régime* ensued from more frequent mails and the institution of the telegraph – an important change which called into being the commission agent. The conveniences of the new system caused rates to be cut finer and finer, and drove the old merchants more and more into company and other business to enable them to maintain their position. But more powerful than this has been the development of the 'compradore system' to a pitch that has seriously affected the profits of those merchants, banks, and houses who have found themselves compelled to resort to it.[7]

Compradore was a Portugese word applied during early European trade with China to a functionary who was something between an interpreter and a steward, and to whom was committed the business of bargaining with the natives in smaller matters.

The loss of British trading hegemony in China is open to many illustrations: for example, whereas 72.6 per cent of raw silk exports from Shanghai was destined for Britain in 1870, this figure fell to 36.8 per cent by 1876, 3.2 per cent by 1895 and 1.3 per cent by 1910; the new destinations being foremost France and the USA. Britain's share of China's imports fell from 23.9 per cent in 1880 to 17.2 per cent by 1905.[8] Yet the impact of competition was sometimes exaggerated, or felt more keenly than the figures justified. At the time of the Chinese revolution in 1910 Britain accounted for some 40 per cent of China's engineering imports worth about £8 million in total. Nevertheless, as Byron Brenan, formerly British Consul-General in Shanghai, commented in 1912:

> the British merchant resident in China was not a very useful representative of the British manufacturer...of new things. The British merchant was quite ready to accept an agency as a side line, and if he was dealing with a well-known thing he would have no difficulty in selling it, but they could not expect him to go out of his way to beat up potential customers and to spend time and money in following up long and expensive negotiations with the prospect of a problematical 5 per cent commission.

He commended instead the arrangement whereby one German firm employed a retired Chinese official in the capital of Manchuria whose only job 'was to watch events and keep on good terms with the officials, and keep his eyes open and inform his principals of possible opportunities of doing business'.[9]

The Chinese attitude to trade seemed unconstructive to westerners. A commercial traveller in Percy Davis's pain-killing patent medicine complained in 1908, 'China fails to understand what "commericals" are and...endeavours to thwart trade never to encourage it...Trade is only [considered] useful as a basis for taxation and for being fed on by herds of expectant officials.'[10] A journalist observed that 'the Chinese are wholly unable to discriminate between good and bad foreigners. They dislike the hardworking capable man who hustles them: they like the easygoing goodnatured careless man who does not interfere with their...passion for squeezing their own government.'[12] For this reason, so the British Commercial Counsellor at Shanghai claimed in 1922, the Chinese generally preferred the 'more conservative and above all more patient business methods of old-established British firms to the hustling, more spasmodic methods of the American'.[12] Another old China hand lamented in 1928, 'The Chinese turn instinctively to monopolies which of course are fatal to all legitimate foreign enterprise'; and Arthur Moore-Bennett, a merchant at

Yunnanfu, noted that 'in China it is an accepted axiom that if news of a contract gets out before the preliminary contract is signed the competition that arises makes the contract practically valueless'.[13] There was ceaseless tension between westerners and Chinese about foreign supervision of expenditure from construction loans and contracts: a tension which rival nationalities exploited in an attempt to win business from one another.

In 1908 Sir John Jordan, the British Envoy at Peking, 'spoke of that curious characteristic of Englishmen – how we worked against each other', and another observer lamented 'that no cohesion of interests can be arrived at between British groups, as...exists between Foreign Groups'.[14] This sense of the disunity and disorganisation of the British business community was pervasive in contrast to the reputedly ruthless efficiency of German mercantile firms such as Carlowitz, Melchers, Siemssen and Arnhold Karberg, or to the mastery of Heinrich Cordes, formerly of the German Legation and chief of the Deutsche-Asiatische Bank in Peking.[15] Claude Kinder, the founder of the Chinese railways, wrote in 1912 of the 'dire and urgent necessity' for the British manufacturing engineer to work collectively in China:

> His foreign competitors are not only infinitely better organised than he for dealing with Chinese contracts, but they have shown a faculty for grouping their interests and systematically tackling the Chinese market that British firms have been curiously reluctant to adopt. British engineering firms are always slow to move, especially when it is a question of combination of interests in any way, yet nothing but an intelligent co-operation between them to overcome the forcesarrayed against them can possibly save the situation.[16]

Similarly Sir Walter Hillier, speaking with forty years experience of China, noted in 1912 that:

> whereas in bygone years the Chinese merchant came to the foreign merchant with demands for the supply of his needs, the growth of trade and the increased competition of numerous rivals in the commercial world of the Far East have practically reversed the old order of things. Now it is the foreign merchant who has to seek out the Chinese buyer, and to seek him over the wide areas which have been opened up by the continued and continuing spread of railway communication. The spread of the railways lines has...created new demands ...Although imports from Britain still head the list in the volume of Chinese trade, our lead is menaced seriously and in new ways in consequence of the greater energy and enterprise of our foreign competitors, who realise apparently more than we have hitherto done the necessity for push and closer touch with the consumer...we cannot hope to maintain a lead by continuing in the old methods. Our German competitors, to mention no others, seem to be beating us in many lines...not...by the superiority of the appliances they supply or necessarily in the matter of price. Their success undoubtedly lies in the enterprise which...is so much keener with them than with us.[17]

References to British divisions and German unity were ubiquitous in the correspondence and conversation of the British in China; yet for reasons which were merely social or personal the British remained fissured and antagonistic. Indeed on many occasions Englishmen who were meant to be close working colleagues shocked or repelled Chinese officials by denunciation and execration of one another, sometimes publicly and on other occasions behind backs. Such conduct made a deplorable impression on the Chinese. 'How British Engineers in China can ever inspire confidence among the Chinese is incomprehensible', G. E. Morrison, the *Times* correspondent at Peking noted in 1911. 'Everyone abuses everyone else, abuses his character, his mental equipment, his morality.'[18]

As to the quality of British business representation in China, its most striking feature was eccentricity. Isolated in a small expatriate community, important British interests were represented by rancorous or neurotic men. Representatives behaved abnormally and wrecked the chances of their principals in Britain. Thus George Jamieson, chief negotiator of the Pekin Syndicate, and previously associated with the British & China Corporation,

> suffers from the delusion of poverty and fears to die poor. He accordingly lives on the smell of an oil-rag and saves several thousands per annum. He goes to see high officials in a coolie cart hired from the street corner for 75 cents and puts his writer in the same cart in order to save expense. The Chinese believe that there is no limit to his gullibility. He is a laughing-stock.[19]

Sir Edmund Backhouse, representative of John Brown the shipbuilders, whose forgeries and sexual phantasies have since been exposed by Lord Dacre of Glanton, was 'always on the verge of a nervous breakdown', 'wonderfully clever but morally unsound'.[20] Edward Little, the ex-Methodist missionary who was Brunner Mond's legendary successful agent of 1900–19, was 'of immense energy, the best [Chinese] public speaker among the English' who knew 'China better than any other merchant...[carrying] more influence over Chinese traders than any other man in China': but he was also a megalomaniac with his self-recommendation for the Nobel Peace Prize, and his numerous applications for decorations, for appointment as Commissioner General of Chinese Commerce and for allotment to him of several thousand square miles of Manchuria.[21]

Equally bizarre was Major G. F. Menzies, representing Lord Cowdray's firm of civil contractors. 'An amiable half-witted fool', formerly tutor to the son of Yuan Shih-kai (Viceroy of Chihli 1901–12, Chinese President 1912–16), Menzies was 'too funny for words' with his 'mysterious investigations' into bomb outrages and his monomanic secretiveness and self-mystification even towards his employers in London.[22] Then again there were cases like John Nind Smith, a schoolmaster at Rugby (1916–24), where his unusual manner earned him the nickname of 'Napoleon' from observant pupils. Smith 'had for some time been a little queer', but after being appointed Professor of Education at Hong Kong in 1924 'became positively dangerous' and caused chaos in 1928 with delusions about railway and road contracts worth £6 million.[23] Lord ffrench, normally cheerful agent of the railway contractor George Pauling, soared into 'the highest degree of nervous tension', succumbed to insomnia and became 'very downspirited and bitter'.[24] Even when the agents left Peking to report in London they remained disorientated: Birch Crisp's financial representative described Vickers' agent visiting London in 1914, 'very full of activity, and disappointed as we all are on these occasions to find that the centre of our little world is not the centre of the world at the other end'.[25]

It was not only British business representatives who became morbid and unbalanced by their isolation in Peking, miserable at the intrigue, 'incessant strain, the late hours, the irregular work, the difficulty of sifting truth from falsehood, the difficulty of understanding Chinese springs of action'.[26] Diplomats also cracked. Dmitri Pokotilov, the overworked Russian Minister in Peking of 1905–8, was 'overwrought and quite unmanned', breaking 'down into bitter fits of weeping'. His successor Ivan Korostovetz eloped in 1911 with the pubescent daughter of Théophile Piry, the French head of the Chinese postal service.[27] After three years as minister Jordan, to the dismay of the British community, was 'much downcast' by the turmoil over railway concessions, 'suffering from mental disquiet [and] half dotty': after 1909 G. E. Morrison and his confidants frequently referred to Jordan's mental exhaustion.[28] Sir Alexander Hosie, the commercial attaché in 1908–12, was 'tottering with alcoholic poisoning', permanently in a 'nervous hyper-excited state disgruntled and shaken...disfigured with a hare lip that has been poorly...restored'.[29] Indeed so lonely and arduous was Peking legation life that one experienced observer regarded it as 'a special punishment for diplomatic criminals' or those 'men who have systematically neglected to endorse or number their despatches'.[39]

In such conditions it was unsurprising that relations between diplomats and businessmen were often envenomed. To the general touchiness of the expatriate community, there was added mutual miscomprehension: according to C. W. Campbell, Chinese Secretary to the Legation 1906–11, 'the diplomats who come here don't know Englishmen', being 'brought up abroad among foreigners, and hence fail to know how to deal with their own countrymen'.[31] There was also snobbery against the bagmen of trade and industry. W. G. Max-Muller, the Legation Counsellor in 1909–11, was regarded by fellow diplomats as 'a cad and a snob': his wife was 'especially disagreeable to the English ladies, and her ill-natured sayings about them are always being quoted', Morrison wrote in 1909. 'I have never known the diplomatic side of our Legation to be so disliked.'[32] Another diplomat, Joseph Addison, 'a supercilious man with a loud voice and an eyeglass', described the Legation as comprising 'a number of nameless nobodies' and complained that he had to meet British subjects whom he 'would not know in England'. In 1909 this 'bounder of the deepest dye' insulted the wife of Henry Beaumont Donaldson, Vickers' agent in Peking during 1908–23. In the following months British society in Peking was rent by rows between Donaldson and his friends on one side, and Addison, Jordan and the Legation on the other, culminating in the resignation of the British Club's committee and a longstanding grudge by Jordan against Donaldson which injured Vickers' interests. Campbell, for one, 'never forgot the mean way in which [Jordan] put up with all Addison's insolences and bullied Vickers' man for not doing the same...I heard Jordan threaten the man and I could hardly believe my ears'.[33] This row came at a bad time for British interests, for in 1909 the Germans were uppermost in securing Chinese arms contracts, and on 22 April George

Askwith of the Board of Trade had officially urged Albert Vickers to combine with Armstrong Whitworth and French manufacturers 'to present a very powerful Anglo-French combination as against the German combination'.[34]

As a former Judge of the Supreme Consular Court in China had written some years earlier:

> Diplomatic society...is apt to degenerate into interminable calls...extreme sensitiveness to imaginary slights, and some jealousies, national and personal. Diplomatists are very feminine in some, if not indeed most, of their attributes. They love dress and scandal, are always on the look out for a slight on themselves.[35]

The vendetta involving Vickers continued for years as several incidents showed. Jordan, keen to retire by 1916, could not do so as this would have passed in wartime the doyenship of the Diplomatic Corps to the pro-German Dutch minister. He instead spent long periods in Europe, during which a 'society poodle', Sir Beilby Alston, acted as chargé d'affaires in Peking. Alston, 'the most incompetent noodle', was dominated by Sidney Barton, the Chinese Secretary at the Embassy in 1911–22. In June 1917 Donaldson all but arranged for the Kiagnan arsenal in Shanghai to build six or eight ships for the British war effort, but needed diplomatic help to surmount the last obstacle, the 'extravagant squeeze' demanded by the naval minister. Alston, disregarding the opinion of the British Consulate in Shanghai, refused to intervene on the pretext that he had not previously been informed of Donaldson's negotiations, and the idea collapsed. The Bartons and Donaldsons were known enemies, and many of the British community felt that Alston's conduct was inexplicable except in terms of the Barton–Donaldson 'social incompatibility'.[36] Further trouble between Donaldson and the Legation followed in 1919 when Vickers supplied Vimy aircraft to China despite an embargo on the supply of armaments which Jordan was vainly trying to impose upon Britain, France, Belgium, Japan, the USA and other suppliers.[37]

The Donaldson row of 1909 coincided with the revulsion of feeling between the agents and diplomats after Germany secured the Canton-Hankow railway contract. Each topic fed ill-feeling over the other, and together they rent the British community in Peking with effects which spoiled subsequent business opportunities. When Jordan did act on behalf of British manufacturers the results could be disastrous. In 1918 he and Barton accompanied A. H. Ginman, Marconi's agent, to a meeting at the Ministry of Communications about a chain of wireless stations from Peking to Kashgar. As Ginman reported, Vice-Minister Yeh Kung-cho

> smiled after Sir John had stated their case and this angered Sir John who ordered Barton to tell Yeh...'His Excellency...may smile but later he will smile at the other side of his mouth'...these were not the exact words but...are a correct paraphrase of the insult...Yeh...shut up with a snap and nothing more has been heard of this scheme.[38]

The wider contrast in Anglo-German business attitudes is shown by the rich but remote Szechuan province in western China. Although Szechuan was within

Britain's Yangtse valley sphere of influence, only one representative of any British manufacturer visited the province in 1909–15 and his visit, coinciding with the rebellion of 1911, was nugatory.[39] No British electrical representative visited Szechuan at all, although it was only a fortnight's travelling by riverboat from Shanghai. In contrast AEG's Chinese agents had a buying agent at Chungking by 1909 when they secured for AEG an order for the power plant machinery for the native Chungking Electric Light Co. About three years later Siemens appointed an agent in Szechuan who soon obtained contracts for wireless stations and electric machinery for the salt mines. A German diplomatic attaché visited Szechuan in December 1912 to explore the hydro-electric possibilities of its irrigation system. Other orders for German electrical machinery (with Babcock & Wilcox boilers) ensued in 1912–14, and only the outbreak of European war made the German electrical giants falter.

Thomas M. Ainscough, a Wigan-born Shanghai merchant who was agent of the Bradford Dyers' Association, was sent to Szechuan in 1915 as a Board of Trade Commissioner to report on the conditions and prospects for trade there. His mission was instigated by the Board of Trade's Advisory Committee on Commercial Intelligence which had been appointed in October 1913. Chaired by the President of the Board of Trade, its members included representatives of the India, Colonial and Foreign Offices, the High Commissioners of Australia, Canada, New Zealand and South Africa, and nineteen businessmen.[40] 'The attitude of the Legation and the Service to my mission is the usual freezing one', Ainscough wrote privately, 'but fortunately I can work far better independently.'[41] In the upshot his long and fascinating report faulted British manufacturers for doing business through Shanghai merchants rather than dealing direct with the natives and for refusing business because the Szechuanese wished to complete payment for machinery only when it was in working order. Ainscough wrote in terms which pinpointed the superiority of German sales methods throughout China.

> The German method is to select a district where foreign plant and machinery is badly wanted, to send down an engineer who is also tactful and possesses the *savoir-faire* required in handling Chinese, and to maintain the representative for a year or so if need be until by dint of acquiring the confidence and goodwill of the buyers, and proving the efficiency of his machines, the contracts are secured. The value of this method has been proved over and over again by the German firms...who have secured almost all of the large electrical engineering plants throughout China...these German firms...played upon the venality of the Chinese by providing two sets of invoices for the goods supplied, the difference in amount being returned to the official who granted the order as his 'squeeze'...it is this close study of the traits and weaknesses of the Chinese character, which has enabled our German competitors to secure a large[r] share of...large contracts in the country than their industrial efficiency warranted.[42]

With such German tenacity and intelligent study of markets, the British were unable to compete, although by 1910, as Table 5.2 shows, the Japanese had emerged as equally serious rivals. In that year, for the first time, China's imports from Japan exceeded those direct from the British Isles, although the gross British total from all sources continued to dwarf all others. (Hong Kong's trade of course was cosmopolitan, but about half of goods passing through were of British Empire origin.)

The Ainscough mission to China reflected wider concern by the Board of Trade Advisory Committee on Commercial Intelligence to modernise the institutional facilities available to British exporters. Thus in 1916–17, following a suggestion from the British commercial attaché in Argentina, they determined to encourage the appointment in South America and similar markets of travelling representatives of associations of manufacturers. The advisory committee envisaged such representatives as being manufacturing experts, selected and paid by their associations, who would investigate the products and methods of Britain's principal foreign competitors and report on new openings for British trade, while recognising the necessity of not prejudicing trade already held by Britons. A sub-committee under Sir Algernon Firth induced associations of manufacturers of jewellery, silverware and electroplate to combine to promote their joint export interests, with travelling investigators in overseas markets (initially South America). The Board of Trade was so keen to encourage export associations of manufacturers of competing products in staple lines that they offered to defray some of the costs of despatching travelling investigators abroad, and miraculously extracted Treasury sanction to spend £5000 on this.[43]

The British Engineeers' Association (BEA), formed in April 1912, was an attempt to improve the British export performance to China. With members drawn from British engineering companies (annually subscribing only ten guineas), its first president was Douglas Vickers the armaments manufacturer (Plate 5.1), of whom his colleague Sir Basil Zaharoff later wrote: 'Mr Douglas Vickers, although not

Table 5.2 To show value and origin of China's imports 1909–10

Country of origin	1909 £	1910 £
Great Britain	9 188 000	9 559 000
British possessions (except Hong Kong)	6 632 000	7 281 000
British total	15 800 000	16 840 000
Hong Kong	13 048 000	14 637 000
Japan	8 074 000	10 333 000
USA	4 378 000	3 276 000
Germany	2 044 000	2 872 000
Belgium	1 454 000	1 548 000
Other countries	10 302 000	12 794 000
Total	55 100 000	62 300 000

Source: S. Ransome, United Empire, vol. 3, p. 53.

Plate 5.1 Douglas Vickers, founding President of the British Engineers' Association (Syndics of Cambridge University Library).

producing a pleasant effect on first sight, is really sound, besides which he is a really first-class engineer, and an acknowledged authority on steel, and...the name of Vickers is worth something.'[44] Its vice-presidents were T. O. Callender the cable maker, Sir Robert Hadfield the Sheffield steel maker, Herbert Marshall (a steam engine manufacturer at Gainsborough), Sir William Mather (of Mather & Platt, textile machinery makers),[45] C. C. Scott (a Scottish shipbuilder, and director of the Leeds Forge Co., rolling-stock makers) and Sir John Thornycroft the shipbuilder. Members of the council included representatives of W. T. Glover Ltd, the Vulcan Foundry, the Eagle & Globe Steel Co., the Hydraulic Engineering Co., Willans &

Robinson, Swan Hunter & Wigham Richardson, the Power Gas Corporation, the Midland Railway Carriage and Wagon Co., British Aluminium, Dick Kerr the electrical company, Stewarts & Lloyds, and Alfred Herbert Ltd, machine tool manufacturers. Other founding members included Babcock & Wilcox, British Insulated & Helsby Cables, Brush Electrical Engineering, and North British Locomotives. Members who joined during 1912 included Sir Charles Parsons the turbine manufacturer and the Cleveland Bridge & Engineering Co., and by the end of the year membership totalled ninety-six. The association's title was literally rendered in Chinese, the British Association of Past Masters in Scientific Manufacturing (Ying Kuo Tsao Shih Hui). The executive committee was chaired by Sir Wilfrid Stokes of Ransome & Rapier, makers of cranes and hydraulic sluices, the company which had built the first railway locomotives for China in 1876. Stokes himself was 'an engineer of proven ability, who...made a name for himself with rotary kilns for cement-making, break-down cranes, railway rolling-stock, and sluices of a type used...in the construction of the Aswan dam'. Later, in 1915, he developed the revolutionary Stokes mortar and trench gun which, after rejection by the War Office, was adopted with success by the Ministry of Munitions.[46]

BEA's secretary was Stafford Ransome (1860–1931), a journalist who had visited Peking at the end of the Boxer Rebellion. In the 1890s Ransome had been a roving foreign correspondent for *Engineer* magazine. His book, *The Engineer in South Africa* (1903), is an inadvertent masterpiece of materialist bombast and racial arrogance, while his businessman's guide to *Japan in Transition* (1899) was of real use to his readers, not least by its lingering descriptions and photographs of geisha girls. Editor of *African Engineering* (1905–12) and of *Eastern Engineering* (1910–12), the latter's editorial column carried a standing notice, 'No Advertisements of Continental or American Manufacturers can be accepted on any terms'. As the American-edited *Far Eastern Review* noted:

> Mr Ransome's journalistic energies were concentrated primarily on an alleged exposure of German trade methods and competition which he openly characterised as the German 'blight' *to be exterminated at any cost*. After Germany, the American manufacturers and their reputed success in China came in for his denunciation...It is quite evident that a purely national organ, appealing to the existing national jealousy against Germany, with the British flag nailed firmly to the mast, and whose policy was a constant insult to Germans and their business methods, and an exhibition of journalistic spleen against all manufacturers other than British, could not hope to be a complete success in the complex international trading community residing in China.[47]

The BEA arose out of a suggestion in *Eastern Engineering*, from which Ransome resigned as editor to become its secretary at the annual salary of £600.[48]

The association's official circular described itself as 'formed for overcoming by collective influence the serious and growing obstacles which tell against the influence of British manufacturing engineers; obstacles which the individual firm, however powerful, cannot hope to overcome. The immediate attention of the Association is devoted to China.' According to Douglas Vickers, addressing the inaugural dinner of

1912 (attended by representatives of the Foreign Office and Board of Trade), BEA had 'to contend against the old principle' of Whitehall 'of allowing British trade to fight its own way'. Although British diplomats at last 'were willing to help' businessmen 'in trade on a big scale with foreign governments', nevertheless Douglas Vickers felt that exporters had been neglected. He also indicted the administrative and political classes in Whitehall and Westminster.

> It all came from old tradition. Sixty or seventy years ago, there were certain 'Mandarins' who held the theory that it was best for trading interests to be absolutely independent. These Mandarins came mainly from the merchant classes. They were not manufacturers, and they had the merchant's instincts. They felt that the capital they had in a business was not permanently in it. They were only carrying the goods on their passage from the manufacturer to the consumer, and if that trade was unsuccessful the merchant could easily transfer his capital elsewhere. The early Mandarins did not think much of the manufacturer. They cared little for the latter's capital, which of course, could not be transferred as the merchant's capital could, nor did they think very much of the working people who were trained to a particular trade, and could not change from one to another.

This phraseology resembled not only the articles of Leo Maxse in the *National Review*, but also the contemporary rhetoric of the Birmingham industrialist Dudley Docker, and his supporters in the Business League movement. Something of the association's nationalist tincture is conveyed by the suggestion of the names of two proconsular imperialists, Lords Cromer and Milner, as suitable honorary members at this time: Ransome himself was a contributor to the *Journal of the Royal Colonial Institute*. According to Douglas Vickers, the BEA 'ought, by gentle pressure, to be able to get the Government to do a great deal more...for British trade, and to break up the old system of allowing the trading interests...to shift for themselves – a policy which was really quite out of date compared with the organisation of the Germans and Americans'. He also wanted the Treasury to look 'with rather a cold eye on loans which did not secure that some portion of the capital raised should be spent in England', and for official pressure 'to get the Chinese Government to adopt the English language and English instructors as far as possible in educating the rising generation of commercial Chinese'. At the same dinner Stokes quoted a letter from Kinder urging 'all reputable British engineering firms to back this movement' as a 'duty...on common sense as well as patriotic grounds'.[49]

Ransome considered that the time was peculiarly ripe for an exports push in China. He wrote that 'in spite of the conflicting reactionary prejudices' hampering foreign trade, it was 'one of the world's great markets'. He welcomed the revolutionary overthrow of the Manchu regime in 1911. 'Whatever the suffering entailed may be, the present outbreak of popular feeling is to be welcomed by those who consider that China is in need of modernisation', he wrote glibly. It mattered little whether the revolutionists won, or the Manchus regained ascendancy: 'the effect will be much the same from the Western standpoint...the China of tomorrow will be one of the greatest, if not the greatest, of our overseas markets, and this fact has long been realised by our foreign competitors'. According to Ransome:

> The Governments, the banks, and the shipping companies of Germany, the United States, France and Belgium leave no stone unturned to forward the interest of their respective manufacturers at home and their compatriots resident in China. The Legations of those countries are constantly using their political influence to obtain orders for their own people and lending their full weight to the financial groups who are endeavouring to obtain concessions and contracts from China. The British Government confines itself to publishing out-of-date, incomplete and often misleading reports concerning matters which are dead and gone by the time they reach the public. They make no endeavour to forward trade interests in any way, either collectively or in the case of the individual.

Ransome did British diplomats a common injustice with these remarks, but was sounder when he criticised British financiers from the exporters' viewpoint:

> The British banker, while as anxious as his competitors in other countries to lend money to China, makes no stipulation as they do to the effect that a portion of the money so lent shall be spent in contracts placed with manufacturers in his own country, and he refuses point-blank to regard a properly authenticated contract as a negotiable asset. Thus at the present day we are faced with the anomaly of our bankers drawing upon the deposits of British manufacturing firms for the purpose of lending money to China to be spent on German machinery. These are a few of the more serious obstacles which stand in the way of Great Britain's trade and prestige in the China of tomorrow...now that Britain has borne the burden and heat of the day our competitors are making herculean efforts to rob us of the harvest which legitimately we should reap, and their lever, financial influence, is a powerful one.[50]

The BEA's formation coincided with the creation of a similar overseas sales and intelligence organisation by the British Electrical and Allied Manufacturers' Association, and was evidence of the mounting awareness by industrialists of the need for combination in export penetration.

In practice the BEA had a narrow function. It was not a trading concern, as its promoters thought it would be impossible for an organisation claiming to represent British national engineering as a whole to discriminate between its members and take contracts favouring one firm over another. Instead it was a missionary society to educate Chinese to adopt British engineering principles and machinery, particularly members' products. Its aims might have been possible if a massive propaganda campaign had been launched in schools, colleges and subsidised newspapers, but was impossible as BEA appointed only one representative in China, in May 1913. This was the 'extraordinarily foolish appointment secured by sheer bluff' of an Irish army officer, Captain Terrick FitzHugh (1876–1939), a 'bibulous incompetent' and 'drunken imposter who drinks...1½ bottles of whisky daily'.[51] In any case his task was hopeless. He was expected to convince the Chinese of British engineering superiority: but in China, as in other markets, the two tests of 'superiority' were a product's price and the credit terms available. As FitzHugh was precluded from quoting prices or terms on individual products he could do no more than quote all the prices of all the British competitors, which hardly made a forcible or lasting impact on the Chinese. The BEA showed the traditional British insularity about foreign weights and measures and postal rates: for example they apparently thought it cost no more to send a letter to Peking than to Croydon and posted their intelligence reports out to China with a twopenny-halfpenny stamp.[52] Ransome also evinced complacency about the overseas marketing of British engineering products. 'Of late years', he wrote in 1913:

> practically every engineering firm throughout Great Britain has been so full of orders, which were obtained without any of the credit conditions which are now necessary in China, that it is hardly likely that it would be necessary for them to go to the extremes which the Germans and other firms have adopted to fill their workshops...much of that trade during the last year or two would not have been worth touching by our firms under the conditions which have prevailed. When such is the case British firms must be content to allow their competitors to obtain such orders.[53]

The merchant Arthur Moore-Bennett, although supporting the BEA, pinpointed its futility. He wrote in 1913:

> how can the association, with one representative, hope to compete with the German American opposition, with their eighty or more fully staffed offices, their highly organised intelligence departments, the loan accounts they keep especially for the convenience of highly placed Chinese officials, the private history accounts of officials used when occasion arises to persuade such officials into line with their requirements, the lever which their position as creditors to minor officials gives them, the strong government backing that Germany never fails to give her houses, the organisation that permits the head of offices in Shanghai and Hongkong knowing months before outsiders do the value of possible contracts, and when others are bidding against them, the knowledge that lets the head office know the value of the opposing bids. Can one man cover ground that it takes the opposition two to three hundred financial and technical experts busy covering?[54]

Moore-Bennett's solution was that Britain should appoint a commercial attaché each to Peking, Shanghai and Canton and that this trio should work jointly with twenty or thirty BEA agents distributed throughout China. Subsequently he formed his own one-man Anglo-Chinese Engineers' Association with this intention. It was clearly true, as a writer in the *Times Engineering Supplement* noted in 1914, that a commercial intelligence bureau, even if properly run, was useless to exporters, 'without an efficient method of placing...wares before the Chinese public'.[55]

A further aim of the BEA concerned specialist personnel. 'Foreign Governments have been forcing the Chinese to accept as advisers, instructors and professors, men of their respective nationalities; the result being that the country is invaded with foreign advisers whose influence is entirely anti-British', so BEA averred in 1913, citing in particular the German dockyard at Tsingtao.[56] Douglas Vickers made great play of this in his speech of May 1913 at a recruitment meeting held in Birmingham to induce Midlands engineering companies to join BEA. In response, it was BEA's declared policy to seek to have only British technical advisers appointed to the Chinese government, and to have British engineering standards and specifications officially adopted in China. The latter they hoped would counteract the effects of the many American and German technical journals circulated to meet Chinese requirements. Ransome lamented in 1912 that 'China is in the hands of moneylenders of all nations', raising industrial loans from seven other countries whose banks (Britain's excepted) stipulated where China should buy goods and whose specialist advice should be sought. Thus, Ransome noted:

the British adviser is ousted in favour of the foreigner, and the foreigner is obtaining a larger and larger foothold as the educator of the modern Chinese...German engineering firms are spending £100,000 on engineering schools in China, conducted in the German language, to be used as trade nurseries for the Vaterland.[57]

However the BEA's efforts to impose exclusively British engineering advisers, standards and specifications were, if anything, counter-productive, arousing Chinese resentment at being dictated to in their appointments, and objections from cosmopolitan commentators such as the *Far Eastern Review*, an influential Shanghai newspaper edited by the American George Bronson Rea.

Other indiscretions were committed. At the BEA's inaugural dinner one of its honorary members, Sir Charles Dudgeon, declared publicly:

Money, of course, would be required. The Association must have its own agents to exploit the field, and in so vast a field they would need many agents. But it was not only for the salaries and travelling expenses of those Agents that money would be required. To get behind the scenes in official China was an expensive matter, and it was essential that the representatives of this Association should know everything that there was to know.[58]

This candid avowal of intent to bribe proved damaging to the BEA, although Dudgeon said no more than what was acknowledged as common truth by everyone.

From April 1913 a series of provincial meetings were held by BEA in British manufacturing centres to recruit new members to the association (which then had 112 members). At the Cutlers' Hall in Sheffield Douglas Vickers 'explained that the most serious obstacle' to exports to China:

was the lack of combination among British manufacturers. This he contrasted with the strenuous efforts of their American and German competitors to get possession of the market. They were not content with the ordinary competition in prices, but sought by educating the Chinese in the language and machinery of their countries to create a more or less unconscious bias in their favour...British firms [also suffered] from the impossibility of getting adequate help from the English government, whose agents were in the difficult position – knowing the jealousy of English manufacturers – of having it said that they were exercising their influence in favour of one to the prejudice of a rival firm. German and American manufacturers, on the other hand, sank their individual interests in the effort to obtain recognition of their country's trade as a whole…much could be done by sympathetic diplomacy.

Arthur Balfour (later Lord Riverdale) described how the Chinese:

saw huge German banks, colleges and offices, equipped in the latest possible style, and this had an enormous effect upon them, impressing them with a conviction that these must be representative of a great Power, whose influence it would be well worth the while of China to cultivate. Unless England followed their example, they would inevitably lose their foothold.

This meeting at Sheffield was followed by others at Manchester, Newcastle, Birmingham and Glasgow which induced about fifty firms to join: some of them small, and others like Firths of Sheffield, Cammell Laird, David Colville & Sons, W. S. Laycock, Yarrow shipbuilders, Birmingham Metal & Munitions Co., Birmingham Small Arms, General Electric, or Wolseley Motors.[59] By June 1914 membership stood at 251.

FitzHugh was far less successful than the foreign trade representatives appointed by the Federation of British Industries in Spain, Greece, and the East Indies from 1919: within a year the FBI's Madrid office was 'in the eyes of all Spaniards an infinitely more important place than the British Embassy'.[60] On the other hand the BEA was no more successful than a marketing and intelligence body set up around the same time by British manufacturers wishing to develop business in Siberia. Part of the explanation for BEA's relative failure was that Ransome, as an ex-journalist, ran the association 'for the interests of newspapers', and was more interested in meretricious publicity than in the spadework of research and analysis.[61] The London office was carelessly managed and wastefully employed; Ransome was proficient at propaganda, paper schemes and deference to BEA's governing committee, but deficient at organising an office or systematically running a long-term campaign. Not only was the BEA, as an effort in export combination, fatally belated, but it was also random and amateur in its methods.

Dr G. E. Morrison, the celebrated *Times* correspondent in Peking, became an honorary member of BEA in September 1912, but took no active part and resigned in December 1914 when he discovered that he was described in its prospectus as its Adviser at a time when he was officially Adviser to the Chinese government. He called this 'an act of sharp practice…designed to delude gullible firms into entering your Association' in expectation of him using corrupt influence on members' behalf, 'a discreditable attempt to prejudice the position of honourable Englishmen'.[62] In subsequent correspondence he told Ransome that BEA's published reports were 'fatuous' and that the association was 'pretence and humbug…a complete failure'.[63]

Similarly Sir John Jordan, in a despatch from Peking in 1915, wrote that the BEA had 'resulted in more harm than good. Its extravagant and tactless pamphlets have caused a feeling of intense irritation among our competitors in China and have placed them on their guard against any organised attempt to "push" British material in the Chinese market'. Jordan cited 'the controversy now raging' over 'indents for material on the Hupeh section of the Huknang Railways'. Americans were 'embittered' because they felt that orders were being apportioned solely according

> to the machinations of the Association who desire to obtain a monopoly for British manufacturers. A like feeling of irritation has been aroused among old-established British firms which have for decades past been doing a legitimate business.
>
> Of constructive work the Association has nothing to its credit. It was…founded for purposes of propaganda and is by its articles of association debarred from selling or distributing the material produced by its members. Its propaganda campaign has not taken the form of educational activity nor indeed any other form which is comprehensible to the Chinese. A campaign for popularizing British engineering products and carried on by means of lectures, the opening of showrooms or even the distribution of descriptive catalogues would have been understood and might have produced satisfactory results. But no activity has been displayed on these lines nor have prospective Chinese buyers who visited the offices of the Association been otherwise then mystified by the refusal of the 'Chief Commissioner' to accept orders…much harm has been done to British commercial prestige by the failure of a combination which boasted that it represented a national effort to capture the Chinese market and let it be generally understood that this effort was being made, if not under the auspices, at least with the full support of His Majesty's Government.[64]

According to the *Far Eastern Review* in 1915, the BEA

> has accomplished nothing and is rarely if ever heard of. The average Britisher accepts it as the usual Association formed for the purpose of enjoying an annual dinner garnished with mutual admiration speeches. It has never been spoken of seriously by any British subjects in China, and when discussed at all it is always with an amused interest in what it accomplishes other than finding employment for a salaried staff, who must bolster up enthusiasm by glowing reports of its work…the open publicity given to the…aims of the Association have placed all other nations on their guard, and whatever chance there might have been of attaining its special ends, has now been destroyed. The mere fact that a candidate for the position of Adviser to the Chinese Government on technical matters is endorsed by the Association, is sufficient to nullify his chances of appointment.[65]

Indeed the French government's reaction to BEA's chauvinist campaign was retaliatory: they decreed that henceforth the French money market should not co-operate with British industrialists in China unless French industry was accorded proportionate participation in the supply of materials. This was a pathetic obituary for the hopes of British engineering exporters.[66]

119

As a result of the European war the BEA's Chinese activities were largely suspended from 1915, although the Peking office was not closed until 1918. The Association during the course of 1915 tried to broaden its basis so as to represent all engineering interests in their dealings with the government; but the executive committee was too slow-moving and impecunious for this attempted re-orientation to succeed. Ransome resigned suddenly, and his successor in 1917 was more preoccupied with the 'revolutionary ferment' of the Shop Stewards Movement than in Chinese markets.[67] During 1916–18 the BEA made unconvincing attempts to compete with the activities of the Federation of British Industries and the Engineering Employers' Federation, before settling in the 1920s as a worthy but sometimes ineffective body offering a variety of services to British engineering exporters. It sent trade commissioners or investigators to Iberia or South America rather than China, but its average annual income from subscriptions in the nine years to 1928 was only £7659.

BEA's inadequacies were perhaps recognised by other manufacturers who joined in 1913–14 to form Representation for British Manufacturers Ltd (RBM). Participant companies included Sir William Arrol Ltd (constructional engineers), John Brown (armaments and shipbuilding), Cravens (rolling-stock), Dorman Long (constructional engineers), Thomas Firth (steel), Hawthorn Leslie (shipbuilding), Hulse of Manchester (manufacturers of machine tools for arsenals, railways and shipyards), W. S. Laycock (makers of rolling-stock fittings), and Simon Carves Coke Oven Co. Several of these firms, four years earlier, had jointly opened representative offices in Turkey, Romania, Greece, Bulgaria and Serbia, and RBM opened a Shanghai office in February 1914 to negotiate for business on account and in the name of member manufacturers. Offices in Peking, Hankow and Canton were planned to follow. The Peking office was to be responsible for business in eastern Siberia, Mongolia, Manchuria, Korea, Chihli, Shansi, Shensi and Kangsu. This initiative by RBM was curtailed by the outbreak of European war, but was a sound conception. Hitherto British manufacturers had mostly done business through Shanghai merchants rather than despatching representatives to deal direct with Chinese natives in the provinces: the price of this indolence had been to lose business to German interests whose travelling agents worked each province thoroughly. As Moore-Bennett wrote, 'Chinese officials do not go to houses for the best technical advice, but expect sellers to come to them, when they invariably buy, not the best machinery, but the machinery that will give the buying official the best cumshaw'.[68] When reporting to the Board of Trade in 1915 Ainscough strongly endorsed Moore-Bennett's view that it was essential for British interests to appoint agents with working knowledge of the individual provinces they covered, and condemned both British manufacturers' reliance on Shanghai merchants and their refusal of business where the Chinese wished to complete payment for machinery only when it was in working order. FitzHugh, clutching his whisky bottle in Peking, did nothing to remedy this deficiency.

Another attempt to organise British industrialists into a Chinese trading syndicate occurred during the post-war reconstruction period, when the Federation of British Industries was seeking institutional reforms as weapons in their planned 'trade war' to capture German international business. In 1919 H. E. Metcalfe, the Asian manager of Babcock & Wilcox, and Colonel W. S. Nathan of the Chinese Engineering & Mining Co., obtained a charter from the government in Peking to open a trade corporation capitalised at £240 000 which would give British traders the right to develop factories in China outside the Treaty Ports. Hitherto, with the exception of a few unscrupulous concession-hunters (including Nathan's employers),[69] foreign businessmen had been prevented from operating factories beyond certain closely defined areas; but the proposed British-China Trade Corporation was intended to enable British and Chinese directors and capital, co-operating on equal terms, to develop factories in China using British machinery and expertise. Metcalfe and Nathan felt that every British-controlled factory in China, though it might compete with individual manufacturers at home, would be a valuable feeder of British trade and industries in other directions. Their idea was supported by the British Legation in Peking, which hoped that the trade corporation would bring about a more coherent and unified exports push in China.

In November 1920 a meeting was held at the FBI offices with Colonel O. C. Armstrong (president of BEA 1918–21), of Greenwood & Batley, in the chair (Plate 5.2). This meeting agreed to seize the chance before the charter was cancelled, and the FBI undertook to co-ordinate this new effort in the Chinese market. A steering committee was appointed comprising three officials of the FBI and representatives of Babcock & Wilcox, Armstrong Whitworth, the British Trade Corporation, United Alkali, Lever Bros., Chance & Hunt (alkali manufacturers) and J. O. P. Bland, then a professional sinologue and previously a disastrous representative of the British & Chinese Corporation in the struggle for the Canton–Hankow railway concession. They worked closely with the Department of Overseas Trade, but the civil war in China and the industrial depression of 1921–2 in Britain robbed them of their impetus and no arrangements were finalised.[70]

Although British businessmen in Peking were often impossibly perplexing it is indubitable that the Legation under Jordan, sometimes following instructions from London, adopted a negative and unconstructive approach to business opportunities. Admittedly the Legation was hobbled by reluctance to use force in business diplomacy. 'It is difficult to see what more we can do than we have done and are doing,' one diplomat wrote in 1906, 'We are trying, ineffectually, to persuade, and we are not prepared to coerce'.[71] Yet many other British in China, led by Morrison, who after all had pressed Jordan's appointment on Lord Lansdowne and Sir Edward Grey in 1905,[72] concluded by 1912 that 'The chief function of the British Legation in Peking is to block British enterprise in China: the chief duty of the Legation staff is to restrict British competition in China and to give special privileges to a favoured few.' Surveying British policy, Morrison concluded: 'We achieve nothing: we only oppose things.'[73] Britain's negative commercial diplomacy in China derived from the fact that after the Sino-Japanese war of 1894–5 and the ensuing international scramble for concessions, Britain was trying to defend in an age of competition what it had taken in an age of monopoly.[74]

The fiasco of the early years of the British Engineers' Association leads to other conclusions. It stresses the extraordinary importance which personal and social

Plate 5.2 Colonel O. C. Armstrong, President of the Federation of British Industries, and of the British Engineers' Association (University of Warwick Modern Records Centre).

factors can assume in overseas marketing, particularly in a small and isolated expatriate community. It shows too that by the late Edwardian period leading British manufacturers were aware of the deficiencies in their overseas marketing arrangements, and were willing to subsume their traditional individuality and rivalry in a co-operative body like the BEA. But their perception of the market position, if the activities of the Association under Ransome are any guide, was coloured by various half-articulated assumptions and inchoate political beliefs. Influenced by the spectacular success after 1890 of some German metallurgical and engineering sectors, by the rhetoric of tariff protectionists from 1903 which had so often taken a Germanophobic form, and no doubt also by recurrent signs of Anglo-German diplomatic tension like the Agadir crisis, they made the BEA an aggressively nationalistic and even crudely xenophobic body.[75] Its anti-German intentions were certainly noted in business circles in that country, and can only have contributed to the political ill-feeling between Britain and Germany that led to Armageddon in 1914.[76]

It was an index of their insecurity about Britain's capacity to retain its commercial lead in an age of competition that the BEA adopted such a combative – almost pugilistic – form. The appointment of a man like Ransome, and the policies that he pursued, suggest entrepreneurial failure as well as political naivety. Apparently the BEA's constituent firms lacked internal resources to organise a concerted marketing effort in China; without the imagination or experience to conceive a strategy of their own, or perhaps unwilling to give time or thought to it, they resorted to Ransome, a man plausible on paper but disappointing in practice. The support of BEA by so many major engineering companies indicates a serious failure of judgment in their business representation in China.

Notes

After the completion of this chapter various lost minute books and other early material of the British Engineers' Association were discovered at the London Business School, and have been deposited at the University of Warwick Modern Records Centre.

1. See, for example, Stephen J. Nicholas, 'The Overseas Marketing Performance of British Industry 1870–1914', *Economic History Review*, 2nd ser., 37 (1984).
2. Sir Theodore Morison and George T. Hutchinson, *The Life of Sir Edward Fitzgerald Law* (London, 1911), pp. 105–8 passim; X, 'A Plea for Cinderella', *United Empire*, 8 (1917), pp. 309–15; J. H. Longford, 'The Consular Service and its Wrongs', *Quarterly Review*, 197 (1903), pp. 598–626; 'How Trade was Lost: Our Consular System; a contrast with America', *Pall Mall Gazette*, 17 March 1910; Percy F. Martin, 'British Diplomacy and Trade', *Quarterly Review*, 215 (1911), pp. 442–61; id. 'British Consuls and British Trade', *Financial Review of Reviews*, 23 (1918), pp. 392–406. For other views see Sir Walter Hearne, *Some Recollections* (London, 1928); D. C. St M. Platt, *The*

Cinderella Service (London, 1971); John McDermott, 'The British Foreign Service and its German Consuls before 1914', *Journal of Modern History*, 50 (1978).

3. The best introduction to this subject is Nathan Pelcovits, *Old China Hands and the Foreign Office* (New York, 1948); cf. G. F. Hudson, *Europe and China: a survey of their relations from earliest times to 1800* (London, 1931), ch. 8; Louis J. Gallagher, ed. and tr., *China in the Sixteenth Century: the Journals of Matthew Ricci 1583–1610* (New York, 1953); J. L. Cranmer-Byng, ed., *An Embassy to China: being the journals kept by Lord Macartney 1793–94* (London, 1962); Michael M. Greenberg, *British Trade and the Opening of China 1800–42* (Cambridge, 1951); W. C. Costin, *Great Britain and China 1833–60* (Oxford, 1937); Teng Ssu-Yu and John K. Fairbank, *China's Response to the West: a documentary survey 1839–1923* (Cambridge, Mass., 1954); John D. Frodsham, ed., *The First Chinese Embassy to the West* (Oxford, 1974).

4. P. A. Chance to G. E. Morrison, 22 November 1898, Morrison papers, Mitchell Library, Macquarie Street, Sydney, New South Wales, hereafter M, vol. 42; C. A. Moreing, 'A Recent Business Tour in China', *Nineteenth Century*, 44 (1898), p. 386. For Morrison's views on extra-territoriality, see his diary 10 January and 16 July 1907. Wider surveys of the subject are G. W. Keeton, *The Development of Extra-Territoriality in China*, 2 vols (London, 1928); Stanley F. Wright, *Hart and the Chinese Customs* (Belfast, 1950), pp. 354, 412–21, 434–58, 742; J. K. Fairbank, *Trade and Diplomacy on the Chinese Coast: the opening of the Treaty Ports 1842–54*, 2 vols (Cambridge, Mass., 1953); W. R. Fishel, *The End of Extra-Territoriality in China* (Berkeley, 1952).

5. Stafford Ransome, 'British Trade Prospects in China', *United Empire*, 3 (1912), p. 56; cf. T. H. Whitehead, 'The Critical Position of British Trade with Oriental Countries', *Proceedings of Royal Colonial Institute*, 26 (1895), pp. 106–63; T. B. Partington, 'British Trade Possibilities in Hong Kong and South China', *United Empire*, 12 (1921), pp. 340–52; Michael Hunt, 'Americans in the China Market: economic opportunities and economic nationalism, 1890s–1931', *Business History Review*, 51 (1977), pp. 278–307.

6. D. C. St M. Platt, *Finance Trade and Politics in British Foreign Policy 1815–1914* (Oxford, 1968), pp. 272–3 and appendix 5; E. V. G. Kiernan, *British Diplomacy in China 1880–85* (Cambridge, 1939).

7. Moreing, 'Business Tour in China', p. 387. Cf. Albert Feuerkwerker, *China's Early Industrialisation: Sheng Hsuan-Huai (1944–1916) and Mandarin Enterprise* (Cambridge, Mass., 1958); Hoh-cheung Mui and Lorna H. Mui, eds, *William Melrose in China 1845–1855: the history of a Scottish tea merchant* (Edinburgh, 1973).

8. Lillian M. Li, *China's Silk Trade: traditional industry in this modern world 1842–1937* (Cambridge, Mass. and London, 1981), p. 84; John Holt Schooling, *The British Trade Book* (London, 1908), pp. 171–2.

9. Byron Brenan, quoted in *Eastern Engineering* (January 1913), p. 212.
10. J. B. Pillow, who also 'was loud in his indignation against the Japanese and their [patent] piracies', quoted, Morrison diary 5 September 1908.
11. Morrison diary 28 April 1909.
12. H. H. Fox to Sir Beilby Alston, 10 July 1922, PRO FO 371/8010. See also D. L. Burn, 'The Genesis of American Engineering Competition 1850–1870', *Economic History*, 2 (1931); S. B. Saul, 'The Market and Development of the Mechanical Engineering Industries in Britain 1860–1914', *Economic History Review*, 20 (1967); R. C. Floud, 'The Adolescence of American Engineering Competition 1860–1900', ibid. 27 (1974); I. W. McLean, 'Anglo-American Engineering Competition 1870–1914: some third-market evidence', ibid. 29 (1976).
13. Sir John Pratt, minute of 20 June 1928, PRO FO 371/13234; Arthur Moore-Bennett, *Times Engineering Supplement*, 26 November 1913.
14. Jordan, quoted Morrison diary 27 October 1908; Arthur Moore-Bennett to Morrison, 10 September 1913, M 76.
15. Morrison to Leo Maxse, 15 November 1912, M 70.
16. Claude Kinder, quoted *Far Eastern Review* (January 1915), p. 295.
17. Sir Walter Hillier, quoted *Eastern Engineering* (January 1913), p. 208.
18. Morrison diary 16 September 1911.
19. Morrison to Arthur Barry, 14 March 1905, M 49.
20. Morrison diary 26 April and 9 October 1908; Lord Dacre of Glanton, *A Hidden Life: the enigma of Sir Edmund Backhouse* (London, 1976).
21. Morrison diary, 18 and 21 July 1918. See also W. J. Reader, *ICI: the forerunners 1870–1926* (London, 1975), pp. 225–6, 335–6, 345–6. See also Morrison to Bland, 16 May 1902: in opposing Lord Inchcape's proposals to reform *likin*, the Chinese transit tax, Little 'in a given time spoke more ill of his fellows, attributed more base motives to those he criticised than any other man I had ever met'. Bland regarded Little as a 'pestilent fellow': letter to Burkill, 9 June 1904, microfilm 1, Bland collection, Thomas Fisher Library, University of Toronto.
22. Morrison diary, 1, 19 August 1902; 26, 29 May 1905; 5 August 1906; 27 June 1913; 15 December 1914.
23. Information from Colonel Vivian Marshall, April 1983; Sir Charles Addis, memorandum of conversation with Sir John Norton-Griffiths, 9 July 1928; W. W. Harnell to Sir George Mounsey, 20 October 1928. PRO FO 371/13234. Nind Smith, 'though obviously mentally unfit' was subsequently a master at Eton. The anonymous reviewer of Nind Smith's book, *China's Hour* (London, 1930), in *Times Literary Supplement* of July 1930 was J. O. P. Bland. See Bland microfilm 8.
24. Morrison diary, 9, 26 March 1909. See R. P. T. Davenport-Hines entry on ffrench in *Dictionary of Business Biography*, II (London, 1984), pp. 350–4; and Cecil Headlam, ed., *The Milner Papers*, I (London, 1931), p. 269.
25. S. Pepys Cockerell to Morrison, 3 January 1914, M 152. On Cockerell, see

Eton College Chronicle, 15 (6 May 1915), p. 788. On Birch Crisp, see R. P. T. Davenport-Hines, entry in *Dictionary of Business Biography*, I (1984), pp. 822–7.

26. Morrison to F. L. Pratt, 10 June 1912, M 65.

27. Morrison diary 21 August 1907, 3, 5 December 1911; Lo Hui Min, ed., *Correspondence of G. E. Morrison 1895–1912* (Cambridge, 1976), pp. 710–11; Korostovsky's appointment in 1912 as Russian Minister at Tangiers was a 'direct insult to every diplomat with whom he may come in contact', Sir William Max Muller minuted, 'He ought to have been shot.' Sir Walter Langley minuted, 'It is an outrage.' PRO FO 371/1345.

28. Morrison diary, 16, 21 June 1909, giving the views of himself, Sir Valentine Chirol and C. W. Kinder.

29. Morrison diary, 15 April 1909; 16 July 1911.

30. Sir Edmund G. Hornby, *Autobiography* (London, 1928), p. 227.

31. Campbell, quoted Morrison diary 21 September 1909.

32. Horace Rumbold, circa 1895–96, quoted Martin Gilbert, *Sir Horace Rumbold* (London, 1973), p. 22; Morrison to Chirol, 12 September 1909, M 150.

33. Morrison diary, 13 October 1908, 1, 16 July 1909; 6, 19 August 1909; C. W. Campbell to Morrison, 12 January 1913, quoted Lo Hui Min, ed., *Correspondence of G. E. Morrison 1912–20* (Cambridge, 1978), pp. 77–8.

34. Sir Vincent Caillard to John Noble, 23 April 1909, Armstrong Whitworth papers 167 (Tyne & Wear Record Office).

35. Hornby, *Autobiography*, p. 231.

36. Morrison papers, vol. 100 fos 113, 115, 117; Morrison to Lord Ronaldshay, 2 August 1914, M 82; Morrison to A. J. Balfour, 29 October 1917, M 95; Morrison diary 27 October 1917. Marcus Samuel (Lord Bearsted) had offered in 1915 to buy Kiagnan arsenal and to utilise it for the war effort at either Kowloon or Hong Kong: see Samuel to Beilby Alston, 11 September, 13 October 1915, PRO FO 371/1915. The motive for Samuel's generosity was his avidity for a peerage, demonstrated in his grotesque correspondence of 1917–18 with Walter Long in Lord Long papers, 947/780, Wiltshire County Record Office, Trowbridge. For continued tension with Jordan over Donaldson's scheme for an Anglo-American Japanese combination to redevelop Kiagnan arsenal, see Sir Francis Barker of Vickers to Sir William Max-Muller, 4, 23 January 1919; and despatch 88 from Jordan, 4 March 1919, PRO FO 371/3688. Barton reputedly inspired Evelyn Waugh's character Sir Samson Courteney in *Black Mischief* (London, 1932).

37. Henry Beaumont Donaldson to Vickers, 11 December 1915, Hewins papers 59/102–112 (Sheffield University Library); J. V. Holt of Peking Aeronautical Dept, to Alston 8, 19 September 1921, PRO FO 228/3558; Sir Vincent Caillard to Foreign Office, 18 February 1922; and Donaldson to Alston, 27 April 1922, PRO FO 228/3559; Caillard to Foreign Office, 27 January, 18 February 1922, PRO FO 371/8010; F. J. Mason, letter in *Financial Times*, 1 June 1923; E. H. Carr, minute of 4 June 1923, PRO FO 371/9205. See also Cecil Lewis, *Sagittarius Rising* (London, 1937).

38. Morrison diary, 11 June 1918, cf. diary, 5 December 1918. The antipathy between British diplomats and Marconi in China continued so long as the company's controversial managing director, Godfrey Isaacs, remained in office. See Sir Victor Wellesley, minute of 9 March 1923, PRO FO 371/9218; and R. P. T. Davenport-Hines, entry on Isaacs, in *Dictionary of Business Biography*, III (London, 1985), pp. 446–52.

39. It should be added that British business in Szechuan was prejudiced by the diplomatic and political wrangle over the mining concession of William Pritchard-Morgan's Eastern Pioneer Co. See George H. Nash, *The Life of Herbert Hoover*, I (New York, 1983), pp. 63–5, 97–8, 238–9; William Stewart, *Keir Hardie* (London, 1921), pp. 166–7, 291; D. A. Thomas, *Rebirth of a Nation* (Oxford, 1981), p. 47.

40. Including Sir Forbes Adam (a merchant in Bombay and Manchester), Sir Alfred Bateman of the Enemy Exports Committee, Sir Hugh Bell the ironmaster, Sir Henry Birchenough, George Cox of Liverpool Chamber of Commerce, Thomas Craig-Brown a textile manufacturer, Sir Algernon Firth (President of the Association of British Chambers of Commerce), Sir Albert Hobson a Sheffield steelmaker, Lord Joicey the coalowner, Sir Stanley Machin, William Mitchell a Bradford spinner, Sir Edward Parkes, MP, a Birmingham ironmaster, Sir Hallewell Rogers of Birmingham Small Arms, Lord Rotherham of the Fine Cotton Spinners & Doublers' Association, Sir Albert Spicer the stationer, D. A. Thomas (Lord Rhondda) the coalowner and Robert Thompson, MP, a Belfast flax spinner.

41. Thomas Ainscough to Morrison, 30 September 1914, M 118.

42. T. M. Ainscough, Report 'Engineering Prospects in Szechuan: an unexploited field for British enterprise', 28 January 1915, M 196. Other interesting correspondence on the mission is in M 118.

43. Paras 29–33, Report to the Board of Trade by the Advisory Committee on Commercial Intelligence (1913–17). Cd. 8815 of 1917.

44. Sir Basil Zaharoff to Reginald McKenna and Dudley Docker, 24 November 1925, Vickers microfilm R315, Cambridge University Library. For the Report by Douglas Vickers of his visit to Peking in 1909, with a further memorandum by Sir Alexander Hosie, see microfilm R307.

45. For an extremely interesting account of Mather & Platt's overseas business arrangements 1890–1919, see Sir John Wormald, 'The Export Trade of our Engineering and Machinery Business', *Ways and Means*, 1 (26 April 1919), pp. 237–8. In the 1890s Mather & Platt dispensed with doing business through foreign merchants and 'proceeded to cover the world gradually with our own branches, installing in each, not only a Commercial Manager, but also a Technical Staff, to which was linked an Erecting Department under British foremen'.

46. J. E. P. Grigg, *Lloyd George: from peace to war 1912–1916* (London, 1985), pp. 276–7; R. J. Q. Adams, *Arms and the Wizard* (London, 1978), pp. 151–4.

47. *Far Eastern Review* (January 1915), p. 285. Both *African Engineering* and *Eastern Engineering* were owned by British Press Ltd, whose proprietors

were Sir William Porter and H. S. B. Brindley, on whom see R. P. T. Davenport-Hines' entry in *Dictionary of Business Biography*, I (London, 1984), pp. 448–50. The two magazines amalgamated in July 1914 as *Eastern and African Engineering*, which in 1915–21 was published as a supplement of the *London and China Express*.

48. See for example the following articles in *Eastern Engineering*: 'The Chinese Republic' (May 1912), pp. 369–70; 'An Important Engineers' Association' (June 1912), pp. 405–6; 'The Merchant and the Engineer in China' (December 1912), pp. 171–2; 'German Ascendancy in Peking' (June 1911), p. 410; 'Our Policy and our Critics' (July 1911), pp. 9–10; 'Progress of British Enterprise in China' (October 1911), pp. 121–2.

49. *Eastern Engineering* (January 1913), pp. 209–10; cf. 'Commercial Organisation of Germany', *The Times*, 31 Jan. 1908; McDonald, 'German Consuls', op. cit.

50. Ransome, 'British Trade Prospects in China', *United Empire*, 3 (1912), pp. 53–6.

51. Morrison diary 11, 18 August 1913; cf. diary 19 August 1913; 7 February 1914; When interviewed in March 1913 an annual salary for FitzHugh of £1000 (to include office expenses and the cost of one assistant) was mentioned. Warwick University mss. 267/1/1/1.

52. Morrison to Ransome, 20 May 1913, M 74.

53. Ransome, letter *Times Engineering Supplement*, 3 December 1913.

54. Moore-Bennett to Morrison, 16 Ocrober 1913, M 76; cf. Moore-Bennett's letter on BEA, *The Times* 26 November 1913.

55. P. Edward Nettle, letter *Times Engineering Supplement*, 29 May 1914.

56. ibid. 12 November 1913; cf. editorial 'British Engineering in China', *London & China Express*, 4 September 1914.

57. Ransome, 'British Trade Prospects in China', pp. 55–6. British manufacturers, including Lionel Hichens of Cammell Laird (a former schoolmaster), were however by 1911 promoting a £250 000 scheme for a Chinese University with English the linguistic medium in applied science. Its first principal however confessed that 'first and foremost' the promoters' object was Chinese welfare: they 'have not initiated their project in the interests of British commerce, nor would they feel it incumbent upon them to devote themselves to such an end, important though it is'. See Revd W. E. Soothill, 'A University for China', *United Empire*, 3 (1912), p. 588. Compare the comment, 'Where the German is, the schoolmaster is abroad': L. Hamilton, 'The German Colony in China', ibid. p. 722.

58. Sir Charles Dudgeon, quoted George Bronson-Rea to Morrison, 29 December 1912, M 131; *The Times*, 16 May, 4 December 1912. Dudgeon also said: 'Britain's competitors in China were not only infinitely better organised for dealing with Chinese contracts, but that they had shown a faculty for grouping their interests and systematically tackling the Chinese markets in a manner that British firms had been curiously reluctant to adopt...nothing but an intelligent co-operation between British firms to overcome the forces

arrayed against them could possibly save the situation...their chief competitors in China were their German friends, whose activities were being evidenced more and more every day – activities backed by government support, and by...powerful syndicates and corporations in the Fatherland. Their work was part and parcel of a far-seeing policy, in which the question of immediate profit was a minor consideration...laying...a solid foundation...to build a mighty edifice of trade.' *Eastern Engineering* (January 1913), p. 211.

59. ibid. (June 1913), pp. 371–7; (July 1913), pp. 13–15.
60. Roland Nugent, Report of FBI Conference on Overseas Organisation, 8 December 1919, FBI Nugent Papers (Warwick University Modern Record Centre). See also R. P. T. Davenport-Hines, entry on Guy Locock, in *Dictionary of Business Biography*, III (London, 1985), pp. 837–41.
61. Morrison to A. G. Cox, 9 February 1919. For example see BEA's protest about the refrigerating machinery bought by the British Legation in Peking, *The Times*, 3 September 1913. For another example of an ex-journalist who was better at meretricious publicity than business, see the account of Sam Evans in R. P. T. Davenport-Hines and J. J. van Helten, 'Edgar Vincent, Viscount D'Abernon and the Eastern Investment Company in London, Constantinopole and Johannesburg', in Davenport-Hines, ed., *Speculators and Patriots* (London, 1986), pp. 48–56.
62. Morrison to Ransome, 16 December 1914, M 131.
63. ibid. 2 March 1915, M 131; cf. Morrison to George Bronson-Rea, 13 January 1915, M 131.
64. Sir John Jordan, despatch 51 of 4 March 1915, PRO FO 311/2329.
65. *Far Eastern Review* (January 1915), p. 291.
66. For relevant *Eastern Engineering* articles at this time, see: 'British Money for German Plant' (February 1913), p. 239; 'The Rapid Progress of the British Engineers' Association' (June 1913), pp. 367–8; 'The British Manufacturing Engineer' (January 1914), pp. 213–4; and list of 235 members (June 1914), p. 385.
67. H. R. Summers, letter *The Times*, 20 October 1917. Douglas Vickers was succeeded by Sir Wilfrid Stokes (BEA president 1915–18); subsequent presidents were Colonel Oliver Carleton Armstrong, of Greenwood & Batley, previously of Beardmores (1918–21), Nevile Gwynne the pump manufacturer (1921–4), Sir Ernest Petter the engine manufacturer (1924–6), H. J. Ward of J. & E. Hall (1926–8), Sir Gilbert Vyle of W. & T. Avery (1928–30), Sir William Reavell (1931–6), and Lord Dudley Gordon (third Marquess of Aberdeen and Temair) of J. & E. Hall (1937–9).
68. Moore-Bennett, *Times Engineering Supplement*, 26 November 1913.
69. Nash, *Hoover*, pp. 125–222; John Hamill, *The Strange Career of Mr Hoover under Two Flags* (New York, 1931), pp. 59–88; Ellsworth Carlson, *The Kaiping Mines 1877–1912* (Cambridge, Mass., 1957, 1971), pp. 2, 68–79 and passim.
70. *London and China Telegraph*, 1, 8 November 1920; *Financier*, 5 November 1920; memorandum of 9 May 1919 by Archibald Rose, Commercial Secretary

at Peking Legation, PRO FO 371/5343; Sir James Kemnal to H. E. Metcalf, 8 April 1921; S. Springer to J. O. P. Bland, 5 July 1921, Bland microfilm 11. Cf. Noel H. Pugach, 'Keeping an Idea Alive: the establishment of a Sino-American Bank, 1910–1920', *Business History Review*, 56 (1982), pp. 265–93; Clarence B. Davis, 'Financing Imperialism: British and American bankers as vectors of imperial expansion in China, 1908–1920', ibid. pp. 236–64.

71. Sir Walter Langley, minute of April 1906, PRO FO 371/19, fo. 346.
72. Morrison diary, 2 October, 18 November 1905.
73. Morrison diary, 7 December 1912; and memorandum inserted in diary (vol. 20) at end of December 1912.
74. L. K. Young, *British Policy in China 1895–1902* (Oxford, 1970), p. 19; Sun E-tu Zen, *Chinese Railways and British Interests 1898–1911* (New York, 1954), p. 7.
75. For the background to this see R. P. T. Davenport-Hines, *Dudley Docker* (Cambridge, 1984).
76. 'A German View of the British Engineers' Association' (from *Technik und Wirtschaft*), *Eastern Engineering* (March 1914), pp. 281–2; A. J. A. Morris, *The Scaremongers* (London, 1984).

6 Marketing the Nettlefold woodscrew by GKN 1850–1939

Edgar Jones

The Nettlefold woodscrew, which held a market dominance in Britain from the 1870s until the early 1970s, was a product with a long and continuously successful life. Technically it altered little during this century, the only major change being the progressive substitution of steel for wrought iron from the early 1880s.[1] Although Nettlefolds periodically experimented with thread rolling machines,[2] the vast bulk of their screws were manufactured by automatic screw-cutting lathes throughout this period. The introduction of more sophisticated heads (principally the reset cross, commonly known as the 'Phillips' head and subsequently called the 'Pozidriv', 'Supadrive' and 'Supascrew' by GKN) began in the 1950s but did not become widespread until the 1970s and 1980s, the traditional nick across the top characterising the woodscrew for these hundred years. In addition the range of screws and gauges by which they are measured remained standard. There was little diversification into other engineering products and scant attempt to devise new techniques of bonding timber together. The mills in which the Nettlefold woodscrews were made in their countless millions experienced virtually no organisational or structural innovation during this period and the machines, though modified and updated to run much faster, were hardly altered in principle from those which had gained the company its British monopoly during the 1870s. Thus a prima facie case may be put forward to say that in the absence of dramatic technical change, marketing and sales policies, whether carefully planned or, on occasion, fortuitously struck upon, were crucial in allowing Nettlefolds to retain their dominant position throughout this period.

Manufacturing by modern methods began in 1854 when the firm of Nettlefold & Chamberlain was established to make woodscrews at their new Heath Street mill in Smethwick.[3] The partnership prospered and given the opportunity to take over several competitors and requiring an input of capital to expand the works, they formed a public limited liability company in 1880 called Nettlefolds Ltd.[4] Although in 1902 they became an integral part of the Guest, Keen & Nettlefolds group set up by Arthur Keen (1835–1915),[5] the name 'Nettlefolds' was exclusively retained for their woodscrews and it was only in the late 1960s that the packaging was altered to include a background containing the GKN logogram. The Nettlefold woodscrew remained one of GKN's leading products and schedules at the Dowlais-Cardiff

Steelworks at East Moors were rearranged so that it could supply pig iron to the Bessemer converters and rolling mills established by Nettlefolds at Rogerstone. However the unsuitability of steel made from Cardiff iron forced GKN to purchase the bulk of their billets from Workington; only round-headed woodscrews, a small proportion of the total, were manufactured from the group's own steel.

Gaining the Monopoly

It should be stated at the outset that Nettlefold & Chamberlain did not obtain their UK monopoly in the manufacture of woodscrews solely, or even primarily, as a result of successful marketing techniques. In essence their ability to undercut their competitors, thereby forcing them into bankruptcy or to become part of the Nettlefold & Chamberlain group, relied on the introduction of modern machinery purchased from the United States and installed in a purpose-built mill at Smethwick.[6] Nevertheless marketing techniques, though possibly more in evidence when they were forced to defend their dominance from rivals setting up factories within Britain or attempting to introduce imports, had their part to play in securing this hegemony.

From the very earliest days at Smethwick, Nettlefold & Chamberlain sold to wholesalers rather than retailers or directly to the public. At this stage Nettlefolds did not seek to open their own shops or to acquire an ironmongery outlet so as to obtain complete control over the chain of sales to the consumer. By dealing with the major wholesalers (who were categorised as Class 'A', 'B' or 'C' according to size), as distinct from the thousands of stores that stocked woodscrews, the company's representatives could build up an intimate relationship with their customers and retain their loyalty by operating a system of discounts (p. 135).

A particular and enduring problem, despite having secured a virtual monopoly of the British market, was the difficulty of obtaining true economies of scale for each gauge of woodscrew. During the period when screws were fashioned individually by hand the public had become accustomed to being offered a large number of sizes. Manufacturers using self-acting machinery found it impossible, or rather, never attempted to break this pattern of demand. Nettlefold & Chamberlain's catalogue for 1871 listed 730 varieties of iron screw and by 1932 the range in steel alone had widened to 1673 types, not including brass screws or those with special coatings, or hooks, rivets, cotters and bolts, which they also made.[7] (Plate 6.1) Although many of the new screw-cutting lathes ran permanently on the same gauge, and some also on a common length, others had to be periodically adjusted to deal with different thicknesses and lengths of wire and all had to be stopped regularly to replace worn cutters. There was apparently little attempt to manipulate the price of woodscrews to encourage popular lines and thereby raise productivity; only in the mid-twentieth century were medium-sized woodscrews, those for which there was greatest demand, priced as low as possible to stimulate consumption. On occasion, and particularly where exports were concerned, exceptions could be made. For example, after requests from their Russian agent in December 1867 Nettlefold & Chamberlain

Plate 6.1 An elaborate display of woodscrews, hooks, cotters and other products prepared for a late Victorian trade exhibition, which illustrates the range and variety of fasteners that Nettlefolds manufactured. Note the 'Castle' trademark decorating the corners of the case (Guest, Keen & Nettlefolds).

agreed to increase the discount on large sizes for sufficiently major orders.[8] This was doubtless in an attempt to boost the volume of these less popular gauges. Nevertheless the British price list remained unaltered from its inception in the 1850s. This allowed the company to introduce a system of discounts offered to wholesalers, as a means of implementing their marketing policy.

The discount system was rigorously and continually employed as the chief weapon against competition whether at home or from overseas. In 1870–1, for instance, as a deliberate challenge to Nettlefold & Chamberlain the Birmingham Screw Co. opened a new screw-making factory at Smethwick adjacent to the Heath Street mills.[9] Joseph Chamberlain (1836–1914) (Plate 6.2), the partner responsible for sales and marketing, responded to this calculated threat with characteristic

Plate 6.2 Joseph Chamberlain (1836–1914) photographed when the partner in Nettlefold & Chamberlain responsible for its sales and marketing strategy (Guest, Keen & Nettlefolds).

aggression and clear thinking. While their neighbours' factory was being built he reduced the discount offered to wholesalers in order to raise his profit margin and amass a capital reserve. These accumulated funds could then be used to finance Nettlefold & Chamberlain when they slashed prices to drive their competitor into insolvency.[10] After taking advice from his friends in the city and discovering as much as he could about the Birmingham Screw Co. Chamberlain produced detailed statistical plans to support his strategy. 'We have got to smash the new company' was his repeated refrain. Accordingly during 1871–2 while the St George's works was being erected by their rivals, Nettlefold & Chamberlain raised prices by as much as 50 per cent; the discount, which was as high as 60 per cent in 1865, was trimmed to a mere 30 per cent by 1872 and from January 1873, when their competitors came into production, was progressively increased reaching its former level in July 1875 (Table 6.1). This action proved sufficient to emasculate the Birmingham Screw Co., which finally agreed to be taken over by Nettlefolds in 1880 when the latter was floated as a public company.

Manipulation of the discount rate offered to wholesalers was also an important weapon in conducting a campaign against rival exporters. In 1881 J. H. Nettlefold (1827–81)[11] reported that 'he had reason to believe that the company's trade was being interfered with by foreign and other competitors' and to combat this recommended that the discount on iron woodscrews be increased from 65 per cent to 75 per cent.[12] Three years later Nettlefolds were shocked to discover that German manufacturers had succeeded in penetrating one of their leading export markets and were selling freely into Australia. To win orders the Germans had skilfully exploited Australian resentment at the higher rates of discount being offered by Nettlefolds to Indian wholesalers.[13] German woodscrews had already obtained a considerable foothold in the Indian market because Nettlefolds had been slow to respond with price reductions, doubtless believing that their established name and the strength of imperial loyalty would counteract any desire to opt for the cheaper German woodscrew. Learning from the earlier misjudgment they decided to act swiftly and increase the discount in Australia from 70 per cent to 75 per cent, which, in turn, 'would render it advisable to take a similar step for South America, where the Germans are already well established, and South Africa, leaving 70 per cent in force for the UK and Canada'.[14] In addition the high level of discounts in operation between 1890 and 1914 was doubtless to counter attempts by Germany to sell within Britain, as evidence presented to the Tariff Commission of 1909 revealed that:

> nails and screws can now be obtained from Germany at about 25 per cent less than the average British price. This refers more particularly to brass screw nails and iron wire nails and is caused by a determined effort on the part of German manufacturers to obtain a sure footing in our market.[15]

Given that the list price of woodscrews remained unchanged it is possible, using the known discounts, to calculate a hypothetical profit series (Table 6.1). Assuming for the purpose of argument that each screw was listed at 100p, of which 25p represented manufacturing costs, the variation in the percentage profit or loss produced by manipulation of the discount rate has been computed and expressed as an index. In April 1853, for example, when the discount was 50 per cent the selling price would have been 50p of which 25p would have been profit, or 25 per cent of the total cost. The figures reveal that the impact of these changes between 1853 and 1939 could be dramatic as the index moves through a considerable range. While the exact figures should not be taken as an accurate numerical measure (the break-even point was probably nearer to a discount of 70 per cent rather than 75 per cent as shown by Table 6.1), they reveal that comparatively small revisions could have disproportionately large consequences for the final profit figure. This in turn suggests that the marketing strategy of Nettlefolds was carefully considered and required considerable subtlety in its operation. If the hypothetical figures are compared with the actual profits recorded by Nettlefolds for 1881–1901 (Table 6.2), a connection seems to emerge. A progressive reduction in the discount rate from October 1888 to April 1893 brought higher profits in both cash and real terms, while an increase in the discount rate from January 1895 until February 1899 corresponded with a fall.

In the period when they were building up their market dominance Nettlefold & Chamberlain paid considerable attention to packaging and the production of a recognisable trade mark. Joseph Chamberlain, the partner responsible for obtaining orders from overseas, was scrupulous in his attention to such details. Always quoting in decimalised weights and measures when dealing with French wholesalers, he ensured that their screws were packaged in the traditional blue wrapping paper (Nettlefold & Chamberlain used green for Britain), with the gauges handwritten in millimetres.[16] By contrast, the Scots, as Chamberlain recorded in his notebook, 'like green labels and printed numbers as they suspect alteration of sizes in the written numbers'.[17] He insisted that their orders were packaged accordingly. To help preserve their major share of the Indian market green labels in Hindi, Tamil or Burmese were affixed according to the destination specified by the export merchant.[18] Such was the importance attached to presentation that a portion of their King's Norton factory (acquired from James, Son and Avery in 1865 for a reported £100 000 after a price-cutting battle)[19] was laid aside for printing presses to produce labels and, when cardboard boxes replaced wrapping paper, for box-making machines. The latter, designed and assembled by Nettlefolds, were so successful that they were able to sell a number to Bird & Sons of Birmingham, and Cadburys of Bournville.[20]

At some point in the 1860s Nettlefold & Chamberlain introduced their 'Castle' trade mark which was to survive unaltered for over a hundred years. The idea had been inspired by their purchase of land at Hadley Castle near Wellington, Shropshire, where they constructed an ironworks and rolling mills.[21] A mock brick turret standing nearby appears to have inspired the design. It proved to be a shrewd choice as the stocky battlemented tower with its three arrow loops appeared to represent an enduring solidity and reliability and at the same time was a typically British symbol.[22] The black 'Castle' was to be seen on every box of screws sold by Nettlefolds and appeared in their catalogues, promotional literature and display boards. In their 1932 catalogue, beneath a specimen label, a warning was printed:[23] 'there are many imitators of our mild steel woodscrews, and nearly all of them use a green label, but the genuine article can be distinguished by the registered design "Nettlefolds" and the Castle trade mark'.

Because they sold exclusively to wholesalers, advertising was highly selective. Space was taken in trade journals and newspapers, such as the *Ironmonger*, the *English Mechanic*,[24] and others, but to no great extent in the popular press. However the company made a determined attempt to enter trade fairs and won prizes in London (1862), Dublin (1865), Cape Town (1877), Paris (1878), Sydney

Table 6.1 Discount rates on Nettlefolds' woodscrews sold in Britain 1853–1939

Date	Discount %	Gross margin index	Date	Discount %	Gross margin index
April 18 1853	50	100	Oct 18 1898	70	40
Nov 17 1853	47½	105	Feb 17 1899	67½	57
Jan 12 1854	45	109	Aug 23 1899	65½	55
Jan 15 1854	47½	105	Nov 14 1899	60	75
Oct 2 1856	52½	95	Dec 2 1905	70	40
Jan 1 1857	57½	82	March 18 1907	67½	57
Oct 1 1857	60	75	March 30 1908	72½	18
April 1 1862	65	47	Sept 28 1912	70	40
Jan 1 1865	70	40	Aug 20 1914	67½	57
Nov 25 1865	60	75	April 14 1915	65	47
Sept 1 1871	50	100	July 7 1915	60	75
Jan 22 1872	45	109	Dec 11 1915	55	89
April 9 1872	40	117	June 7 1916	50	100
June 22 1872	30	128	Oct 6 1917	45	109
Jan 18 1873	40	117	Feb 9 1918	40	117
July 1 1874	50	100	May 4 1918	35	123
July 1 1875	60	75	Aug 24 1918	30	128
April 25 1876	65	47	Nov 9 1918	25	133
Jan 8 1877	70	40	Dec 23 1919	15	141
Sept 20 1877	72½	18	Feb 10 1920	5	147
March 21 1879	75	0	April 13 1920	Net	200
Jan 17 1880	65	47	March 1 1921	10	144
March 28 1881	75	0	June 1 1921	25	133
Oct 7 1881	72½	18	Jan 2 1922	35	123
Dec 24 1881	70	40	Jan 1 1927	45	109
Feb 17 1886	75	0	Sept 6 1932	50	100
June 23 1888	72½	18	March 22 1934	47½	105
Oct 8 1888	67½	57	March 18 1937	40	117
March 18 1889	62½	67	May 1 1937	37½	121
Nov 11 1889	57½	82	Jan 2 1939	40	117
April 26 1893	67½	57	Nov 1 1939	37½	121
Jan 1 1895	72½	18			

Note: These percentages refer in the first instance to wrought-iron screws, though steel was substituted during the 1880s.
Source: 'Woodscrew Discounts from 1853' (typescript sheet, May 1954), courtesy of Sela Fasteners Ltd, Leeds.

(1879), Melbourne (1880), Adelaide (1881) and Calcutta (1883–4).[5] Elaborate displays composed of thousands of screws and hooks of various sizes and metals stitched on to boards to create patterns or pictures, were exhibited, while smaller versions framed behind glass were presented to ironmongers to be hung in their shops. Advertising campaigns mounted by Nettlefolds appear to have made no attempt to undermine the quality of rival products being designed merely to keep the

Table 6.2 Profits earned by Nettlefolds Ltd 1880–1901

		£	Adjusted £
To 31 March	1881	64,204	64,853
	1882	57,240	56,673
	1883	57,634	57,063
	1884	56,925	59,921
	1885	57,260	65,068
	1886	47,534	57,270
	1887	40,415	49,895
	1888	38,418	45,736
	1889	67,830	80,750
	1890	91,739	105,447
	1891	112,130	130,383
	1892	143,096	174,507
	1893	101,569	123,865
	1894	136,830	184,905
	1895	111,555	154,938
	1896	101,871	139,549
	1897	97,876	132,265
	1898	99,111	127,065
	1899	89,619	106,689
	1900	93,133	102,344
	1901	92,265	107,285

Note: Figures are after tax and after deduction of dividend.

Source: Nettlefolds Ltd, General Meeting Minute Book, June 1880 – February 1902. Figures adjusted by the Rousseaux Price Index 1800–1913, average of 1865 and 1885 = 100, Mitchell and Deane, *Abstract of British Historical Statistics*, pp. 472–3.

company name in the minds of wholesalers and retailers and to indicate the range and quality of their products in an undemonstrative fashion.

Defending the Monopoly

In 1865 Birmingham as a whole was producing 130 000 gross woodscrews a week of which 69 per cent, or 90 000 gross were manufactured by Nettlefold & Chamberlain.[26] By 1873 their weekly output had risen to 150 000 gross, representing an annual figure of 7 200 000 gross.[27] In 1880 after they had taken over the Birmingham Screw Co. and several other smaller manufacturers, Nettlefolds Ltd secured a virtual monopoly of the UK market. Hence they were particularly secure in 1891 when the American Screw Co. announced that they were to build a rival factory in Leeds, and thereby break their unchallenged eminence.[28] Importing modern machinery from America, a purpose-built mill was constructed in Kirkstall Road and commenced operations under the style, the British Screw Co. Ltd, in 1892 (Plate 6.3). With a weekly output

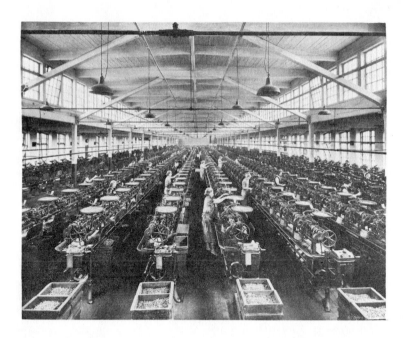

Plate 6.3 The upper floor of the British Screw Co. in Leeds during the interwar period when it was a secret subsidiary of GKN. Not as extensive as the Heath Street mills belonging to Nettlefolds it nevertheless shows how self-acting machinery could be operated by a comparatively small number of semi-skilled workers. The clerestory roof was a typically American feature and reflected its original ownership (Sela Fasteners Ltd).

of around 60 000 gross and making the complete range of woodscrews, they were in a position to present real opposition to Nettlefolds. Characteristically the latter increased its discount from 57½ per cent to 67½ per cent in April 1893 in an attempt to drive the British Screw Co. out of business and in January 1895 a further price reduction was ordered. With some patriotic bias the *American Manufacturer* observed that:

> Nettlefolds Ltd, of Birmingham, announced on New Year's day, an increase of 5 per cent in the discount [to 72½ per cent] from list prices of iron woodscrews. This is equal to a reduction on the net price of 10 to 15 per cent and may be regarded as a further attempt...to crush the American Screw Company...Nettlefolds are the last people in the world to reduce prices unless compelled by competition from outside sources.[29]

Finally a depression in the screw industry brought the American Screw Co. into financial difficulties[30] and in October 1898 Nettlefolds acquired the Leeds factory. In that year they published a profit figure of £121 173[31] and having created a secret reserve of over £50 000 in 1894[32] could well afford the transaction. As a marketing ploy they decided that the subsidiary should continue to operate under the title

139

British Screw Co. and that its products should continue to be sold under that name. A brief history of the GKN Group including all its constituent and associated parts, compiled in about 1925, deliberately omitted any reference to the Leeds factory.[33] It was said that employees never guessed that they were part of the same organisation as Nettlefolds and believed that they were their genuine rivals. In this way GKN were able to preserve the illusion of competition long after Nettlefolds had in fact restored their monopoly of the UK woodscrew market. The high discounts in force from 1893 to 1895 were swiftly reduced during 1899 when three cuts brought the percentage down to 60 per cent (Table 6.1).

When competition from overseas became severe Nettlefolds resorted to a further defensive strategy, the formation of cartels. In January 1881 Nettlefolds had come to an agreement with the American Screw Co. under which the former promised to sell no more than 5000 gross screws a week to Canada, provided the Canada Screw Co. gave them 'preference for any screw and screw-rods' they wished to purchase.[34] In return the American Screw Co. were not to attempt to sell screws to Britain, Norway, Sweden, Germany, Holland, Denmark, Belgium and France. In effect it was a means of preventing Nettlefolds from penetrating the North American market while protecting north-west Europe from any transatlantic competition. Further clauses determined that second-quality screws were only to be exported to South America and Mexico. Elsewhere, that is those European nations upon whom no embargo had been placed, together with Africa, Asia, Australia and New Zealand, the American and Canada Screw Companies both agreed to sell at the prices and terms offered by Nettlefolds.[35]

More serious proved to be competition from Germany. In February 1886 in order to finance another round of higher discounts a 10 per cent reduction in wages was imposed on the Heath Street mills.[36] This was seen as an interim measure for in May 1886 meetings were held with their German opposition in an attempt to establish a cartel. The discussions continued until June 1888 when Edward Steer (1851–1927), a director and from 1920 chairman of GKN, helped to establish an experimental International Union in Brussels composed of the leading British, French, Belgian and German manufacturers. The parties agreed to sell at the English price (72½ per cent discount) and a system of fines was devised for those who exceeded this limit.[37] Cartels remained notoriously difficult to enforce and in 1902 the GKN board was forced to consider the consequences 'of the low prices which German manufacturers of screws were quoting in the English, Indian, Australian and other markets'. The agreement covering these regions had fallen through in 1893 and Nettlefolds had been compelled to respond by increasing their discounts.[38] However it was not long before the various European manufacturers returned to the negotiating table and in 1905 a new International Union of Screw Makers was established, Charles Steer, a director of GKN, being its first president.[39]

Throughout the hundred years under discussion Nettlefolds maintained tight control over their products. There was no attempt to introduce cheaper lines; the emphasis was consistently on a high quality woodscrew. Unlike the British Screw Co. at Leeds, Nettlefolds did not sell seconds, which they disposed of as scrap to steelworks. Diversification was limited and in so far as it was pursued with any vigour proceeded no further than the nail and nut and bolt trade. Nails were manufactured simply to consume wrought-iron, and later steel, rod which was not of sufficient quality to be drawn for woodscrews. Nettlefolds did not make anything like the full range of nuts and bolts but confined themselves to those gauges and types that could be conveniently produced from the available supplies of rod and wire. In so far as diversification proceeded beyond the fastener market, they also made Storer's patent lubricators (for engines) and Weston's patent differential ratchet braces, but these, together with their fleeting excursion into the realm of steam engines for small boats in 1888,[40] were sidelines.

Having decided to concentrate their attention on a relatively narrow band of products (albeit highly divided and specialised) Nettlefolds sought to contain the number of producers. Unlike their neighbours in Smethwick, the Patent Nut & Bolt Co., which bought and sold patents and licensed overseas manufacturers to use machines of their invention,[41] Nettlefolds consistently refused to deal in manufacturing technology. In May 1881, for example, they had received an inquiry from a Mr Tillmans whose factory in Russia had recently been destroyed by fire, wishing to purchase their machines. A refusal followed with the suggestion that Nettlefolds would be agreeable to 'make some working arrangement...for supplying the Russian market with screws'.[42] Further inquiries of a similar nature (from John M. Sumner & Co. of Manchester, wanting machines for Sweden; and Rabone Brothers of Birmingham, for Russia)[43] received the same response. By retaining the secrets of their manufacture within the business and not engaging in the secondary market of machine technology, Nettlefolds were able to maintain a firm hold on their monopoly within Britain.

In about 1925 the details and conventions of the company's marketing policy were revised and formalised in a plan which remained in force until the 1960s.[44] In essence it distinguished between the hardware factors (or large wholesalers), retailers (local ironmongers) and the customer. The hardware factors were asked to sign an agreement by which they were to stock all the articles listed in the Nettlefolds catalogue and buy exclusively from them. In return Nettlefolds undertook not to supply either ironmongers or consumers direct, apart from special exceptions which would be settled in advance. In addition they signed an agreement with virtually every ironmonger in the country which specified the factor or factors that would supply them and bound them to buy and stock exclusively from Nettlefolds all articles listed in the catalogue. On top of the published discount rate, factors were allowed an extra discount of 5 per cent. Further a rebate system, based on the loyalty agreement, was introduced by which both wholesalers and retailers were rewarded. Ironmongers received a 5 per cent rebate at the end of the year if their orders from factors had exceeded £100, which was not a difficult target to meet, while larger ironmongers could qualify for still higher percentages. The factor received a rebate in the form of a 10 per cent discount on their purchases and this was paid quarterly. Since the stock was often delivered direct from the factory to the shop, the factor could win this rebate for little more than collecting the order from the ironmonger and passing it on to the screw manufacturers.

Because Nettlefolds had direct agreements not only with hardware factors but also with virtually every ironmonger, they were able to remain in close touch with market developments. The consumer benefited because he had guaranteed access to supplies of good quality fasteners from an enormous number of retail outlets. The company maintained a high level of stock in its warehouse (orders were never executed directly in the works) so that deliveries were both quick and reliable. This marketing policy probably raised the cost of the woodscrew marginally but the customer continually exhibited a preference for quality and availability rather than low price.

The nature of their customers also assisted Nettlefolds in safeguarding their market share against competitors. The major consumers of woodscrews were first the building trade and secondly furniture manufacturers. By virtue of their large orders both categories of commercial customer could negotiate special discounts from the wholesalers. Woodscrews under 2 inches in length were boxed by the gross in cardboard cartons. Larger sizes were packed more elaborately in strong brown paper secured by string and also sold by the gross.[45] This method suited both the building and furniture trades which consumed woodscrews in large numbers and a wide variety of sizes and types; while the ironmonger could sell smaller quantities loose from the box to members of the public as they were required.

Although sales to the general public remained subsidiary, it was argued that national characteristics, in particular the belief that an Englishman's home was his castle and the desire to undertake carpentry tasks oneself, contributed to the continued success of the woodscrew. In the garden shed or workroom an Englishman might typically be expected to keep small boxes of Nettlefolds woodscrews; many would remain unused, but would be stored for contingencies and to demonstrate the owner's standing as a handyman. The established name and appeal of the green labelling ensured that the Nettlefold screw remained a symbol of good quality workmanship, while the maintenance of a monopoly made it difficult to purchase an alternative screw should the public decide that they might be poorly manufactured or overpriced.

Summary

On the demand side Nettlefolds were fortunate that in the period 1850 to 1939 new technology and working practices did little to disturb the woodscrew as a primary means of holding together pieces of timber. Other types of metallic or plastic fastener, or powerful adhesives, were not developed during these years and the building and furniture trades loyally continued to buy woodscrews in ever greater quantities. The problem was that they had become accustomed to being supplied with a myriad of gauges, types and coatings. Although output rose it was difficult to gain economies of scale for all sizes of woodscrew so long as machines had to be adjusted for new lengths, widths and different shaped heads. Although attempts were made to introduce thread-rolling machines (which ultimately came to the fore in the mid-twentieth century), the screw-cutting lathe, despite having to be stopped regularly to replace worn cutters, remained the most efficient means of mass-producing woodscrews in this period.

The market dominance secured by Nettlefolds during the mid-1870s was gained by adopting the latest technology and aggressively pricing competitors into insolvency or take-over. This monopoly was subsequently defended against overseas competitors by increasing the discounts but when faced with manufacturers in Germany, America, Belgium and France using equally advanced machinery, this policy produced a ruinous stalemate. Accordingly cartels were established to restrict competition to specified neutral countries, leaving their respective home markets unmolested.

Throughout this period Nettlefolds placed a consistent emphasis on quality and there is no evidence that they set out to exploit their monopoly by overcharging or manufacturing sub-standard woodscrews. Their attitude to their customers remained somewhat paternalistic, understandable in so far as the relationship had been established during the Victorian period. The marketing strategy of Nettlefolds was not the result of a master plan researched in detail on the basis of surveys of customers and economic trends; it evolved as the business grew and relied on the accumulated judgment and experience of the company's managers and salesmen. Formalised in the mid-1920s, it revealed a complexity and sophistication which lay at the root of the consistently high profits earned by Nettlefolds.

Acknowledgements

For their comments on an earlier draft of this chapter I am most grateful to Sir Trevor Holdsworth, Mr J. F. Howard, Mr S. Lloyd, Miss Elizabeth Rowbottom and Sir Anthony Bowlby. Any errors that remain are the author's responsibility alone.

Notes

1. Nettlefolds Ltd, Directors Minute Book, No. 1 (1880–6), 1 March 1881, p. 88.
2. 'Recollections of the Screw Dept' (typescript compiled by Nettlefolds in 1927), Mr Thomas Burns, p. 5; Nettlefolds Minute Book No. 2 (1886–94), 5 November 1889, p. 159; 6 January 1891, p. 217.
3. *Ironmonger* (10 February 1923), p. 96; *Hardware Trade Journal* (25 May 1934), p. 304.
4. D. J. Jeremy and C. Shaw, eds, *Dictionary of Business Biography*, hereafter *DBB*, III (1985), Edgar Jones, 'Arthur Keen', pp. 570–4.
5. Nettlefolds Minute Book No. 1, op. cit. 8 March 1880, p. 1.
6. For a detailed discussion of this story, see Edgar Jones, *Guest, Keen & Nettlefolds, Innovation and Enterprise, Volume One, 1759–1918*, (London) (forthcoming).
7. *Nettlefold & Chamberlain Catalogue*, 2nd edn (1871), pp. 1–15; *Nettlefold Ltd Screw Dept, Catalogue*, 18th edn (1932), pp. 8–104.
8. Birmingham University Archives, Chamberlain Papers, JC 1/18/2, Joseph Chamberlain's Business Notebook 1864–74, 21 December 1867.
9. Birmingham Screw Co. Ltd, Drawing No. 31, Cross Section and Transverse Plans, October 1870.

10. *DBB*, I (1983), Peter T. Marsh, 'Joseph Chamberlain', p. 646.
11. *DBB*, IV (1985), Edgar Jones, 'J. H. Nettlefold', pp. 428–31.
12. Nettlefolds Minute Book No. 1, op. cit. 23 March 1881, p. 91.
13. ibid. 7 October 1884, p. 317.
14. ibid.
15. British Library of Political and Economic Science, Tariff Commission Collection, TC 1 4/1 *Report from the Tariff Commission* IV (1909), para. 756.
16. 'Recollections', op. cit. Mr A. Weare, p. 9; Mr J. Dinnis, p. 22.
17. Correspondence with Mr Stephen Lloyd, former GKN director, November 1985.
18. Birmingham University Archives, Chamberlain Papers, JC 1/18/2, op. cit. 14 November 1865.
19. *The Engineer*, Vol. XX, 14 July 1865, p. 16; 'Recollections', op. cit. Mr R. Earp, p. 28.
20. ibid. p. 29.
21. *Guest, Keen & Nettlefolds Ltd, an outline history of this Group of Companies* (c. 1925), p. 49.
22. ibid. illustration of all GKN's trade marks, p. 66.
23. *Nettlefolds Ltd, Screw Dept, Catalogue*, Birmingham (1932), p. 10.
24. *English Mechanic and Mirror of Science* (1 January 1869), p. vii.
25. *Nettlefolds Ltd, Catalogue* (1900), front cover.
26. *Birmingham Daily Post*, 4 July 1914.
27. G. Phillips Bevan, ed., *British Manufacturing Industries* (London, 1878), W. C. Aitken, 'Wood Screws', p. 63.
28. *Practical Engineer*, 'A New Industry for Leeds', 10 July 1891.
29. *American Manufacturer* (18 January 1895), 'Our English Letter'.
30. *Evening Telegram*, Providence, 10 March 1898.
31. *Birmingham Daily Post*, 23 June 1898.
32. Nettlefolds Minute Book No. 2, 1 August 1893, p. 375; Nettlefolds Ltd, General Meeting Book 1880–1902, 25 September 1894, p. 50.
33. *GKN: an outline history*, op. cit.
34. Nettlefolds Minute Book No. 1, 2 November 1880, p. 76; 4 January 1881, p. 83.
35. ibid.
36. ibid. 2 February 1886, pp. 379–80.
37. ibid. 1 June 1886, p. 397; Nettlefolds Minute Book No. 2, 22 June 1888, op. cit. p. 389.
38. GKN Minute Book, I (1900–5), 6 March 1902, item 429.
39. ibid. II (1905–16), 5 October 1905, item 1173; 2 November 1905, item 1185; 7 December 1905, item 1207.
40. *Engineer*, lxvi (26 October 1888), p. 349.
41. Patent Nut & Bolt Co. Directors Minute Book No. 1 (1864–9), 3 October 1866, item 8; 8 April 1868, item 692.
42. Nettlefolds Minute Book No. 1, 3 May 1881, p. 96.

43. The plan outlined in a letter from Sir Anthony Bowlby, retired director of GKN, December 1985.
44. Nettlefolds Minute Book No. 1, 3 April 1883, p. 208.
45. *Nettlefolds Ltd, Screw Dept Catalogue* (1934), p. 2.

7 The British marketing of armaments 1885–1935

R. P. T. Davenport-Hines

Introduction

The arms business has several unusual characteristics. Unlike other industrial work the demand for armaments is volatile and unpredictable, not following any economic cycle, but moving in the thrall of international tension. The private armourer must adapt to fluctuations of peacetime orders without sacrificing his power of swift and immense wartime productive expansion. Above all armaments companies operate in a market with monopsony conditions: they serve 'one class of customer only, namely Government',[1] a client with no civilian equivalent in power or ruthlessness, and moreover do so in competition with the client's own factories (in Britain, the Royal Ordnance factories included Woolwich for artillery, Enfield for small arms and Waltham Abbey for explosives). The marketing of armaments has few features in common with the other industrial products considered in this book. As one company director wrote in 1931 of his relations with the Admiralty, 'there is no real salesmanship required, but very delicate negotiations are continually taking place'.[2] The aim of this chapter is to explore the nature of such negotiations and the marketing methods used by British armaments companies under these conditions of monopsony.

Trebilcock has coined the phrase 'special relationship' to describe the private armaments manufacturers' relations with the government's procurement officers, and has described in detail the mechanics of that relationship before 1914.[3] Here, the evolution of the 'special relationship' is considered over a longer period and on an international basis, with an attempt to assess the quality and organisation of the salesmanship which British armaments companies deployed at home and abroad.

The First World War will be shown as a watershed in the British marketing of armaments. The 'special relationship' which had evolved in 1888–1914 was shattered: the government's carefully created rings of private suppliers proved inadequate to meet national munitions requirements, the financial bases of the 'special relationship' were knocked asunder, and the informal personal contacts on which the relationship had relied were forced into a more impersonal institutional framework. Although the private manufacturers had suffered a severe dearth of

146

orders in 1907–11 the large surpluses of equipment and capacity left after the First World War, coupled with the disarmament policy of the British government in 1920–34, created an unprecedented paucity of business, which strained the 'special relationship'. With the clarifying vision of hindsight, the government's relations with its private suppliers before 1914 failed because few anticipated that, in an age of railways and industrialisation, a war between the European powers would require the total mobilisation of industry far in excess of the resources of a few specialist companies. After 1918 these relations were even less satisfactory: for economic and political reasons the government was unwilling to undertake all arms development and production themselves, and instead relied on a shrinking nucleus of specialist companies for both designs and supplies, with the result that rearmament, through shadow factories and other civilian manufacturers after 1936, was (in Trebilcock's phrase) a perpetual crisis.

From 1869, when the Admiralty's separate department of contracts was set up, until the early 1880s, the directors of contracts at the service ministries dealt with private suppliers through civilian agents. But during 1882–5 George Rendel of Armstrongs sat as an 'expert' Civil Lord at the Admiralty, while in 1885 Sir William White was recruited from Armstrong's warship department to become the Admiralty's Director of Naval Construction. These appointments inaugurated closer personal and financial links between businessmen and civil servants: increasingly thereafter the Admiralty and War Office eliminated middlemen to deal directly with manufacturers, inviting tenders in an open market on receipt of a requisition. Lists of approved suppliers were compiled for the vast range of commodities required by the armed forces, but for a small number of high-technology products, such as armour-plate, weaponry or explosives, the procurement officers operated a selective tendering policy intended to create a nucleus of proven and specialist suppliers.

According to the aphorism of Lord Fisher, favouritism was the key to efficiency. By 1908–13 the service departments were placing orders with twenty-one private arms manufacturers, of whom nine produced shells, seven produced explosives, five made small arms ammunition, four produced guns, and three produced small arms. These were conditions of oligopoly, with manufacture concentrated among only a few producers who encouraged the erection of entry-barriers to newcomers and preserved a high rate of profit among themselves. Procurement officers kept orders within this limited group of industrialists, believing that other manufacturers lacked the expertise for high-precision technology. Relations between these privileged manufacturers and their client were a strained mixture of wary collaboration and mutual exploitation. The procurement officers sometimes tried to outwit contractors, and directed the bulk of orders in lean times to government arsenals (Tables 7.1, 7.2, 7.3), starving the private manufacturers of business while expecting them to have staff and facilities in readiness when demand increased. As Floud has described the cartridge and torpedo departments of Greenwood & Batley:

> the firm was catering almost entirely for government orders, on which payment was often long delayed, and was in a market situation [where]...the

Table 7.1 To show Admiralty expenditure on armaments and percentage of money spent on naval armaments supplied by private industry 1905–12 and 1920–35[a]

Year	Total naval expenditure on armaments	Spent in government factories	Spent with private industry	Percentage of total amount spent on industry
	£	£	£	%
1905–06	2 553 000	1 347 000	1 206 000	47
1906–07	2 444 000	1 361 000	1 083 000	44
1907–08	1 818 000	1 220 000	598 000	33
1908–09	1 688 000	1 121 000	567 000	34
1909–10	2 080 000	1 286 000	794 000	38
1910–11	2 438 000	1 350 000	1 088 000	45
1911–12	3 351 000	1 521 000	1 830 000	55
1920–21	6 049 000	1 833 000	4 216 000	70
1921–22	4 009 000	1 723 000	2 286 000	57
1922–23	2 406 000	1 281 000	1 125 000	47
1923–24	2 680 000	1 321 000	1 359 000	51
1924–25	2 668 000	1 432 000	1 236 000	46
1925–26	2 649 000	1 483 000	1 166 000	44
1926	2 235 000	1 124 000	1 111 000	50
1927	3 070 000	1 366 000	1 704 000	58
1928	2 911 000	1 689 000	1 222 000	42
1929	2 606 000	1 568 000	1 038 000	40
1930	2 336 000	1 502 000	834 000	36
1931	2 160 000	1 283 000	877 000	41
1932	2 039 000	1 176 000	863 000	42
1933	2 520 000	1 333 000	1 187 000	47
1934	2 773 000	1 481 000	1 292 000	47
1935 (Forecast)	4 126 000	2 140 000	1 986 000	48

[a]Figures for 1913–19 omitted as distorted by the First World War.

Source: Evidence of Sir Maurice Hankey to Royal Commission on Private Manufacture of Armaments.

government attempted, by placing orders with selected companies, to persuade them to instal machinery to make a particular type of arms; once the machinery was installed, and the first order was completed, no further orders would be placed, all peacetime demand being supplied by the government factories, the government reasoning that the private firm would be unwilling to scrap its investment in new machinery, which would therefore be available in time of emergency need.[4]

The dominion of government procurement offices is incontestable. 'The power possessed by the Director of [Army] Contracts would appear to be unique in any business transaction', it was stated in 1901. 'His department is the largest purchasing

Table 7.2 To show army expenditure on armaments, and percentage of money spent with private industry 1905–13 and 1920–35[a]

Year	Total expenditure	Ordnance factories production for army	Trade balance (approx.)	Trade
	£	£	£	%
1905–06	2 681 053	1 279 770	1 400 000	52
1906–07	2 397 826	1 154 794	1 243 000	52
1907–08	1 869 345	1 125 771	744 000	40
1908–09	1 677 103	1 161 314	516 000	30
1909–10	1 466 022	919 458	547 000	37
1910–11	1 452 188	966 074	486 000	34
1911–12	1 512 466	893 344	619 000	41
1912–13	1 682 336	841 528	841 000	50
1920–21	b	1 414 061	—	—
1921–22	1 381 143	1 274 461	107 000	8
1922–23	1 841 843	1 360 938	481 000	26
1923–24	2 364 526	1 206 573	1 158 000	50
1924–25	2 569 986	1 602 906	967 000	38
1925–26	2 267 848	1 504 568	763 000	34
1926–27	1 949 812	1 243 222	707 000	36
1927–28	1 787 454	1 123 811	664 000	37
1928–29	1 946 350	1 025 361	921 000	47
1929–30	2 124 941	1 096 065	1 029 000	50
1930–31	1 555 494	976 984	579 000	37
1931–32	1 740 751	1 092 086	649 000	37
1932–33	1 556 299	987 073	569 000	37
1933–34	1 714 254	1 076 147	638 000	37
1934–35	2 293 809	1 016 652	1 277 157	56
1935–36 (Forecast)	4 800 000	1 363 360	3 436 640	72

[a]Figures for 1914–19 omitted because of the First World War.
[b]This figure was £5 742 204 but included large transactions from earlier years.

Source: Evidence of Sir Maurice Hankey to Royal Commission on Private Manufacture of Armaments.

department in the world.'[5] But as Oliver Lyttelton, a businessman who became a government official, concluded after describing the methods by which the Director of Army Contracts tried to buy 50 000 tons of copper during the Abyssinian crisis in 1935, 'the ignorance of Government Departments of the "market", or of the impact of quite simple transactions upon it, is only matched by their brazen commercial methods'.[6] Procurement officers seldom felt compunction about their methods or broken promises, as Lyttelton observed, 'no doubt secure in the knowledge that the Public Accounts Committee would applaud their efforts to get away with half the minimum charge'.[7] Thus in 1888 George Curzon, a director of Hadfields, was

Table 7.3 To show division of naval expenditure (1889–1905) on contracts with some major firms in £000

	1889–1893	1895–1897	1889–1900	1900–1901	1902–1903	1903–1904	1904–1905
Fairfield	–	132	835	903	823	657	829
John Brown[a]	356	351	581	873	340	950	679
London & Glasgow Co.	119	106	122	200	524	532	183
Vickers[a]	114	292	729	1017	876	1303	1575
Thames Ironworks	99	4	381	760	228	534	400
Cammell Laird[a]	235	29	152	340	225	514	260

[a]Including predecessors and constituent firms.

Source: S. Pollard, 'Laissez Faire and Shipbuilding', *Economic History Review*, 2nd series, 5 (1952), p. 108.

'frequently assured' by the War Office 'that so long as we could ensure punctual delivery, we were not likely to suffer from want of orders but that on the contrary we should have as much as we could do'. Hadfields therefore invested £10 000 in new shell-making plant, only to receive negligible government orders, so that by 1890 Curzon was complaining that Hadfields were 'in a worse position than at the start'.[8] Then again, in 1891, when Hadfields tendered for a contract for 6 inch shell, they obeyed a War Office suggestion to reduce their price in return for getting an enlarged order of 15 000 shells, but were then outraged to receive only an order for 7250 shells over two years (1892–4), at the reduced price. 'This reduction in orders amounts very nearly to a breach of faith on the part of the WO, who appear to have cajoled us into a substantial abatement of price and then to have given us the go-by', Curzon fulminated.[9] Similarly fifteen years later, in 1906, Birmingham Small Arms bought the Royal Small Arms factory at Sparkbrook from the War Office, the contract specifying that BSA would consequently receive a quarter of all trade orders for Lee Enfield rifles during 1906–9, such orders to be worth at least £20 000 until 1907. In the event the War Office reneged, and BSA found themselves saddled with major overcapacity in rifles until 1914.[10]

Other examples of this kind are provided by the Coventry Ordnance Co. As a reaction to an alliance in warship construction agreed in 1903 between Armstrongs, Beardmore and Vickers, John Brown of Sheffield, Cammell Laird, and Fairfields of Glasgow formed Coventry Ordnance jointly in 1905. 'The absolutely indispensable condition for the existence of the new concern was a flow of contracts from the Admiralty and the War Office', and the two service departments encouraged the creation of this new specialist supplier both to 'cover some of their requirements and act as a check on prices charged by the other private contractors'. Coventry Ordnance was initially guaranteed orders on condition that it avoided all price rings and renounced all arrangements (other than those of supplier or customer) with Vickers and Armstrongs, but the company 'soon learned the dangers of dependence' on government promises or orders. The Admiralty indicated that it wanted Coventry Ordnance to supply 9.2 inch guns in turrets: 'the company tooled up and had just completed installing and equipping the production lines when the Admiralty changed its mind about the turrets', and gave orders for larger turrets to Coventry Ordnance's competitors. Next, in 1909, Colonel H. H. Mulliner, Coventry Ordnance's managing director, became embroiled in a campaign about German naval preparedness directed against the Liberal government by J. L. Garvin, editor of the *Observer*. Contracts for large naval mountings had been promised to Coventry Ordnance, as Mulliner later wrote. 'However, the orders did not arrive, and at a board meeting several of my co-directors explained how they had been approached directly and indirectly by Admiralty officials, with a strong hint that these orders would not come until I left the works.' Mulliner promptly retired and Coventry Ordnance 'a few days afterwards...received the contract which we had been daily expecting for the past three months'. His successor as managing director, Sir Reginald Bacon, was recruited by Coventry Ordnance from the Admiralty, where he was Director of Naval Ordnance.[11]

Rings

Unpredictable demand made businessmen averse to erecting plant and maintaining it unused for hypothetical future crises, especially as orders receded once the emergency was over. As industrialists told the Royal Commission on the War in South Africa of 1903, large War Office orders before 1899 would have financed factory facilities together with a trained nucleus of personnel, and thus have facilitated wartime productive expansion.[12] Similarly the Director of Naval Construction advised in 1920 that if 'an approximate programme for the next five years could be foreshadowed', as happened with the Naval Defence Act of 1888, 'it would probably be possible to make much more satisfactory financial arrangements with the contractors by offering them a regular sequence of work...than by suddenly placing large orders as has usually been done'.[13] This uncertainty of demand under monopsonist conditions, coupled with the high cost of equipment, led to the evolution of compensatory mechanisms, which would make it absurd to portray the private armourers wholly as dupes or victims.

Specifically, after the Naval Defence Act of 1888 when the decision was taken to widen the number of private armaments manufacturers, the system of 'rings' was developed with official cognisance. There was no other industry in which it was so crucial for government to control its range of suppliers, whose number it consequently preferred to be small. But as the government found that a few suppliers acting as 'a tightly-grouped reserve of private manufacturing capacity' tended to increase prices, it retained some element of competition and other instruments of price control. 'As a client sufficiently powerful to play price-maker rather than price-taker', the British government 'could manipulate prices with some freedom', according to Trebilcock. 'However energetically the armourers might employ "ring" tactics to drive up prices, they still depended on the government's *acceptance* of their price – there was no alternative source of demand within the home market once the service ministries had declined to do business'.[14] In one authoritative description of 1913:

> The orders of a given year must be distributed so as to maintain private factories in efficient condition, during periods of limited demand. Capital must be maintained intact, and staffs must not be dissipated even when orders are so scarce as to require but a skeleton of full output conditions. Individual companies would be tempted to seek salvation by cutting prices so as to secure a disproportionate share of orders when these are not plentiful enough to go round. The victims of any such attempt naturally respond by a further drop in prices, and...the impossible combination of scarcity of orders and low prices supervenes. The object of a ring is to regulate personal greediness in the common interest, so as to maintain manufacturing facilities intact for the time when the strain of exceptional demand arises. Government officials approve any machinery for the peaceful division of orders in proportion to the relative scope of individual firms, this course only being possible when prices are standardised by mutual agreement...any undue inflation of prices would bring new firms into the business.[15]

As Floud has shown there was by 1889–90 longstanding price fixing and market sharing, to which procurement officers were not privy, among suppliers of machine-tools for government armaments requirements. Collusion between companies which were component suppliers to arms-makers rather than fully integrated armaments manufacturers themselves may have persisted for some years; but for those companies which directly supplied weaponry to the British government the penalties for transgression of ring etiquette were severe. In 1907 Cammell Laird was struck off the list of Admiralty and War Office contractors after falsifying figures at their Sheffield factory: in the ensuing crisis the chairman and two managing directors resigned, and although the company was subsequently restored to the list it remained on the brink of closure for several years.[16] Similarly after 1924 the Air Ministry was involved in negotiations with Hawkers about their Hart, a two-seater flight reconnaissance aircraft. 'We have found them exceedingly difficult in the matter of price negotiations', the Directorate of Contracts wrote in 1930, 'until they are passed over on account of price, this attitude will persist.' On one occasion when tenders were put out, both Hawker and A. V. Roe returned identical prices for their Hart and Antelope machines, so when Hawkers and Faireys both put in prices of £3500 for their Hart and Fleetwing machines in May 1930, the Director of Contracts determined to make an example of them.

> There is nothing actually wrong in collusive identical tenders – *force majeure* compels us to tolerate it from the Great Oil Companies – but there is no reason why we should acquiesce in...a bare-faced attempt by two prosperous and important firms who have done well out of the Royal Air Force, to stifle

competition in a peculiarly sheltered industry at the expense of its only large patron and foster parent, particularly when it enjoys the unusual advantage of free trade and protection [he minuted to the Air Minister]. I propose to decline both tenders and when the machine has been selected to call for a single tender which will be liable to costing... Another course would be for both firms to be...warned as to the impression produced on the whole [Air] Council by their conduct and invited to reconsider their tenders which in no case would be accepted as they stood.[17]

Armour plate provides one example of the long-term development of a ring. Here the Admiralty negotiated with five contractors who co-operated fully with one another over the price and proportionate distribution of orders. The costliness of the plant required, and the impossibility of its conversion to civilian use, justified this arrangement, which worked relatively smoothly until the First World War. During the munitions crisis many other non-specialist manufacturers produced armour plate, and after 1918 orders shrivelled. When the Washington naval conference of 1921 between Britain, Japan and the USA agreed a ten-year 'holiday' in capital ship construction, the Admiralty cancelled orders for joint capital ships recently placed with Fairfields, John Brown, Swan Hunter, and Beardmore. The British delegation at Washington expected that during the naval holiday, 'Government should take over manufacture of all warship specialised industry', while the Cabinet accepted the need to keep all 'necessary plant in existence by subsidies [during] the ten years' holiday'.[18] As a contribution to their establishment charges the armour plate makers sought a government subsidy including £41 365 for Cammell Laird, £49 078 for Brown, and £86 000 each for Vickers and Armstrongs: the Admiralty indeed considered paying £46 000 each to the former two companies, and £35 000 each to the latter, but pressure to economise after the Geddes axe on services expenditure prevented agreement being reached on a subsidy.[19]

The armour plate ring was coaxed and cajoled by the Admiralty to maintain their plant almost unused throughout 1921–5, but then exploded with wrath when an order for deckplate was given to Colville, who had submitted a cheaper price, and who had learnt their expertise from members of the ring during the war. As Brown's managing director complained, his company maintained plant worth £1 million, whereas Colvilles carried plant worth only £100 000. Brown with 'their heavy burden of overhead charges' therefore faced 'unfair competition', and could not 'supply at an economic rate' unless the Admiralty granted expenses for the maintenance of plant. 'Up to 1931 they would carry a burden of overhead charges out of all proportion to the orders that could be placed with them...at present they were losing orders through no fault of their own.'[20] The Admiralty then suggested reducing the armour ring to three members – Armstrongs, Vickers and one other – but the quintet counter-proposed that instead of a maintenance allowance of £71 340 to each of three companies, that total of £214 020 should be divided between the quintet, but deducting £15 for each ton of armour ordered. The five companies calculated their actual costs of maintaining staff and plant for armour plating as £81 713 for Armstrongs, £116 633 for Beardmore, £91 678 for Brown, £59 155 for Cammell Laird, and £147 196 (later revised to £74 896) for Vickers.

Eventually in 1926 the ring agreed with the Admiralty a price of £190 per ton for cemented ship armour up to 2500 tons, with £136 per ton for higher quantities; depending on the amount ordered, the price for non-cemented armour varied from £160 to £184 per ton. The ring agreed to rebate £21 per ton of armour ordered by other home buyers, and £15 per ton of foreign armour, the amount recoverable by the Admiralty being limited to £85 000. The ring's membership and capacity were diminished by the fusions between Armstrongs, Cammell Laird and Vickers in 1927–8 (creating the English Steel Corporation in 1929), and armour plate prices were re-negotiated in 1930, with ESC recovering 60 per cent of orders, and the Admiralty price being effectually a subsidy. As late as 1935 Britain needed only about 7000 tons of armour plate, but despite expansion by ESC, Beardmore and Firth Brown in 1936, it was calculated in 1937 that production for the next three years would be 65 000 tons short of needs. Indeed the Admiralty considered seeking supplies from Schneider, Krupp or Carnegie-Illinois, and 12 500 tons were received in 1938–9 from Vítkovice, a Czech factory under German control.[21]

Financial Facilities

Just as the assumption before 1914 that selected private manufacturers would satisfy national productive needs in any emergency did not survive the First World War, so the financial basis on which manufacturers sold armaments to the British government was also transformed by the events of 1914–18. As one director of Vickers lamented in 1928, 'before 1914' armaments companies 'made a great deal of money', but 'for their ultimate welfare the money was perhaps too easily made'.[22]

Wartime expansion to meet the demand for munitions often proved ruinous. One of the few metallurgical companies to pay ordinary dividends during the 1920s was the South Durham Steel & Iron Co., which had disagreed with the munitions authorities during the war and undertook little armaments work. Without big wartime extensions to adapt, they did not issue new capital after 1918 and enjoyed greater flexibility than most competitors.[23] Similarly one of those involved in the collapse of Armstrongs bewailed in 1926, 'if we could set the clock back, and have been able to see the future when in negotiation with the Government for the [wartime] expansion of the plant, we would have flatly refused to have entertained the Government's proposals.'[24] This view was confirmed in 1926 by the Ministry of Munitions' former Controller of Iron and Steel Production: 'great extensions have since completion been either partially standing, or if working, losing very vast sums of money with little chance...of any change in the near future'.[25]

Notwithstanding the facilities provided by the government to finance war expansion, or write it down after the cessation of hostilities, the addition of emergency plant could be cripplingly expensive. In particular, because 'war-like stores are a high-class engineering job involving heavy overhead expenses',[26] the

154

costs of specialist armourers (and consequently their prices during the First World War) were often higher than those of factories which were mobilised to munitions production during 1914–18, but usually geared to satisfying a stable civilian demand requiring lower overheads. Greenwood & Batley, for example, had maintained productive capacity exceeding fourfold or fivefold the amount of cartridges ordered, and during a short period of high demand wanted to recover its previous susbstantial outlay: they warned the War Office in September 1914 that 'in view of the present urgent demands, all manufacturers are increasing their plant very considerably, and therefore when normal conditions again prevail, the large increases made to the now existing plant will become useless'. Because of these 'temporary and abnormal conditions' contractors sought to 'protect themselves against probably very heavy loss of capital by asking rather higher prices'.[27] Notoriously these factors led to many discrepancies and disagreements over the costs and prices of the specialist manufacturers, especially during the earlier period of the war. As the deputy minister of munitions wrote in 1916, 'Trevor Dawson [of Vickers] metaphorically shrouded himself in the Union Jack and almost wept as I expostulated that these great patriotic firms were charging too much.'[28]

Attempts were made to meet this problem at the time. From October 1914 onwards the War Office placed 'assisted contracts', whereby munitions manufacturers received grants or advances of money usually worth the total estimated cost of extensions required to reach a given maximum output by a given date. In earlier 'assisted contracts' these extensions were to remain the property of the companies: subsequently, when the extent of post-war over-capacity was clearer, the latter agreed that subsidised plant would remain government property.[29] From 1915 the government eased manufacturers' liquidity with advances and banking loans worth 80 per cent of the value of the arms, paid on delivery; and partial remittance of the company's tax bill so as to assist their capital expenditure incurred in expanding armament output. This became the general practice during 1918 and postulated that the company was prepared to bear at least some of the risk, that the new fixed assets would be useful after the war, and that there would be sufficient profits to make an appreciable obligation under Excess Profits Duty.[30] These postulates were not always present. After 1918 many fixed assets proved hard to convert to peacetime industrial production, while conversion costs fell as a heavy charge on future profits, as the example of the Skefko ball-bearing factory at Luton demonstrated.

Until the outbreak of war in 1914 Britain imported some 2 250 000 bearings from Germany annually, and the capital cost of the Luton factory was about £50 000. At governmental urging, after August 1914 Skefko spent £500 000 on buildings, plant and machinery, and imported manufactured stock from its Swedish parent company until its indebtedness to the latter reached £465 000. The government provided writing off allowances at 40 per cent of cost for buildings, and 50 per cent for cost of plant (£240 300), and financed £525 000. This left a balance of £284 700 on loan, repayable during 1922–4. Other firms were expanded by the Ministry of Munitions, such as Hoffman, Rudge Whitworth and Ransome & Marles. By 1921, when both Hoffman and Rudge Whitworth were 'entirely shut down' under government ownership, the average monthly sales of ball bearings in Britain were worth £70 000, which Skefko could absorb threefold, or Hoffmans twelvefold. Skefko calculated that their fixed assets had cost £289 000, and their stock in trade £720 000, whereas a factory suitable for their post-war requirements would have cost £175 000 with stock of £300 000. Of the difference of £500 000 between these totals, £300 000 was recoverable by forced liquidation of stock, leaving a balance of £200 000 which was a dead loss.[31] Owing to government limitation of prices, Skefko made little wartime profit, and recorded a loss for 1921 of £120 000.

Skefko was an extreme case of the adverse effects of war production on industry, but many other companies were left with comparable grievances. Thus in 1920 Rolls-Royce claimed £388 000 from the Ministry of Munitions, but accepted £370 000 for a swift settlement. BSA a few months later laid a Petition of Right for £135 090 against the Crown for unfulfilled rifle contracts. In 1922 Cammell Laird made a Petition of Right for £565 560, but settled for £290 000 in 1923.[32] Vickers, whose wartime transactions with the Ministry of Munitions were estimated at £100 million, submitted in 1920 a claim of £7 008 214 which was later settled for £1.75 million.[33] Although often these were a small proportion of the total value of contracts received from the government the amounts involved were critical to financing the manufacturers' transition to peacetime civilian production.

The risks which business met in extending its productive capacity, especially involving outside borrowing, were acknowledged in rearmament policy of the late 1930s. An agreement of 1936 concerning the Air Ministry's expansion programme for 1935–9 provided that if the contractor found during 1939–41 that he had seriously excess capacity, he could claim compensation for the difference between the cost of capital assets written down by depreciation at income tax rates, or any higher rates conceded in Air Ministry contracts, and the market value of such assets at 31 March 1941.[34] Other 'capital assistance schemes', where the government partly or wholly provided the fixed capital for rearmament extensions, were agreed from 1937. In cases like shipbuilding where it was possible that building extensions would have post-war utility capital, assistance schemes sometimes included a contributory element from the firms concerned.[35] Indeed such was the magnitude of the problem of fixed capital for wartime expansion that Vickers in 1936 stated publicly that in another major war they would be happy for their ownership to be taken over by the government for the duration of hostilities, as was done with the railways in 1914–18, with management left under the directors' control, with dividends paid to shareholders, and with allowances for depreciation and an agreed payment for obsolescence when the factories were returned to private control.[36]

As a result of the blows to the 'special relationship' administered during the First World War, most of the specialist private armourers of 1914 left the sector within twenty years. Coventry Ordnance in 1919 merged with three other businesses to form the English Electric Co. The armament side of John Brown's business merged in 1930 with their Sheffield neighbour, Firths; and by 1936 Firths were capable of meeting only small orders for hardened shell. Birmingham Small Arms largely left armament *manufacture* by 1925, although dealing in second-hand material. Beardmore was reduced to an armament nucleus, capable in 1936 of meeting small orders for naval guns. The Projectile Co. could cope with various shell orders, and

156

Hadfields had a considerable capacity in hardened shell.[37] The Darlington Forge Co. went into voluntary liquidation in 1933. Armstrong's armament side was merged into Vickers in 1927, as was part of Cammell Laird's in 1928. Although this loss of capacity was regretted in Whitehall, it was the dispersal of research, development and production specialists within the companies, and the loss of their records and traditions, that caused the keenest anxiety to procurement officers.[38]

Domestic Marketing

Relations between the service departments and their private manufacturers were altered in other ways by the First World War. In 1907 one Admiralty official described his department, Armstrongs and Vickers, as 'rather a trinity',[39] and in 1913 it was said that 'precious little of what comes out of the Admiralty construction department by the front door has not previously entered at the back'.[40] Many companies tried to emphasise or enhance the intimacy of their official relations by the choice of directors or managers drawn either from the nobility or senior official class. The young politician George Curzon was given a board seat by Hadfields worth £250 a year when his crony St John Brodrick was at the War Office, although his attempt to exert special influence strained their friendship without succeeding in either by-passing officials or extracting more orders. Beardmore's board was joined in 1904 by the Marquess of Graham, young heir to a Scottish dukedom, who proved an enthusiastic but not brilliant recruit, and in 1908 by a more experienced administrator, Colonel O. C. Armstrong, formerly of the Indian government's Military and Finance Department; Rear-Admiral T. B. S. Adair served as superintendent of its gun department (1907–28) after being court-martialled when the battleship *Montagu* under his command was shipwrecked; while an obscure and impecunious Irish baronet, Sir John St George, was employed to represent Beardmore at meetings of the armour plate ring. Many other examples could be adduced.

One director of Armstrongs, Lord Rendel (Plate 7.1), described his company as 'not only an essential auxiliary of the Government but...itself essentially dependent ...upon its relations with the Government'. Rendel in fact argued to political friends 'that *one* constructing firm, capable of supplying *all* naval requirements was the cheapest policy...as the profits of only one business would have to be provided'. As part of his strategy to give Armstrongs pre-eminence as 'a semi-Governmental enterprise like Krupp',[41] he tried to obtain Lords Milner or Kitchener as chairman and from 1911 successfully recruited to the board officials like Sir George Murray of the Treasury and Sir Charles Ottley of the Committee of Imperial Defence, and colonial administrators like Sir Percy Girouard or Lord Sydenham. The chief result of this policy was not to enhance Armstrong's official relations, but to pack the board with elderly men lacking business experience who presided over the company's financial catastrophe of 1921–5.

The Edwardian workings of the 'special relationship' are epitomised by Trevor Dawson of Vickers. A sailor who was Experimental Officer at Woolwich Arsenal when recruited to become Ordnance Superintendent at Vickers in 1896, he was a power on

Plate 7.1 Lord Rendel, the director of Armstrongs, who wanted to establish his company as a semi-governmental monopoly enterprise (BBC Hulton Picture Library).

the board throughout 1898–1931. Heavily involved in research, development, production and commercial liaison, the service departments always found him 'amenable and handy', and he was restored to the naval list in 1902. His personality and contacts became integral to the organisation of British national defence. During the Anglo-South African war, he recruited a secret agent for the government, in 1904 he fed the War Office with details of Russian policy in Tibet and later he skated through the ice-bound Kiel dockyards spying on German naval shipbuilding for the Admiralty. At the height of Anglo-American naval rivalry in 1920 he sent the First Lord of the Admiralty data 'very secretly obtained from absolutely reliable sources' on new US government orders for 97 914 gross tons of armour plate, to strengthen the First Lord's hand in demanding Cabinet approval for large naval estimates.[42] Yet even Dawson fell out with the War Office in 1904 when he told Arthur Balfour, the Prime Minister, that Vickers' artillery contract had been delayed by the War Office's non-delivery of drawings, and was promptly cited by Balfour 'as a witness to the delays and improvidence of the War Office'. The Secretary of State furiously contested Dawson's allegations, and had a long stormy interview with 'this clever but somewhat slippery gentleman'.[43]

It might be thought that the First World War enhanced this intimacy by the secondment to Whitehall of industrialists known as Lloyd George's 'men of push and go'. In fact the opposite occurred, as indicated by Sir Eustace Tennyson-d'Eyncourt, the retiring Director of Naval Construction, in 1924. There was no suitable candidate outside the Admiralty to succeed him, he wrote:

> The conditions now…are totally different from those subsisting before the war, when most of the information held by the Admiralty was, to a very large extent, available for shipbuilders and naval architects outside. When the war began, immediately an immense amount of special information was accumulated, including all the experience gained during naval operations, and all the confidential experiments made…All this later information has been kept very strictly within the walls of the Admiralty, and no-one outside has the special knowledge required to enable the best design and construction work to be done to meet the new conditions.[44]

For this reason every British warship (except submarine repair depots) constructed after 1918 by private contractors was designed by d'Eyncourt or his successor, and not by private shipyard designers such as Sir George Owens-Thurston, Vickers' naval designer.[45] Moreover the allegations of political radicals that merchants-of-death were subverting procurement agencies undoubtedly constrained official relations with businessmen, although as an admiral in naval intelligence wrote in 1926, 'we are doing everything possible in the Admiralty to assist the armament firms'.[46] These tendencies to more anodyne relations were enhanced by the elaborate procurement bureaucracy which evolved after 1918.

After the three service departments had wrested back their supply duties from the Ministry of Munitions in 1920, an inter-departmental Contracts Co-ordinating Committee was formed, to be replaced in 1924 by a new organisation, the Principal Supply Officers Committee (PSOC). This was put under the aegis of the Committee of Imperial Defence, and was intended to fend off the administrative convulsion of creating a Ministry of Supply, while preparing plans for increasing supplies during a national emergency. In 1927 the PSOC was reconstituted under the President of the Board of Trade, and a Supply Board was created to study national war requirements in raw materials and manufactured products, and to allocate Britain's productive capacity accordingly. The Supply Board was subdivided into seven committees, each with a speciality like armaments, engineering stores or shipbuilding, and a nationally ramified organisation, of sizeable proportions, developed. 'At a level of administrative planning Britain had never been better prepared for a major war than…in September 1939';[47] but the system had none of the subjective personal ingredients that characterised the heyday of Lord Fisher and Sir Trevor Dawson. There was no part for flamboyant individuals: only a demand for well-oiled administrative apparatus run by anonymous civil servants.

The post-Armistice character of the 'special relationship' is conveyed by Vickers' experience with land armaments. The huge surplus of munitions left after 1918, and the political impossibility of large Army Estimates in the 1920s, meant that poor demand persisted. Until 1927 Dawson handled liaison with the War Office, and supervised Vickers' foreign policy, with the support of three colleagues, H. J. Morriss of the Ordnance Department (director 1919–26), the gun designer Sir George Buckham (director 1919–28) and Colonel W. C. Symon (director 1919–26). The technical staff at Vickers House sometimes performed poorly, the sales staff lacked push, and foreign clients occasionally complained that they could not get models or detailed figures of what Vickers had to sell.[48]

One Vickers' bagman at this time was Major Ferdinand Cavendish-Bentinck, an Old Etonian, who was severely wounded at Mons in 1914 and invalided out of the army in 1919. He was Liberal parliamentary candidate for South Kensington, and worked for a paint company until it went into liquidation, whereupon in 1923 his father used influence with Sir Edmund Wyldbore-Smith (director of Vickers 1921–8) to procure him a berth as assistant to Murray-Baillie covering Belgium and France for Vickers from Brussels. Later Cavendish-Bentinck settled in Kenya, where he became a fanatical if charming spokesman for white settlers' interests. Always impecunious, he was unique among members of the Kenyan Legislative Council for depending upon politics for his income, and was later made its Speaker so as to secure his financial position in old age. Surviving until 1980 as the eighth and penultimate Duke of Portland, he epitomised the indigent but better-class and often more effective bagmen employed by Vickers during and after the First World War.

The indifferent management and sales initiative of Vickers military armaments during 1918–27 were transformed when General Sir Noel Birch was recruited as director in charge of land armaments sales from the War Office, where he had been Master General of Ordnance. This extrovert soldier took to his second career with zeal and zest. His military experience gave him mastery of client-contacts at home and abroad, and he hectored War Office brass-hats with the freedom of an old friend. While Vickers' Barrow naval yards were described as 'a shop to which the Admiralty came for what it wanted, and if there was a difference of view about what was best, the customer was always right',[49] Birch treated the War Office as if he was still a member of the Army Council. Thus in 1929, with his co-directors' concurrence, he wrote to Field Marshal Milne, Chief of Imperial General Staff, about the 'serious' position of industrial mobilisation: 'The War Office complains that our prices are high. When you get shops working at fifty per cent of their capacity, the prices can be nothing else. After all the shareholders must have some consideration even if they are rash enough to take shares in a national concern.'

Concerning the War Office veto on Vickers selling current weaponry types abroad in case such sales jeopardised the secrecy of British research and development, Birch urged Milne:

Release every model as soon as it is accepted, whether it is gun, tank, rifle or instrument of any sort for war. It is only by selling new things that we can hope to live as an armament firm. Releasing can do the Empire nothing but good, and it will increase our power of mobilisation, and we are not near enough to war to make it dangerous.

He complained of the practice, arising from the manner in which the Service Estimates were put before parliament, whereby government work 'as a rule ceases on 1st April and does not begin again until June', causing slack periods of uneconomic working. Birch continued:

If we are honest as a nation we must pay just as much attention to the industrial mobilisation for war as we do to our armed forces and act accordingly…British outside armament firms…should get the same proportion of orders and the same facilities as the Arsenal has for continuous work… To put it plainly we are being had for fools. Other nations are pushing all they know how to get orders for their armament firms for two reasons. One is to produce their own armaments cheaply, and the second is to keep their armament firms alive. Further, they cannot be unmindful…that they are incidentally reducing the fighting power of the British Empire…the next war will be won in the workshop.

If private manufacture continued to run down, Birch asked, 'where will be the force behind diplomacy?'[50]

Birch believed that profits from armaments 'should be looked upon as windfalls', and that Vickers' future profits lay with commercial work.[51] Nevertheless he put a tremendous effort into marketing organisation, and until 1929 there was 'great deal of strafing'.[52] Birch dismissed several staff, like General Guy Livingston, Vickers' volatile agent in Argentina, Paraguay, Peru and Uruguay. Livingston had been recruited in 1920 at an annual salary of £4500 to win aeronautical business in South America (after a stormy spell as first aviation correspondent of *The Times* during 1919).[53] Something of the official attitude to him, and to Vickers before Birch's arrival, is conveyed by a letter from an attaché to naval intelligence in 1926:

He is a Jew boy, I should imagine very much alive and a thoroughly good businessman. I am told he started life as a ranker but I cannot vouch for this. He is quite a nice fellow to meet in the ordinary way…The trouble out here (and it is really the same at home), is that all the Vickers people seem to be rather slippery, rather what shall I say, not perhaps quite the right class. This opinion may be wrong, but it is certainly held at the legations.[54]

Birch immediately recruited men of better stamp: three artillerymen who had won the DSO in the First World War, Colonel Gerald Kinsman, Colonel Rupert Ryan and Colonel Charles Bridge. Kinsman had joined the Royal Artillery in 1896 and was chief instructor in gunnery during 1918–19. In 1921 he was seconded to the Chilean army, and was British military attaché to Chile and Brazil in 1923–7. A fluent speaker of Spanish, he took charge of Vickers' armament business in South America in 1928 and remained with the company until 1945. He made tours of South America, using the first in 1928 to select and appoint various new agents, and leaving memoranda of his visits with the Admiralty, Foreign Office and War Office.[55] Ryan had Irish, Macedonian and Australian roots; was educated at Harrow and Woolwich; and after distinguished war service, was British Deputy High Commissioner on the Rhineland Commission at Coblenz, 1920–8. His wife was an earl's daughter,[56] and after their divorce in 1935 he entered Australian politics. His commanding manner and artillery expertise made him a good salesman, and his overseas travels for Vickers included spells in Bangkok and Moscow. Regular officers, like Ryan, who served on the Rhineland Control Commission, were convinced, as one of them wrote, that Germany 'never has been disarmed, materially or morally' and 'has never acknowledged her responsibilities, has never accepted defeat, is determined to rearm in any event, and is merely biding her time'.[57]

Bridge (Plate 7.2), who was a nephew of the most able opponent of Lord Fisher's naval policies, Admiral Sir Cyprian Bridge, was a former military attaché at Washington, Warsaw and Prague, who joined Vickers rather than accept the offer of the same post in China. He spoke French, German and Italian, with a smattering of central European languages, and left Vickers in 1934 to become founding Secretary General of the British Council. Appointed Head of the British Military Mission to Poland in 1940, like Cavendish-Bentinck, he subsequently settled in Kenya, until driven out by the Mau-Mau. 'A difficult man...with a very hot temper', who was prone to throw *Who's Who* at his secretaries, Bridge was an apparently conventional man with unexpected streaks of idiosyncrasy. 'In addition to the energy and exactitude of a first-rate staff officer, the courtesy and knowledge of the world expected of a military attaché, and the dash and choler proper to an Irish cavalryman, he possessed...[an] indefinable mixture of devilry and charm.'[58] He proved crucial in improving the co-ordination of Vickers' land armaments sales and in laying the foundations for British rearmament.

Bridge and Ryan 'were both exceptionally intelligent people, and would have risen to high rank had they remained in the Army'.[59] Part of Bridge's job was privately 'to refute the statements made by sloppy pacifists that we and Schneider, Škoda and Bofors farm out all armament orders between us',[60] and together with Birch he was responsible for publicity and propaganda. He was a proponent of mechanisation, respected by men such as Sir John Carden, the tank designer, or progressive soldiers like Sir Frederick Pile.[61] Apart from his correspondence with military attachés and agents he accompanied Birch on a Baltic tour in 1932, and visited Berlin in 1933 in search of Chinese orders.[62] Bridge, like Kinsman and Ryan, was recruited at an annual salary of £1000 and also drew retired army pay. Vickers (particularly Bridge) worked cordially but discreetly with British Intelligence,[63] one of whose officers wrote to Birch from the War Office in 1928:

Our M[ilitary] A[ttaché]s do what they can to assist the sale of British war material: we here realise only too well how you are handicapped in

Plate 7.2 Charles Bridge, who gave Vickers' military sales organisation much-needed efficiency and respectability in the 1930s, photographed when military attaché at Washington (Mr Christopher Bridge).

competition with foreign armament firms by the fact that the latter receive Govt: assistance in more ways than one – but you can rely on us in M[ilitary] I[ntelligence] to assist in any way we can.[64]

Indeed their Romanian representative for almost all of the interwar period, Edwin Boxshall (1897–1984), was in charge of British intelligence in the Balkans for much of that time, and was later an important figure in the Special Operations Executive. Men like Bridge and Ryan, with their first-hand knowledge of German and Czech economic mobilisation,[65] were a far cry from lurid merchants-of-death legends about Sir Basil Zaharoff, propagated in this period, but represent more accurately Vickers' armament business after the early 1920s.

When Birch took over, Vickers' military sales could scarcely have been in a sorrier condition. In February 1928 they had only two foreign land artillery orders (for Lithuania and Bolivia) and felt routed by Schneider and Škoda.[66] Birch's new team held that another war was inevitable: the 'only chance' of achieving the necessary industrial mobilisation was 'by selling munitions abroad'.[67]

Holding these beliefs they attacked their new work with energy and resource. The marketing problems confronting Birch were typified by Vickers' experience with machine-guns. During the First World War some 71 355 machine-guns of Vickers type were produced (in addition to 133 104 Lewis machine-guns of BSA type), but the company was not complacent, and in 1918, at Dawson's behest, bought the rights of a new machine-gun designed by a Frenchman, General Berthier. During the next sixteen years over £100 000 was invested by the company in developing the Vickers-Berthier machine-gun, but until 1923 they had only one order, for sixty guns, from Spain.[68] By 1928 only Latvia and Bolivia had adopted it, while the British army's actual machine-gun stocks in that year were 11 860 Vickers, 37 760 Lewis and 31 692 Hotchkiss, compared with estimated needs respectively of 2774, 1740 and 1368.[69] Internationally Vickers faced fourteen competitors (Colt, Belgium; Brno and Škoda, Czechoslovakia; Madsen, Denmark; Darne and Hotchkiss, France; Simpson, Germany; Fiat and Breda, Italy; Star and Trapote, Spain; Führer, Oerlikon and Solothurn, Switzerland), and were 'competing for work that would not keep a cat'.[70] Finally in 1929 the Indian army ordered Berthiers, but anticipated contracts from the War Office never materialised, as by the early 1930s the Berthier had lost its technical lead to other guns, notably Brno's, which was 30 per cent cheaper than the Berthier.[71] Vickers and Brno had in fact discussed a three-year agreement to collaborate over tender prices in 1928 and to give one another a free shot at securing orders: it is unclear whether the agreement was actually signed, but in any case it expired by 1931.[72] Vickers' annual drawing office expenses on machine-guns had reached £10 000 in 1934, while their Crayford factory was equipped to produce weekly 1000 guns within eighteen months, but the Berthier was beaten internationally by the Brno, which began British production in 1937 at Enfield as the Bren gun.[73]

Vickers' aviation armaments had little more success than in land weaponry, and also committed major marketing errors in the 1920s. Without a contract signed in October 1919 to supply forty Vimy aircraft to China, Vickers would have closed the

164

Aviation Department, which was anyway absorbed into the Ordnance Department in the summer of 1920. All of its London staff were dismissed[74] except for three secretaries, Captain Peter Dyke Acland, the head of the department, Brigadier W. B. Caddell (late Director of Aircraft Equipment at the War Office), responsible for developing foreign sales, and the chairman's son, Oliver Vickers. Acland was a handsome cavalry officer whose influence was based on social contacts rather than technical expertise:[75] when Lord Trenchard, Chief of Air Staff 1918–29, was hired by Vickers to report on their aviation business in 1930 he criticised Acland, who left Vickers shortly afterwards.

Together Acland and Oliver Vickers made a marketing blunder which damaged Vickers' reputation for technical leadership. During the 1920s the life of RAF aeroplanes in service was not supposed to exceed five years: in the fourth year of life competitions were called to decide upon replacements. Therefore when 1925 proved an important year for replacements, it was obvious that 1930 would also be critical. In 1925–6 Vickers sold seventy-eight big heavy machines (Vernons, Virginias and Victorias) to the Air Ministry, but only nineteen in 1927, sixteen in 1928 and none in 1929. From drawing board to production of a new type took three years, yet in 1930 Vickers had no replacement in stocks. Trenchard called this 'a definite lack of endeavour to provide new machines to replace the old ones where obsolescence should have been foreseen'. In 1928 Vickers bought for about £400 000 Supermarine Aviation, specialists in flying boats and high-speed aircraft, whose chief designer in 1920–37 was the Spitfire's progenitor R. J. Mitchell. In 1925 Supermarine had sold six Southamptons, followed by fourteen in 1926; ten in 1927; sixteen in 1928; and two in 1929. 'It should have been obvious after the first one or two production orders that the time would come when the machines would die out', but again, Trenchard complained, nothing was done.[76]

Foreign Marketing

In Britain, as elsewhere, the development and production costs of armaments always exceeded government funds for military use. The cost of maintaining facilities for such elaborate and expensive production was high, as were the production costs on the small output required to meet peacetime domestic demand, although 'rings' and other domestic price-fixing arrangements raised or maintained some export prices. Arms exports were essential to reduce labour and material costs per unit of production, and to support the maintenance of skilled employees. Exports enabled research and development costs, and other special expenses, to be distributed over longer production runs, and were thus crucial to maintain productive capacity.

In the international arms market, the First World War was as much a watershed as in the domestic market. There was a proliferation of production, which not only left the world with huge excess capacity after 1918 but also with large surpluses of weaponry, which cut the demand for new products for more than a decade. The periodic interwar economic crises and dislocation of foreign exchange meant that the financial terms offered by companies in arms contracts were often more important than the technical superiority of the weapon. The British government became less sympathetic, in some respects, to supporting their arms exporters, and as British prestige and self-confidence faltered after 1921 difficulties increased for the bagmen of arms companies, as political nuances were crucial in deals of this sort. After 1919 British armourers were struggling in a diminished market against competitors who had increased in number and expertise, on political and economic terms which were far more adverse than before 1914. Following the war all Great Powers were arms producers, and according to figures compiled by Noel-Baker in 1936 purchased 78 per cent of all arms manufactured in the world. Other producing and non-producing allied States accounted for another 12 per cent, which left only 10 per cent of the world for free competition: specifically South America, China, the Baltic and some Balkan States, especially Turkey and Greece.[77]

Vickers' difficulties in competing for a share of this free market were conveyed by Birch, writing in 1930: 'Quite apart from the world depression in buying power, our prices in many cases are such that unless we are technically ahead of our rivals and produce work of outstanding excellence, we cannot hope to gain a paramount position in supply.'[78] Vickers were by far the most successful British arms exporter of the interwar period: the international dispersal of their major contracts in 1926–34, together with their worth, are shown in Table 7.4.

The relations of a company like Vickers with the Foreign Office were always those of a government supplier dealing with a department of its main customer. There was deference, and the Foreign Office always dictated the pace and direction of events.

Table 7.4 To show distribution of Vickers' major armaments export orders as percentage of Vickers' total annual armaments exports 1926–34

	1926 %	1927 %	1928 %	1929 %	1930 %	1931 %	1932 %	1933 %	1934 %
Bolivia	–	39.5	0.1	–	–	–	11.3	–	3.7
Brazil	–	–	–	–	–	–	–	17.2	–
Chile	–	10.1	18.6	4.0	4.7	–	–	–	–
China	–	–	–	–	6.8	–	5.1	10.2	10.2
Esthonia	–	–	–	–	–	–	–	–	30.7
Japan	1.9	4.9	11.9	3.5	9.1	4.4	49.6	6.2	–
Netherlands	–	0.5	12.0	6.2	12.4	–	2.9	–	–
Poland	1.9	3.3	–	0.6	4.9	11.0	2.5	4.4	–
Portugal	0.5	–	–	–	–	58.5	1.8	34.8	–
Russia	0.5	–	–	–	29.9	–	4.1	–	–
Siam	–	–	–	12.8	4.9	–	11.0	11.0	–
Spain	56.3	26.8	24.8	25.2	3.7	–	–	2.5	–
Turkey	–	–	–	35.8	4.3	–	–	–	–
Vickers' total armaments exports in £ million	1.8	4.5	0.9	1.7	0.8	1.6	0.7	1.8	1.2

During Bridge's period personal relations were sometimes intimate, as when the British envoy in Chile wrote:

> Things are rotten out here and for the moment there is nothing we can do for you. We haven't got the Chileans to pay for what has already been bought, and they certainly can't afford to order anything else. It has been a hard year and I am worn out with protests and requests. It is like banging one's head against a brick wall.[79]

Alternatively some officials grew irritated with the extra work which foreign arms contracts generated. At the height of an imbroglio over Romania an official of the Central European Department of the Foreign Office minuted in 1929, 'The more we see of Vickers, the more helpless they seem.'[80] Nor was Whitehall squeamish in confronting unsuitable agents: when Captain Gerald N. Deane, Vickers' 'very capable and energetic man' who visited Argentina, Brazil and Chile in 1925, proved 'lackadaisical..."fresh" and far too pleased with himself', both the Foreign Office and Department of Overseas Trade told Vickers so plainly, and months later Deane left to join Handley Page.[81]

Vickers' foreign salesmanship, though not flawless, was more experienced and extensive than other British armourers. Beardmore, for example, suffered greatly from the autocracy of its chairman Lord Invernairn, who arrogated all power and, perhaps unwittingly, stifled his managers' initiative. Vansittart of the Foreign Office found Beardmore's Overseas Department 'naive', and wrote of a lost Chilean order in 1927: 'Beardmore's are perfectly hopeless people and deserve very little support...this kind of thing is prejudicial to British interests as a whole'. Even the company's man in Santiago complained to his principals, 'you have made my position as an Agent rather ridiculous...you do not answer my letters'.[82] In May 1919 Beardmore bought a controlling interest in the London engineering export house of John Birch, as a sales organisation to push their civilian and other products worldwide; and two years later they took one-third of the £3000 capital of Associated British Engineers Ltd, of Calcutta, newly formed to sell British engineering products on the Indian sub-continent. Then in 1925, apparently with encouragement from Whitehall, the Beardmore Overseas Corporation was registered as a marketing agency for the company's products, particularly in Russia, where since 1921 their Colonel Bonner had been chasing locomotive and other orders. However the corporation was suspended in confusion in 1926 when it emerged that its managing director had perpetrated an elaborate fraud, inventing both non-existent negotiations and staff.[83] Another Beardmore fiasco occurred around 1926 in Chile, where the agent, Plaza, was a retired admiral, ill-chosen, as retired admirals had the reverse of influence. Beardmore also sent out their sales manager, a naval commander who 'behaved in such a way as to make his firm lose all chances of securing the [order]...his...slander...coupled with his conduct at dances etc. made his trip a complete fiasco', even before Beardmore sent Plaza 'a stupid letter' refusing 'to have anything at all to do with the Chilean Government'.[84]

BSA pursued a comparable policy to Beardmore's investments in John Birch and Associated British Engineers by buying control in 1919 of Burton Griffiths, an engineering export house familiar with the USA market, which was intended to develop its civilian business in motor cars, bicycles, machine tools and special alloys. This tactic was only a mixed success, probably because of the poor co-ordination between production and marketing which long characterised the parent company. Certainly the chief marketing brain of Burton Griffiths, who joined BSA's board after the merger, retired from it within a few years and held jaundiced views about his colleagues' capacities.

The factory tours provided by armourers for foreign clients were an important piece of marketing, as indeed with other engineering companies. Well before 1914 Vickers commissioned a cinema film about the growth of the company and the range of its activities: one distinguished visitor who watched it with Albert Vickers recalled that it depicted:

> thousands of workers pouring out of the works in Barrow or Sheffield; the monster Dreadnoughts in either Japanese or British waters that had come forth from the works; the terrific guns that were to spread death and defeat among the serried masses of the German troops – though at that moment we neither of us thought of such a collision between the two great Empires as within the range of possibility; and all the other products as overwhelming in their size and magnificence almost as the events in which they were soon to take a part.[85]

The use of films was subsequently developed by Vickers, and for example one taken by Kinsman on his South American sales tour of 1928 was 'attended with great success'.[86]

Competitive demonstrations of equipment were also important, although stories abound of ways in which wily salesmen like Zaharoff of Vickers were able to subvert or circumvent the results of such trials.[87] In some markets they seem to have served simply as a way for officials to gather together representatives of all the foreign businessmen from whom they hoped to extract bribes. These competitive demonstrations were often an expensive futility, so that in 1908 Škoda suggested 'an arrangement among the leading firms' to eschew gun trials in those countries where they had to make 'a very serious outlay without any certainty of proper treatment'.[88]

With the proviso that they could not favour the interests of one British manufacturer against another, British diplomats usually supported armaments companies abroad: but there were limits to such support. Thus in 1925 when Sir Vincent Caillard (director of Vickers 1898–1927) wrote to the Foreign Secretary, Sir Austen Chamberlain (whom he had known since they campaigned together for tariff protection twenty years before), asking that the Prince of Wales on his forthcoming Argentine visit should support Vickers' current arms tender there, he was told 'that it is out of the question for the Prince of Wales to have any personal connection with this matter, but apart from this we shall continue to do all we can to endeavour to obtain the contract on behalf of your firm'.[89] Similarly in 1929, when Peru was on the brink of giving considerable naval orders, Vickers' agent Luis Aubry approached the British envoy in Lima, who reported:

> Juan Leguia, the President's favourite son...is courted and flattered by those

who want to get something out of his father. He is...to share in the thirty thousand pounds which...Aubry is to receive if he pulls off the contract. But the Americans want to supply submarines and will most certainly press for these instead of Destroyers from Vickers. They too will probably bribe Juan...and very likely outbid Vickers...Juan Leguia...would very much like a KBE ...Please consider whether we might not let it leak out...that the President will get another British decoration or his son some recognition...I cannot myself advocate thus casting the King's Pearls and I think that the British here would be shocked if we were thus to pander to the mammon of unrighteousness on Vickers' behalf. The question is however how far are you prepared to go in support of Vickers?

The Foreign Office replied that they were unwilling to go any distance: 'not only on the general principle that "purchase by decoration" should not be countenanced, but also...[as] Juan Leguia is a notorious rascal'.[90]

One experienced diplomat, writing in 1919 of recent French supplies of aircraft accompanied by expert advisory missions to various Balkan countries, emphasised 'great political influence...can be secured through such missions and contracts'. Whitehall officially encouraged the despatch of Vickers' aviation experts to Peking in 1919 as much as, say, the Admiralty's naval missions to Greece of 1921–3 and 1929.[91] As to diplomatic intervention in foreign armament contracts, one of Vickers' most experienced international bagmen, Lancelot Leveson, prepared a memorandum on this subject in 1930, which Kinsman and other colleagues endorsed.

The British Naval, Military and Commercial Attachés are helpful with propaganda, but they do it in a dignified way as compared with their Italian and French colleagues who have been known to go and present the armament tenders of their countries in full uniform. In some countries the latter procedure is resented, but in many countries it helps...when it comes actually to negotiating the contract Italian and French attachés have no hesitation in...abusing their position in support of the firms in which they are interested and from whom, in some cases, they...receive commission.

The main handicap that we have experienced...is the unwillingness exhibited by the British diplomatic representatives to take full advantage of a political situation to reap the material gain...wherever a French Military Mission is sent any armament firm, other than French, has the greatest difficulty in obtaining orders whereas British Missions, while helpful individually, consider themselves to be temporarily in the service of the Government to which they are attached, compelled to give entirely impartial advice and not in any way to insist on their advice being taken.[92]

Bagmen were discouraged from meddling in foreign politics as counter-productive. Vickers' Belgrade man in 1910 urged the Serbian Prime Minister to buy at least one gunboat worth £120 000 ('un veritable Dreadnought de rivière') for use on the Danube and Save, where, he wrote, Austrian monitors 'menacent [sic] constamment la capitale même'; he also assured the Serbs of official British sympathy for their riparian and maritime ambitions. To the distress of British diplomats the Austrians immediately obtained a copy of this indiscreet missive. In the following year his successor was sacked when he 'exceeded his instructions and made promises aligning his employers with the Serbs and against the Dual Monarchy'.[93] Henry Drummond-Wolff, Armstrongs' man in Greece and later a Conservative MP, espoused the Royalists against the Venezelists so vigorously that although he secured some aeroplane orders under King Constantine's regime of 1920–2, his 'foolish' indiscretions 'enraged' other Greeks. Drummond-Wolff's presence in Greece was judged 'highly undesirable' by the new King George II; and the British envoy in Athens, who thought Armstrongs would lose contracts because of their bagman, was 'relieved' for Wolff's own safety when he left Greece in 1923 when Constantine's ex-ministers were shot.[94] Another case was Major J. T. S. Barnes, an Old Etonian cousin of Lytton Strachey and British expert on Adriatic affairs at the Paris Peace Conference, who became a votary of Mussolini when Rome correspondent of the *Financial Times* in 1924–6. On the staff of Armstrong's Puzzuoli Co. (1925–7), and as Vickers' aviation salesman in north-east Europe (1930–3), he got 'the reputation of being completely mad',[95] and was notoriously erratic in negotiations. Inevitably some bagmen willing to exile themselves in remoter parts of the world proved mercurial, and from 1928 the company sought to maintain its 'excellent arrangements with the Foreign Office...and...reputation as straight and open dealers' by appointing established merchant houses as agents or retired officers as salesmen.[96] The latter category was typified by Brigadier R. E. T. Hogg, resident armament representative in Serbia 1923–5, with his artillery and aeronautical expertise.

Foreign Competition

Political adventurers like Drummond-Wolff and Barnes were exceptional. As Esthonia's finance minister told BSA in 1923, 'business relations' with Britain were preferred by many States as being 'genuine business relations without any aim of political, intellectual or national hegemony' which, for example, characterised 'German economic penetration'.[97] In the French case in particular, both business and diplomatic representatives worked in intimate and ruthless co-operation, admitting few distinctions between the interests of private capital and the French State. The British envoy to Bolivia in 1927 called his colleague from Paris 'a commercial tout', who 'was most annoyed when he failed to secure the order for armaments for Schneider's'.[98] The British military attaché in Romania and Greece told Bridge in 1929:

> French interests and influence are strong, and are worked for all the French are worth. Their highest representatives appear to work on definite instructions to urge that specific orders are given to French firms – and the benevolence of the French God – or its displeasure – appear to depend on the result.[99]

In 1930, during the London Naval Conference, the French chargé d'affaires approached the Japanese Foreign Minister 'urging Japan to hold out' against proposals for submarine limitation which the French disliked, and 'suggesting possibility of French credits as part of the bargain'.[100] Kinsman wrote of Uruguay: 'Schneiders do not depend much on their agents, but look to the French Government for assistance'.[101]

In addition to France there was strong competition from other nations, such as Spain for South American naval orders, or Italy. During the era of sham Caesarism after Mussolini came to power in 1922, a policy prevailed of official subsidies for arms exports or the provision of long-term credits, which often meant that Italian equipment was sold at prices which 'ruined' the market for other countries.[102] Italian success owed little to technological superiority. One British admiral attributed the Italian grip on building for the Romanian navy to 'the paper performance of Italian ships; and secondly the greatly superior finish of the Officers' Quarters'.[103] The great Italian naval yards of Odero-Terni-Orlando (which took a great deal of business from Britain after 1920) were one of the competitors, which provoked the President of the Board of Trade to warn a Cabinet committee in 1933: 'it was well known on the Continent that British armament firms were in a dying condition'.[104]

Another new if smaller competitor was Bofors, which until 1919 was occupied in supplying the Swedish navy and did little armament work. But the Versailles Treaty's prohibition of German arms exports forced Krupp, which had previously agreed to supply twelve six-inch guns to the Netherlands Marine Department, to transfer the contract to Bofors.[105] Subsequently the Swedes acquired some of Krupp's plant and designs (thirty skilled men were transferred there from Essen in 1921), and took artillery orders from Japan, Spain, the Netherlands and South America.[106] Their 100 kroner shares stood at 122 kroner in 1920 and paid a dividend (1919–20) of 6 per cent, but by 1923 the price was only 28 kroner, and dividends were passed until 1925. During the crisis of 1923 Vickers sent Leveson to visit Bofors and discuss working agreements on naval fire-control and armour plate over 4 inches, and as late as 1928, when Bofors employed 1,500 workmen and had annual production worth about 12 million kroner, it had difficulty in raising capital to increase capacity (issued capital was then 19.8 million kroner).[107] The total value of their ordnance orders was £2 574 000 in 1924–7 and £2 250 000 in 1928.[108] 'The firm of Bofors in Central Sweden has recently advanced to a position among the leading armaments firms in the world and can now claim, except for products of the heaviest calibre, to range in the same class with Schneider, Škoda and Vickers-Armstrongs,' the British envoy at Stockholm reported in 1929. 'The best foreign customers of Bofors are Holland, Finland, Turkey and the South American republics.'[109] By 1933, as Birch wrote after being beaten for a Bolivian ammunition order, 'Bofors' influence is getting very strong everywhere, and someone is putting money behind them, I presume Germany';[110] though with Hitler's ascendancy the Swedes limited the German role of Bofors.

Export Licences and Embargoes

Czech, French, German and Italian firms all enjoyed more intimate and aggressive co-ordination with their governments' international policies than Vickers did in Britain. Indeed during 1919–39 British private armourers faced two types of government discrimination which hindered foreign competition: export licences and export credit guarantees. Legislation empowering the prohibition of armament exports dated from 1672. The Customs and Inland Revenue Act of 1879 empowered the prohibition of arms exports by order or proclamation, but such prohibition had to cover export to all destinations. In 1900 the Exportation of Arms Act was passed, giving power to prohibit exports of arms to specific destinations: the powers were primarily intended to stop British forces, or their allies, from facing British arms in the hands of Boxer insurgents in China. Extended powers, valid in wartime only, were included in Acts of 1914–18 but lapsed in peace. The Finance Act of 1921 extended the 1879 and 1900 Acts to munitions of every description, as well as to firearms and ammunition which were not war weaponry. This was partly done to meet the spirit of the Arms Traffic Convention signed in 1919 by Britain and other nations, but never ratified. From 1921 war material fell under an order which carefully defined fifteen classes of armament; a new general order of 1931 added bayonets, swords, lances and aircraft to take account of provisions in the Arms Traffic Treaty,[111] signed in 1930 by France, Italy and Abyssinia and ratified by all four countries. Under these orders of 1921 and 1931 all weaponry for overseas markets required export licences, although during 1921–32 there were only seven cases where manufacturers were refused export licences,[112] and five occasions when export licences were granted but revoked. Of these five revocations only the first had substantial international consequences. Under the minority Labour government of 1924 BSA were licensed to supply Soviet Russia with 200 newly manufactured Lewis guns worth £19 992, but the succeeding Conservative government imposed an embargo on arms exports to Russia, and revoked the licence in January 1925.[113] The number of licences issued and refused in 1929–35 is shown in Table 7.5.

Table 7.5 To show number of export licences for armaments issued and refused 1929–35

| Year | Number of licences | |
	Issued	Refused
1929	325	5
1930	411	3
1931	435	1
1932	410	3
1933	413	–
1934	413	7
1935[a]	309	7

[a]Figures up to 30 September 1935 only.

Source: Minutes of Evidence to Royal Commission on Private Manufacture of Armaments (1935–6), p. 340.

The Department of Overseas Trade had a liaison officer who worked with a counterpart in the War Office's Military Intelligence section 1.b to operate the licensing system and scrutinise other aspects of arms exports. The DOT concluded by 1930 that considerable 'inconsistency' had 'arisen from trying to apply to the whole world an uniform procedure', and would have preferred more flexible criteria adaptable to local market circumstances.[114] British armourers could thus do little abroad without government consent after 1921 as all export had to be processed through the official licensing system. Significantly Vickers' chairman, General Sir Herbert Lawrence (director 1921–37), favoured the existence of formal supervision as removing popular or political suspicion of abuses.[115]

A Cabinet Committee which examined the condition of private armourers in 1933 strongly recommended a change in the licensing system, and this was accepted by the Cabinet in December.[116] They agreed, as the First Lord of the Admiralty said, that

> the existence of a system of export licensing was the main deterrent to foreign purchasers...we had been internationally hoodwinked, as this system was self-imposed and...though...an example to other countries, had certainly frightened away possible purchasers. The present prosperity of Škoda and other Continental firms showed that while there were plenty of orders about, the amount coming to this country were negligible.[117]

However Ramsay MacDonald, the Prime Minister, thought the proposed change (to give open export licences to approved manufacturers of national importance) would prejudice disarmament discussions elsewhere, especially as Britain had advocated specific licences at recent international conferences; and he prevented any revision of the rules. Britain continued its unilateral practice of specific licensing, while giving a private assurance to major armourers that licences would be given with minimum delay and would be revoked only exceptionally. This compromise was not ideal: private assurances seemed to foreign customers an unreliable guarantee of continual supply.

Procurement officers also sometimes prohibited the export of up-to-date types, although their exercise of these powers was by no means equable. In 1902–13, for example, the Admiralty gave Vickers a virtual monopoly of submarine orders conditional on foreign powers not being supplied, but as Vickers were working under licence from the Electric Boat Co. of the USA, which was not similarly bound, this prohibition had little effect. Similarly with tanks, in 1918–36, Vickers and the Royal Ordnance factories were almost the only contractors. Other companies would not touch the work without 'a more or less certain guarantee of a production order later', but available funds 'barely sufficed' to support 'a very narrow field of research and experiment' by the ROF and Vickers.[118] The latter therefore desperately needed foreign orders to spread overheads, and in 1930 a Russian order for 6 ton tanks and tractors, obtained 'entirely due' to the Chief of Imperial General Staff, 'saved the situation' for Vickers-Armstrong.[119] But the War Office refused to release modern types for export, with results of which Bridge complained to the Master General of Ordnance in 1932:

> The firm is in some difficulty now. There is not a single tank in the British

Service that they can sell, except the old Mark II, which the Poles three years ago rudely described as "junk"...they have been spending about £32 000 a year on development, but...there is no certainty that when they have spent a good deal of money in creating a new model, that the War Office will release it for sale. We soldiers here know that you are just as keen on industrial mobilisation as we are...Vickers-Armstrongs are now very much handicapped by other foreign firms in the tank market.[120]

Apart from the licensing system Britain also operated foreign embargoes. The diplomatic representatives of the western powers in Peking in May 1919 agreed not to supply munitions to the forces of the contending provincial warlords in China. This local embargo was animated by the British envoy Sir John Jordan, and although it proved inoperable, both because of the huge amount of second-hand arms coming over the border from Russia and because it was systematically flouted by Italy and Japan,[121] Britain adhered to it until 1929. One result of the Chinese embargo 'was to foster the arms industry of the smaller States', especially Czechoslovakia, which seized hold of the vacant Chinese market and retained a seriously competitive position in Far Eastern business well after 1929.[122]

An embargo on supplies to Greece and Turkey was also enforced in 1922–3. The Greek naval programme of 1923 again showed that the British government was less opportunistic in such matters than other manufacturing powers: whereas the French were happy to provide credits for a five year programme for a battlecruiser, ten destroyers and sixteen submarines, plus anti-aircraft and other equipment, the British government exercised its powers under previous refugee and League of Nations loans, which were conditional upon the Greek government not contracting more external debts, to prevent Greece from borrowing from France or anywhere else. They did this although Armstrongs, Palmers, Whites of Cowes, Whitehead Torpedo, and other British interests were frontrunners for the contracts: Curzon the Foreign Secretary even considered demanding France's payment of the interest on its war debt to Britain unless the French desisted from extending armaments credits to minor powers.[123]

The most famous case was Britain's unilateral action during the Sino-Japanese war in 1933. 'The embargo in the Far East probably weakened our national defence, increased unemployment and made other nations laugh', Birch wrote. 'What good did it do?'[124] The effects of stopping arms exports to China and Japan were listed by an official of the Committee of Imperial Defence as:

(a)   to help Japan, who alone have the stocks
(b)   to down our own industry
(c)   to get us unpopular with Japan and laughed at by all others. Sentimental folly, with a nasty element of risk.[125]

Vickers at Barrow alone lost Japanese orders worth £500 000 during the fortnight of the embargo,[126] which was a diplomatic failure, quite apart from commercial considerations.

Less famous, but more effective, was Britain's lead in 1934 of an embargo on supplying munitions to Bolivia and Paraguay. The British Cabinet had agreed in

March 1933 not to join an embargo on these warring neighbours unless the USA was party to it. On becoming President in 1933 Roosevelt finally obtained powers from Congress to declare an embargo, which he did in May 1934. Thereafter, as the British Foreign Secretary announced on 4 June, licences in Britain were held up pending the conclusion of an embargo agreement.[127] There was no formal embargo, and neither Vickers nor ICI were prevented from shipping armaments under licences already granted. The Foreign Office simply delayed the issue of current licences.[128] While Britain maintained the embargo through the summer of 1934, Czech, Belgian, Italian and Japanese competitors supplied the belligerents, and it was not until winter that the main manufacturing States, having exploited the lack of Anglo-American competition, finally joined the embargo. By that time the situation between Paraguay and Bolivia had altered, and in January 1935 all the Powers raised the embargo. Although Britain played 'the part of the prying moraliser',[129] its self-denial did not stop arms supplies to the belligerents; but the embargo bit during the last six weeks of 1934, and if it had lasted long into 1935 both Bolivia and Paraguay could scarcely have protracted hostilities.

Export Credits and Loans

Generally armourers concentrated on preparing bids and accepting low-margin initial orders so as to get essential experience to qualify them for larger and more lucrative orders. As a result subsidies or export credits could be critical to the success of overseas marketing. Typically a Purchasing Commission of the Portuguese Naval Air Service, which visited Britain, France and Italy during 1928 with a remit to order six seaplanes, told Supermarine Aviation that their prices were about double those of their French or Italian competitors, prompting an official of the Air Ministry to lament, 'Naturally in the face of foreign competition (direct subsidies) our firms do not stand much chance.' Continental firms often had assistance from their governments to secure initial low-margin orders, including export guarantees, conditional loans to the foreign purchasing government, or subsidies. Thus in 1931 the French government guaranteed to the Sauter Harle Co. some 70 per cent of all payments due from the Romanian government on mines (whether manufactured in France or Romania), and provided Sauter Harle with facilities to take payment from the Romanians over seven years. This was usual French practice.[130] On other occasions alluring financial terms were offered in conjunction with associated financiers. If the Austrian small arms firm of Steyr was exceptional in being wholly owned by the Credit Anstalt Bank,[131] nevertheless continental competitors consistently beat the British to initial and replacement orders by the involvement of bankers in foreign marketing policy.

In contrast British makers were under a special disadvantage, they felt, because under the Trade Facilities Act of 1921 munitions were exempted from Export Credit Guarantees, though the prohibition did not extend to armed aircraft, or their parts. Manufacturers constantly pleaded for the repeal of this. It was mentioned at many of Vickers' annual general meetings and in representations to government.

The Department of Overseas Trade argued in 1930 that the export of British weaponry 'does not rest on price or terms of credit, but on special design and suitability', but this was a contentious opinion. The Army Council wanted the relevant section of the Trade Facilities Act to be revoked,[132] and in 1931 the President of the Board of Trade in the Labour government made enquiries, with Cabinet sanction, whether Baring's or other merchant banks would furnish assistance to armourers equivalent to the 1921 Act. This initiative was rebuffed, and British industrialists continued to feel at a disadvantage against Italy, France and other manufacturing powers.

As Chamberlain, the Foreign Secretary, wrote in 1929, 'loans by foreign Governments and financiers [are] the most potent instrument in deflecting orders from this country'. He urged that British banks should pursue 'a less exclusively financial policy and one more calculated to facilitate the capture of foreign markets by British industry'. One disadvantage met by British banks 'vis-à-vis their competitors in raising loans for foreign countries' was the stamp duty chargeable on bearer bonds on foreign loans which was raised in Britain from £1 per cent in 1920 to £2 per cent. In 1927 Barings' agents in Argentina reported that the Minister of Finance required a loan of £3 million for naval armaments. The Argentines, whose government had placed in New York loans worth US$138.6 million since June 1925, offered to undertake that two-thirds of the total would be spent in Britain: on Barings explaining that the British stamp tax made it impossible for them to accept the loan, Argentina actually offered to leave half of the loan's proceeds with Barings for three to five months at 2 per cent: Barings still declined to help, and the Argentines eventually accepted a Spanish loan of 100 million pesetas.[133] 'Spain got the loan and sold two destroyers', Sir Malcolm Robertson the British Ambassador in Buenos Aires commented. 'We, for the sake of £30 000 lost £30 000 stamp duty, lost the loan, lost prestige and lost £2 000 000 of work definitely promised.'[134] Similarly in 1929 Turkey ordered two destroyers from Italy worth a total of £645 000, because although Vickers' tender price had been lower by £100 000 the Ottoman Bank in London refused to discount Turkish Treasury bonds, and Vickers then failed to seek support in another obvious direction, the Turkish Ish Bankasi, which as the government bank could scarcely have declined to discount such bonds.[135]

Robertson in Buenos Aires attributed the collapse of British trade in Argentina to companies' 'preference to stay at home and wait for business to come to them, in the intervals of their golfing weekends, instead of sending their principals out here'. He warned that Britain must 'attack this market root and branch, horse, foot and Vickers-Armstrong artillery, with all the resources at our disposal, or...lose the little that is left of what once was ours'.[136] Though Vickers were superior in their foreign selling organisation to a competitor like BSA,[137] their export drives often reflected the comment of a man who was a director of both companies, 'We are ill-organised as a people...the three great divisions of the business world, industrial, mercantile and financial — pay little regard for one another's interests.'[138]

Bribery and Conspiracy

Correlli Barnett, commenting on inter-war British foreign policy, has written of 'parsonical belief in the powers of moral reprobation...accompanied by an equally parsonical dislike of "immoral" forms of pressure, such as bribery, threats or force', adding that there was 'insufficient understanding of the bargaining process' and over-reliance on the 'meeting of minds in good faith'.[139] Any generalisation courts contradiction, but Barnett's remarks frequently seem applicable to the conduct of British overseas salesmanship, whether by those bagmen who did forsake their golfing weekends, or by the diplomats who often had to rescue such trade negotiations. The British often shrank from the more ruthless imperatives of international salesmanship. This of course is not to pretend that British armourers recoiled from bribery in those countries where 'it was customary and conventional in all departments of trade'. As Trebilcock writes, bribery was not a 'particular adjunct of the arms trade' or 'sales specialism of the armourers' but 'part of workaday business practice'; Vickers' official historian comments that in some markets, 'Bribery was not accidental or occasional, but essential and systematic in every factor of commerce'.[140]

Lavish bribery was often seen as counter-productive, although in 1905 at a time of acute Russo-Japanese tension Vickers paid commission of £86 000 to their foreign bagman Basil Zaharoff, much of which doubtless passed to other intermediaries. Normally however, as Vickers instructed a newly appointed agent to Romania in 1912, before quoting prices the company required to know 'the amount which may have to be included in our prices for satisfying the requirements of friends, sub-commissions, etc.' as 'in view of the serious competition which now exists in war material, it is of the utmost importance that...all sub-commissions should be kept to the lowest possible limits without endangering the chances of success'.[141] Similarly in 1933 when a Vickers employee in China who was suffering from brain concussion seemingly offered a bribe of £50 000 for a tank contract, he was immediately ordered home, and Vickers' agents reported to London, 'In including such enormous commissions, which we would never consider in the ordinary way, we expose ourselves and you to grave danger, and which, if discovered would have disastrous reactions not only on all our varied business activities here, but also on our joint reputation.'[142] Vickers were subsequently examined *in camera* about this incident by the Royal Commission on the Private Manufacture of Armaments in 1936. Two directors explained that their agents worked on commission, and as they had 'to hand in our actual quotations', could not themselves load Vickers' prices; 'any palm-greasing has to come out of his commission'.[143] Not much grease was permitted by the level of commission. For example Lieutenant-General Sir Edwin Atkinson, the former Master General of Ordnance in India who represented Vickers in China in 1931–2, and had commission of 1 per cent on all orders, to a minimum of £1000, and received monthly general and subsistence expenses of £100. Vickers also undertook to reimburse 'entertainment or other special payments by you' which 'have, wherever possible, been first approved by us'.[144] Typically Brigadier W. C. E. Rudkin, an artillery officer (previously ADC to King George V) who was Vickers' world-wide representative for military artillery in 1920–3, received an annual salary of £2000 and commission of 5 per cent on technical fees paid by the Spanish government; 4 per cent on machine guns; 2 per cent on guns up to 4.7 calibre; and 1 per cent on guns of higher calibre.[145]

Companies learned to be cautious not only about the scale but the methods of bribery. The payment of 'Commission Notes should be effected only when we have received the first instalment of any order', Caillard of Vickers wrote of a Chinese naval cruiser order in 1910. 'Any contract actually signed is of really no use to us unless it has been confirmed by the actual payment of the first instalment'; even then so many technical and political problems, factitious or otherwise, might arise, that the company preferred to ensure good behaviour and forestall attempts to extort further bribes by paying commission on amounts over £5000 in instalments pro rata on the contract price received.[146]

When Atkinson wrote from Tientsin in 1931 reporting Chinese attempts to reduce 'squeeze', Bridge replied, 'the same thing is happening in other countries where the men at the top have announced that there is to be no more, but when one really gets down to brass tacks, it is almost impossible to do without it'.[147] Although Livingston, Vickers' aviation bagman in South America in 1920–8, claimed, 'In my numerous travels I have discovered that nearly everyone is amenable to reason if put forward in a practical way', Bridge wrote of a Polish count's claim, forwarded by the military attaché in Warsaw, that he could 'ensure' the placing of a machine-gun order with Vickers, 'No-one can ensure this; the matter is far too important.'[148]

Whitehall was candid in its acceptance of the practice and necessity of bribery. In 1925 the War Office appointed BSA as their foreign agents in second-hand rifles and machine-guns with commission of 5 per cent plus 5 per cent on the sale proceeds above the minimum price agreed. This commission was to 'cover local payments which obviously should not appear in the War Office accounts'; as the War Office wrote, 'the pernicious system of "commission"...inseparable from these deals ...makes it impossible for us to carry out except through private firms'.[149] Similarly the British envoy in the Baltic reported in 1929 that France had won a Latvian order for two submarines because '(1) the special agent of Vickers was an idiot of the name Savitsky, who bungled the whole matter, spent his time chattering in bars and was unable to arrange for the necessary cumshaw; (2) HMG refused to allow Latvian officers to be trained in England'. Vickers' price for each submarine had been £285 000 payable over four years. The envoy, Joseph Addison, whose vendetta with an earlier Vickers' agent in Peking is described in Chapter 5 (p. 108), contended that Savitsky's successor Sakovsky was equally distrusted:

> because he chatters too much and does not keep...promises...to distribute ...money to the persons interested...It is quite useless for...any...firm to imagine that they are going to place the order for these two submarines unless they are prepared to pay...for services rendered. This of course will form a part of the price of the submarines. Sakovsky is such an ass in his own business that he actually went to somebody I know here and asked him whether he could introduce him to Admiral Keyserling and fix up the proper bribe. Anything more idiotic I cannot imagine. This is obviously a matter about which I must look as if I know nothing at all, but I think I can ascertain before the question comes to a head exactly who the person is to whom...Vickers...should go on arrival here and offer the appropriate sum for his valuable assistance in

negotiating the order, in short, sign an open commission note for so much per cent.[150]

Part of this message certainly reached Vickers, who shortly afterwards told the Foreign Office orally that their director Sir Trevor Dawson was ready to visit Riga to try to salvage negotiations and limit the damage done by Sakovsky, to whom Vickers were bound by contract.

The British government frequently urged that British manufacturers should work in export combinations. In 1909, for example, the Board of Trade recommended Armstrongs and Vickers to co-operate with French industrialists in order to beat the Germans in competition for Chinese contracts; in the following year Vickers were officially advised to combine with their French competitors if they wanted a chance of Serbian orders.[151] Similarly in 1925 the British envoy in Chile deplored that there, was 'no expert technical agent' in Santiago representing the private armourers: 'they should, if possible, work in altogether so as to avoid competition between themselves which might be unfortunate…[as] the Italians are making very advantageous offers'. Following this hint, Armstrongs and Vickers instructed their agents to work openly together; although Beardmore preferred 'to keep independent and take their chance', unless the orders were worth over £6 million, when 'there would be enough for everyone'.[152] Even in these international arrangements however the First World War was a watershed. On several occasions before 1914 Vickers and Schneider privately collaborated over prices in specific foreign markets. There was, for example, a working arrangement in 1907–10 between Schneider, Vickers and Armstrongs 'to stop competition' and ensure 'remunerative prices' on Turkish tenders for warships and their armaments;[153] but in 1928 when Schneider proposed to Bofors and Vickers that they should reach a secret agreement on pricing and apportioning Turkish orders, with the possibility of further such collaboration on a wider international basis, Vickers declined the overture. As Birch wrote at the time:

> Eventually any combine must get to our Government's ears. The same sympathy and help could not be extended to us when that moment arrives. They would rightly tell us, 'We cannot help a combine of European interests'…if this had been a suggested combine of steel, linen or anything of that sort which had no connection with any government, I would have gone for it. In armaments we deal entirely with governments and so it behoves us to be wary of taking any step that might antagonise them, or in spite of temporary advantage, lead eventually to loss of trade…I do not think for one moment that secrecy is possible, and so it is well to think over now what the attitude of the various governments will be when they hear of it, and particularly what effect it will have on our present excellent arrangements with the Foreign Office, Admiralty and War Office, and our reputation as straight and open dealers.[154]

This quotation conveys the pressure which the British government was able to exert from its position of monopsonist power, and confirms that much of the latitude in pricing and marketing which manufacturers enjoyed before 1914 was lost as the 'special relationship' became more formalised and depersonalised in the 1920s.

Conclusion

This chapter has tried to show that the marketing of armaments diverged in many features from those of civilian products. Overseas it was a highly political trade, sensitive to the ebb and flow of national prestige: the confident remorseless arms marketing before 1914 mirrored the national mood in that period when, as one Vickers director wrote in 1905, there was 'an empire in the making';[155] similarly the hesitation and retreat of 1918–39 reflected Britain's new position as the Carthage of the North Sea. It is not coincidental that the Washington naval disarmament treaty of 1921, which many have ranked with the fall of Singapore or Indian independence as the turning points of twentieth-century British imperialism, was also a cataclysm on the fortunes of private armaments manufacturers, from which several never recovered.

Even in 1913 the Foreign Secretary Sir Edward Grey and one of his most experienced diplomatists, Sir William Tyrrell, felt that without 'a cessation of armaments...our present civilisation would eventually be destroyed...an armament trust was forcing all governments not only to pay excessive prices, but was creating war scares – they being the only people having any interest in having the different governments keep up large expenditures for war purposes'.[156] Although this interpretation has rightly been contested by diplomatic and other historians, an understandable reaction against international arms dealing occurred in Britain after the carnage of the First World War: the licensing system, embargoes and credit provisions which were manifestations of this reaction undoubtedly dulled British international competitiveness, although there is also no denial that private manufacturers continued to receive valuable official support in other aspects of foreign marketing.

At home in Britain the government's position in a monopsony market, with the related development of oligopolistic suppliers, created an unusual marketing environment. It was not the case, as Noel-Baker claimed in 1936, that 'governments do not hesitate to scrap their existing weapons' to buy with their 'virtually unlimited resources' newer and more efficient weaponry: still less were governments 'a clientele to whom money [was] no object'.[157] Instead, before 1914 the British government developed arrangements to obtain 'a leaven of the greatest [possible number of] skilled men everywhere', especially in 'private works [where] their skill can be used for civilian and private work when they are not actually doing the war material for the government'.[158] Such arrangements were justifiable when, as the Secretary of the Committee of Imperial Defence noted in 1925, private armourers were receiving 'huge orders' from British and foreign governments, equivalent to 'a giant subsidy, which carried the overhead charges', but they were an evident failure at other times. While in August 1914 sixty warships for the Royal Navy and thirty for foreign navies were being built in private British yards, the corresponding figures in August 1924 were sixteen British warships and one gunboat for Siam.[159] Although the private manufacturers did try to exploit their oligopolistic advantages in the prices they charged to governments, this could be partly defended in terms of the irregularity of orders. The extraordinarily poor survival rate of armaments companies – some such as Hotchkiss or Coventry Ordnance going out of business, others like Armstrongs and Beardmore only being saved from extinction by Bank of England intervention, and even Vickers writing off capital of almost £12.5 million in 1926 – demonstrates unanswerably that despite the occasional solicitude of Whitehall, companies supplying a monopsony market faced a hostile and even fatal environment.

Notes

1. Memorandum by Lord Rendel, 25 October 1911. Armstrong Whitworth papers (hereafter AW), box 164, Tyne and Wear County Record Office, Newcastle.
2. Sir Charles Craven, memorandum of 28 March 1931, Vickers microfilm R212, Cambridge University Library.
3. Clive Trebilcock, 'A "special relationship" – government, rearmament and the cordite firms', *Economic History Review*, 2nd ser. 19 (1966), pp. 364–79.
4. Roderick Floud, *The British Machine Tool Industry 1850–1914* (Cambridge, 1976), p. 126.
5. Evidence to Sir Clinton Dawkins' committee on War Office organisation, Cd. 580 of 1901, QQ. 2367–8, quoted Clive Trebilcock, *The Vickers Brothers* (London, 1977), p. 6.
6. Viscount Chandos, *Memoirs* (London, 1962), p. 150.
7. ibid. p. 149.
8. George Curzon to St John Brodrick, 3 June 1890, Earl of Midleton papers, British Library, Add. 50073.
9. ibid. 3 April 1891.
10. BSA to War Office, 1 February 1908; and Kenneth Davies to Henry de la Bere, 31 April 1909, BSA papers 3/3/9 and 10, Warwick University Modern Records Centre; R. P. T. Davenport-Hines, *Dudley Docker* (Cambridge, 1984), p. 49.
11. Maurice Pearton, *The Knowledgeable State* (London, 1982), pp. 150–1; H. H. Mulliner, 'The Admiralty and the Navy', *National Review*, 54 (1909–10), p. 883; id. 'Germany's Opportunity', ibid. pp. 345–6; Philip Noel-Baker, *The Private Manufacture of Armaments* (London, 1936), pp. 449–510, which should however be read in the context of A. J. A. Morris, *The Scaremongers* (London, 1984), pp. 164–84; Sir Charles Ottley to Reginald McKenna, 25 Febraury 1909, McKenna paper 3/14, Churchill College, Cambridge; on Mulliner's later work for the Mineral Oil Production Department and as chairman of the Inter-Allied committees on Petroleum Economy, see Sir John Cadman to Walter Long, 2 May 1919, Viscount Long papers 947/795, Wiltshire County Record Office, Trowbridge.
12. David French, *British Economic and Strategic Planning 1905–15* (London, 1982), pp. 44–5.

13. Sir Eustace Tennyson-d'Eyncourt to Sir Frederick Field, 17 May 1920, DEY/28, Tennyson-d'Eyncourt papers, National Maritime Museum, Greenwich.
14. Trebilcock, 'Special Relationship', pp. 364–5; id. 'Radicalism and the Armament Trust', in A. J. A. Morris, ed., *Edwardian Radicalism* (London, 1974), p. 185.
15. *Arms and Explosives*, October 1913; for an account of the Admiralty preventing Coventry Ordnance tendering for large mountings, see Mulliner, 'The Admiralty and the Navy', p. 881.
16. Floud, *British Machine Tool Industry*, pp. 178–83; R. P. T. Davenport-Hines, entry on Lionel Hichens, in D. J. Jeremy and C. Shaw, eds, *Dictionary of Business Biography*, III (London, 1985), hereafter *DBB*, pp. 198–205.
17. Directorate of Contracts to Air Marshall Sir John Higgins, 29 April 1930; C. R. Brigstocke to Lord Thomson of Cardington, 22 May 1930, PRO Air 5/395.
18. PRO Adm 116/2149; *Documents of British Foreign Policy* (hereafter *DBFP*), 1st ser., 14 (London, 1966), pp. 475–6. For some background to this see Sir Vincent Caillard to Albert Vickers, 26 October 1917; Albert Vickers to Caillard, 27 October 1917; J. W. Allan (Browns) to Caillard, 14 January 1919, microfilm R246.
19. W. St D. Jenkins, Director of Naval Contracts, 19 August 1925, PRO Adm 116/3351. For an account of the Geddes committee in action, see John Vincent, ed., *The Crawford Papers* (Manchester, 1984), p. 416.
20. Sir William Ellis at conference of 15 July 1925, PRO Adm 116/3351.
21. PRO Adm 116/3351; memorandum of meeting at Vickers House on armour plate, 25 September 1930, microfilm R334; Norman Gibbs, *Rearmament Policy* (London, 1976), p. 358; D. P. R. 258, 270, 271, 293, 299, PRO Cab 16/143; D. P. R. 306 of 19 April 1939, PRO Cab 16/144.
22. Sir Noel Birch to Sir Herbert Lawrence, 3 January 1928, microfilm R334.
23. J. C. Carr and W. Taplin, *History of British Steel Industry* (London, 1962), p. 360.
24. Sir Peter Rylands, quoted in *Economist*, 2 October 1926; cf. R. P. T. Davenport-Hines, entry on Rylands, in *DBB*, IV (London, 1985), pp. 1004–10.
25. Sir Charles Wright to Winston Churchill, 12 February 1926, PRO T 172/1549.
26. Report of inter-departmental committee on alternative work in the Royal Ordnance Factories, 22 April 1930. Chaired by Sir Warren Fisher of the Treasury, para. 9. PRO Adm 1/8739/38.
27. *History of Ministry of Munitions* (London, 1920), I, pt 1, p. 76.
28. Dr Christopher Addison, diary 8 February 1916, Bodleian Library, Oxford.
29. *History of Ministry of Munitions*, III, pt 3, pp. 1–3.
30. ibid. p. 17.
31. Memorandum by Skefko, 10 January 1922, PRO, Mun 7/142. For the comparable case of the Baldwin steelworks, see Sir Charles Wright to Churchill, 30 September 1926, PRO T 172/1549.

32. PRO Mun 4/6319; PRO Mun 4/6408; PRO Mun 4/6439.

33. Sir Sigmund Dannreuther to Treasury, 29 August 1922, PRO Mun 4/7015.

34. William Ashworth, *Contracts and Finance* (London, 1953), pp. 200–1. For other perspectives, of varying value, on these subjects, see Robert Shay, *British Rearmament in the Thirties: politics and profits* (Princeton, 1977); and George Peden, 'Arms, Government and Businessmen 1935–45', in John Turner, ed., *Businessmen and Politics* (London, 1984), pp. 130–45.

35. Ashworth, *Contracts and Finance*, pp. 197–228.

36. Royal Commission on Private Manufacture of Arms, Cmd. 5292 of 1936, *Minutes of Evidence*, pp. 347, 357. Samuel Roberts, MP, a director of Cammell Laird, said on 21 April 1915 that if the armament firms were brought under 'the kind of control' which the railways had, 'we of the armament firms shall not oppose it'. House of Commons Debates, LXXI, col. 310. Cammell Laird's chairman, Lionel Hichens, was the most politically sensitive armourer of the period, and his thinking was usually in advance of his counterparts in other companies.

37. See confidential evidence of Sir Maurice Hankey to Royal Commission on Private Manufacture of Armaments, 8 and 21 May 1936, PRO Cab 16/126.

38. At the time of Armstrongs' collapse, see report proceedings and memoranda of Cabinet committee on armaments mergers, July 1927, PRO Cab 27/353.

39. Evidence of E. G. Pretyman to the Murray Committee (1907), Q. 1200.

40. *Arms and Explosives*, October 1913.

41. Lord Rendel to Lewis Harcourt, 12 July 1912, AW box 163; cf. R. P. T. Davenport-Hines, entries on Sir P. Girouard and Sir G. H. West, in *DBB*; Samuel Evans to Sir Percy FitzPatrick, 20 May 1904: 'Girouard possesses a certain superficial smartness; he is unreliable and, I am afraid, a little unscrupulous'. Eckstein papers 136, Barlow Rand Archives, Johannesburg.

42. Sir George Murray to Lord Rendel, 6 March 1912, Rendel box 166, Tyne & Wear Record Office; Lord Fisher's endorsement of Albert Vickers to Trevor Dawson, 4 January 1906, Campbell-Bannerman papers, Add. Ms. 41231; diary of Oakeley Arnold-Forster, 30 May 1904, Add. Ms. 50338; Dawson to McKenna, 3 May 1909, McKn 3/14; and McKenna to Asquith, 30 June 1910, McKn 3/22; Dawson to Walter Long, 1 November 1920, Long papers 716/1.

43. Arnold-Forster to Arthur Balfour, 21 December 1904; Arnold-Forster diary, 16, 20 December 1904; Add Ms. 50342.

44. Tennyson d'Eyncourt to Admiral Sir Cyril Fuller, 9 February 1924, DEY/26.

45. Though Owens-Thurston visited Turkey in October 1927 in connection with the naval programme, Vickers found increasingly little work for him, and retired him against his wishes less than three years afterwards, with an annuity of £1250. In 1911, when Watts was retiring as Director of Naval Construction, Dawson pressed Thurston's claims as his successor against d'Eyncourt.

A. Vahid Bey to Thurston, 18 November 1927; and Thurston to Jenkinson, 4 November 1927, microfilm R340. Jenkinson to Craven, 27 July 1934, microfilm R334. Dawson to McKenna, 1 September 1911, McKenna papers 3/22.

46. Admiral Alan Hotham to R. G. Vansittart, 25 February 1926, PRO FO 371/11122.

47. Gibbs, *Rearmament Policy*, p. 782.

48. Birch to Lawrence, 10 February 1928, microfilm R286.

49. W. Parker to J. D. Scott, interview September 1959, Vickers file 115.

50. Birch to Field Marshal Sir George Milne, CIGS, April 1929, microfilm R286. See my entry on Birch in *DBB*, I (London, 1984), pp. 333–5.

51. Birch to Lawrence, 10 February 1928, microfilm R286.

52. Charles Bridge to Capt. Ronald Botterill, 26 November 1929, microfilm R309. Botterill was Vickers' agent in Bulgaria but operated from Warsaw. He afterwards became agent for Chetwood safes in India. Botterill to Yapp, 6 March 1933, microfilm R300.

53. See Livingston's bombastic autobiography, *Hot Air in Cold Blood* (London, 1933). Sir Beilby Alston to G. R. Warner, 4. December 1924, described Livingston as 'a live wire but...not lacking in the characteristic assurance of his race'; while he 'seems no great stickler for truth', *pace* R. G. Vansittart, minute of 26 June 1926, both in PRO FO 371/10604. There is an excellent obituary in *Aeroplane*, May 1950.

54. Capt. Salmond to Cdr Lang, 24 January 1926, PRO FO 371/11122.

55. A. V. Bunbury, minute of 23 November 1928, PRO FO 371/12733. On Kinsman see despatch 38 of Sir Thomas Hohler (Santiago), 20 February 1925, PRO FO 371/10612.

56. See Rupert Furneaux, *The Murder of Lord Erroll* (London, 1960); James Fox, *White Mischief* (London, 1982); Ryan's father-in-law, the twentieth Earl of Erroll, was British High Commissioner in Rhineland 1921–8.

57. Lt-Col. Charles Hordern, late of Control Commission, to Brigadier J. H. Morgan, late of Inter-Allied Military Mission of Control in Germany, letter 11 October 1933. Quoted J. H. Morgan, *Assize of Arms* (London, 1945) p. xv. There are many interesting references to Ryan in *DBFP*, ser. 1a, vols I, II (London, 1966–8). Another Vickers official with such experience was Major P. L. Teed, RNAS who after the Armistice was Head of the Gas Chemistry Section of the Inter-Allied Mission of Control in Germany, before becoming principal assistant to Barnes Wallis in the Airship Guarantee Company (1924), a Vickers subsidiary. Teed was metallurgist and chief of the mechanical testing department at Vickers Aviation, Weybridge, 1931–8, becoming Chief Inspector of Materials at the Air Ministry, 1939. Later Deputy Director of Aeronautical Research & Development at Vickers-Armstrong Aircraft Ltd in 1950s.

58. Lady Donaldson of Kingsbridge, *The British Council* (London, 1984), p. 44; Bridge was also described as 'a most excellent fellow in every way': Rex

Leeper to J. D. Gregory, n. d. [Dec. 1927], PRO FO 371/12645. See also correspondence in PRO FO 371/4612 & 12909.

59. General Sir James Marshall-Cornwall to writer, 17 July 1978.

60. Bridge to Colonel J. Russell Kennedy, 20 September 1933, microfilm R310.

61. Sir Frederick Pile to Bridge, 19 December 1933, microfilm R310.

62. No arms orders were then being placed abroad by Chinese without reference to military advisers in Berlin. Bridge to Birch, 16 May 1933, microfilm R307.

63. See Sir Basil Thomson to Emile Cohn, 21 April 1921; memorandum on state of Russian industry in 1920 by Weintraub, Chief Officer of Russian Inland Water Transport, who escaped to the West in January 1921, microfilm R346.

64. Colonel A. T. MacGrath, Military Intelligence, to Birch, 15 Febraury 1928, microfilm R286; Sir Kenneth Strong to writer, 16 July 1978. Captain G. S. Courtney, who worked for Vickers-Armstrong from October 1934 until July 1938 as personal assistant to Birch, was with the Military Intelligence department of the War Office 1918–19. *Vickers News*, September 1938.

65. See Appendix V, 'The State of German Disarmament in January 1925', in Morgan, *Assize of Arms*; Col. James Marshall-Cornwall, Report on military activities in Germany, dated 9 December 1929, in *DBFP*, ser. 1a, vol. VII (London, 1975), pp. 275–85.

66. Birch, memorandum of 24 February 1928, microfilm R286.

67. Birch to Sir Hugh Jeudwine, 29 March 1933, Vickers file 124.

68. Minutes of Peace Products Committee, book 3, p. 64, Vickers file 308; Birch to Hew Kilner, 21 March 1934, microfilm R307.

69. Birch, memorandum of 3 May 1928, microfilm R286; 27th interim report of Committee on Mobilisation, Equipment and War Reserves, 27 September 1928, PRO WO 33/1175. Cf PRO WO 33/1209.

70. Birch to Neilson, 14 March 1936, Vickers file 154.

71. Bridge to C. A. Larssen, 12 December 1930, microfilm R309; Birch quarterly report on armament to 31 December 1930, file 32.

72. Agreement between Vickers-Armstrong and Bofors, 19 February 1928, microfilm R286.

73. Bridge to Col. W. A. C. Saunders-Knox-Gore, 3 March 1933, microfilm R307; Bridge to Birch, 1 March 1934, microfilm R308; Birch, note of February 1936, file 374.

74. Caillard to Acland, 11 June 1920. Acland to Caillard, 21 June 1920, microfilm R275. Sir Arthur Whitten-Brown who flew a Vickers aeroplane in the first crossing of the Atlantic in June 1919 was apparently one of those dismissed. He had previously been employed by British Westinghouse (Metrovic). Pilots and those on foreign missions (such as Livingston) were not dismissed.

75. Harald Penrose, *British Aviation: the adventuring years 1920–9* (London, 1973), pp. 531–2. Acland became assistant manager of the Aviation Department in February 1918 at an annual salary of £1000 plus 2 per cent

commission on aviation profits from Weybridge and Crayford. In March 1919 Acland became manager of the department at an annual salary of £2500, plus 3 per cent commission on net aviation profits. In April 1920 his annual salary was reduced to £1500 plus special annual entertaining allowance of £1250. Vickers papers, box of agreements AA-AM.

76. Lord Trenchard, Report to Board of Vickers on Aviation, August 1930, microfilm R275. Caddell retired from Vickers-Armstrong in 1939.

77. Philip Noel-Baker, 'The Private Manufacture of Armaments' vol. II, unpublished typescript, United Nations Library, Geneva. See pt. 2, ch. 1, p. 24. Cf. his table to show totals of national defence expenditure 1929–32 (pt. 1, ch. 3, p. 4).

78. Birch, quarterly report on air and land armament sales, to 31 December, file 32. Cf. PSO 361. Report on Private Armaments Industry in Foreign Countries (chaired by Sir E. F. Crowe), 13 March 1933, PRO Supp 3/43. Other aspects of this transition are described in R. P. T. Davenport-Hines, 'Vickers as a Multinational before 1945', in Geoffrey G. Jones, ed., *British Multinationals: origins, management and performance* (London, 1986).

79. Sir Henry Chilton to Bridge, February 1932, microfilm R310.

80. C. H. Bateman, minute of 24 April 1929, PRO FO 371/13695.

81. H. Wiswould to C. J. W. Torr, 5 August 1925. Sir Edward Crowe of Department of Overseas Trade to Sir Robert Craigie, 26 November 1925, PRO FO 371/10609. cf. Crowe to Vansittart, 22 March 1926, PRO FO 371/11122.

82. Sir Robert Vansittart, minute of 7 June 1927; Thomas C. Sargent to Beardmore, 24 June 1927, PRO FO 371/11980; cf. Sir Edward Crowe to Vansittart (recounting conversation with Cdr H. S. Harrison Wallace of Beardmores), 30 January 1926, PRO FO 371/11122.

83. John Hume and Michael Moss, *Beardmore* (London, 1979), p. 172; *DBFP*, 1st ser., XX (London, 1976), p. 794.

84. Julius Hudson (agent of Bofors, Bristol Aviation and Thornycroft in Santiago) to H. W. Wiswould, 13 February 1928, PRO FO 371/12751. Matters at Beardmore improved after Lord Invernairn was succeeded by H. A. Reincke, on whom see Sir Arthur Steel-Maitland to Lord Tyrrell, 31 December 1926, PRO FO 371/11957.

85. T. P. O'Connor's obituary of Albert Vickers, *Daily Telegraph*, 16 July 1919; for a Chinese tour of Beardmore, see Duke of Montrose, *My Ditty Box* (London, 1952), pp. 152–3.

86. Sir Christopher Steel, minute of 26 October 1928, PRO FO 371/12733.

87. Sir Hiram Maxim, *My Life* (London, 1915), pp. 186–204, 233–6.

88. D. Merry del Val (Santiago) to Vickers, 31 December 1908, microfilm R307, reporting the proposal of 'Mr Hochstetter, one of the heads of Škoda'.

89. Caillard to Sir Austen Chamberlain, 23 April 1925. Chamberlain to Caillard, 5 May 1925. PRO FO 371/10604. Cf. Vansittart to Sir Patrick Hannon, 12 February 1927, Hannon papers, House of Lords Record Office, H 31/1.

90. Sir Charles Bentinck to Sir Robert Craigie, 8 August 1929, Sir Thomas Maitland Snow, minute of 30 September 1929, PRO FO 371/13507.

91. Sir Eyre Crowe, despatch 1423 of 26 July 1919, PRO FO 371/3601; on the Greek naval missions, see FO 371/8831, 8832, and PRO Adm 116/2635.

92. L. I. G. Leveson, memorandum on diplomatic intervention in government contracts abroad, 14 January 1930, microfilm R300. It was not only French and Italian diplomatic attachés who had such links. In 1921 A. C. Temperley, British military attaché in the Hague, reported to the Director of Military Intelligence that Major von Dimer, previously assistant military attaché to the German Embassy in the Hague, was now Škodas' agent in Holland where Škoda was on the verge of becoming 'universal provider to the Dutch Army' instead of Krupp. 'From a national point of view this would be a great pity'. Letter of 30 August 1921 in PRO FO 371/7091. British businessmen were strictly forbidden to wear uniform when on overseas business, as shown by the persecution of Royal Dutch Shell's Bucharest representative, Col. J. W. Boyle. Despatches 153 and 140 of Frank Rattigan, 2 September 1919; 29 May 1920; Queen Marie to Sir George Barclay, 13 May 1920; PRO FO 371/3601; William Rodney, *Joe Boyle, King of Klondike* (Toronto, 1974), pp. 249–59.

93. Despatch 42 of Sir James Whitehead (Belgrade), 6 June 1910, PRO FO 371/982; PRO FO 368/580; Clive Trebilcock, 'The British Armaments Industry 1890–1914: false legend and true utility', in Geoffrey Best and Andrew Wheatcroft, eds, *War, Economy and the Military Mind* (London, 1976), p. 90.

94. Sir Charles Bentinck to Sir Miles Lampson, 13 November 1923, PRO FO 371/8832; for other criticism of Drummond-Wolff, see C. H. Bateman to Sir David Waley, 14 June 1926, PRO FO 371/11418. Vickers' man in Bucharest at this time was Dr Edward D. Madge, the royal obstetrician, who however was apparently denounced in 1919 by King Ferdinand and Queen Marie as 'endangering the throne' by his intrigues. Sir Lancelot Oliphant, secret memorandum of 11 April 1919, PRO FO 371/3597.

95. Lawrence Collier, minute of conversation with British Adviser to Latvian air force, dated 8 January 1932, PRO FO 371/16292. Barnes (1890–1955) was Secretary General of the International Centre for Fascist Studies at Lausanne 1927–9 and Reuter's correspondent with the Italian army in Abyssinia 1935–6. His entry in *Who's Who's* was removed (1943), and misstates his year of birth, as was Barnes's wont. On his abortive Albanian tobacco concession of 1922, see *DBFP*, 1st ser., XXII (London, 1980), pp. 869–70.

96. Birch, memorandum of 15 November 1928, microfilm R338.

97. Davenport-Hines, *Docker*, p. 220.

98. Sir Robert Michell, despatch of 14 January 1927, PRO FO 371/11962.

99. Colonel Goodden to Bridge, 31 March 1929, microfilm R309; cf. R. P. T. Davenport-Hines, 'Vickers and Schneider: two new multinational strategies

1916–25', in Alice Teichova, ed., *Historical Studies in International Corporate Business* (Cambridge, forthcoming).

100. *DBFP*, 2nd ser., I (London, 1946), pp. 265–6.
101. Colonel G. R. V. Kinsman, Report on Uruguay, 20 September 1928, microfilm R338.
102. Telegram 57 of Sir Ronald Graham, Rome, 26 February 1925, with minute of Charles Peake, 9 March 1925, PRO FO 371/10975.
103. Rear-Adm. Bertrand Watson, Report of visit of 3rd cruiser squadron to Turkey, Bulgaria and Romania, September and October 1932, para. 8, PRO Adm 116/2914.
104. PA (33), 1st meeting, Walter Runciman, 7 December 1933, PRO Cab 27/551.
105. Despatch 368 of Sir Ronald Graham, the Hague, 25 May 1921, PRO FO 371/5876; Naval Inter-Allied Commission of Control at Berlin to Admiralty, 17 August 1921, PRO FO 371/5878.
106. Report on Bofors by Colonel W. Robertson, Stockholm military attaché, 30 August 1921, PRO FO 371/5879.
107. Report on Bofors by Robertson, 19 March 1923, PRO FO 371/9379; memorandum on Bofors, 14 January 1928, PRO FO 371/13326; report by Colonel J. H. Marshall-Cornwall, 23 August 1929, PRO FO 371/14055.
108. Report by Marshall-Cornwall, 26 February 1929, sent to Bridge, microfilm R308; cf. Military Intelligence Directorate to FO, 12 June 1925, PRO FO 371/10607.
109. Annual Report of 1929, quoted Department of Overseas Trade memorandum, 4 October 1930, PRO BT 60/26/7.
110. Birch to Craven, 28 September 1933, microfilm K612.
111. Cmd. 414; Cmd. 3707.
112. In 1926 BSA was refused a licence to export 5000 .303 rifles worth £12 500 to Nicaragua on the grounds that Britain did not recognise the Nicaraguan government. In 1927 Nobel's were forbidden a licence to export powder for rifle ammunition worth £3500 to Britain's ex-enemy, Bulgaria. In 1928 BSA were refused a licence to export rifles and cartridges worth £1232 to an arms dealer in Afghanistan who was not acting for the Afghan government. In 1929 Vickers were refused a licence to export 12 machine-gun barrels worth £36 to a German firm, and similarly, in 1930, a revolver worth £4 to a private Austrian citizen, because they were ex-enemy nationals. ICI were refused a licence in 1931 to export 100 000 tons of TNT to the insurrectionary Cantonese provincial government, and in 1932 were refused a licence for rifle and machine-gun cartridges worth £13 000 ordered by the State of Sao Paulo, Brazil, where there was a revolution.
113. At the same time, in January 1925, the government refused to renew licences already issued to BSA on Russian orders for machine-gun tools and spare parts worth £17 068; as also a contract between Russia and Vickers for machine-gun parts worth £9100. In 1927 a licence granted to a London dealer to supply to Nicaragua 250 Lewis guns (War Office surplus worth £10 000)

was revoked after ten days when Scotland Yard found that the guns were not destined for the Nicaraguan government. Following the decision of a new Labour government in 1929 to suspend the sale of surplus government arms to foreign governments, two licences were withdrawn that December, permitting BSA's sub-agents, the Soley Armament Company, to supply Latvia with War Office surplus Lewis guns, anti-aircraft guns and shells worth £18000. Finally in December 1932, following withdrawal of oil concessions by the Persian government, a licence to Vickers to export newly manufactured practice bombs worth £1056 was recalled. The case was reconsidered and in February 1933 the licence was re-issued. This account of the licensing system is taken from PRO Supp 3/43. There is a good deal about the principles governing sales of munitions to foreign governments in PRO WO 32/4956.

114. Department of Overseas Trade memorandum, 4 October 1930, PRO BT 60/26/7.
115. *Minutes of Evidence*, p. 367.
116. C. P. 289 (33) Report of Committee on Private Armaments Industry, 8 December 1933. PRO Cab 27/551; PRO Cab. 69 (33) conclusion 6(a).
117. Eyres-Monsell to 258th meeting of CID, 6 April 1933, PRO Supp 3/43 and Cab 2/5.
118. DPR 128. 'The Tank Situation', memorandum of 19 October 1936, by Duff Cooper, Secretary for War, PRO Cab 16/141.
119. Birch to Sir Ronald Charles, 14 July 1931, Vickers file 374.
120. Bridge to Charles, 17 June 1932, microfilm R307.
121. This is extensively documented in PRO FO 228/3102, FO 228/3103, FO 228/3559; also FO 262/1551, FO 262/1267, FO 262/1604 and FO 262/1674.
122. Hankey to Neville Chamberlain, 2 March 1933, PRO Cab 63/46.
123. Curzon, minute of 21 November 1923, Harold Nicolson minutes of 12, 21, 27 November 1923, PRO FO 371/8831; *DBFP*, 1st ser., XXIV (London, 1983), pp. 890–2, 898–900.
124. Birch to Sir Hugh Jeudwine, 29 March 1933, Vickers file 124.
125. Brian Bond, ed., *Chief of Staff* (London, 1972), I, pp. 12–15; cf. *DBFP*, 2nd ser., XI (London, 1970), pp. 379–462.
126. Craven to Eyres-Monsell, 2 March 1933, microfilm R334. Cf. Hankey to Runciman, 3 March 1933; Sir Ernle Chatfield, First Sea Lord, to Ramsay MacDonald, 6 March 1933 (with enclosed Admiralty memorandum), MacDonald papers, PRO 30/69/1/519.
127. House of Commons Debates, CCXC, col. 552; cf. Thomas Wewege-Smith, *Gran Chaco Adventure: the thrilling and amazing adventures of a Bolivian air cabellero* (London, 1937); David H. Zook, *The Conduct of the Chaco War* (New York, 1960); Herbert S. Klein, *Parties and Political Change in Bolivia 1880–1952* (Cambridge, 1969), pp. 156–94.
128. Minute of Philip Broad, 13 June 1934, PRO FO 371/17450; cf. C. P. 196 (34). Memorandum by Sir J. Simon, Foreign Secretary, on Bolivia-Paraguay Arms Embargo, 18 July 1934, PRO Cab 24/250. One of Hankey's fears of

embargo proved groundless: that Britain would lose 'the supreme advantage conferred by sea-power', namely obtaining munitions from abroad during major wars, by the USA or other nations demurring from such supplies and citing British embargo precedents in the 1930s. Hankey to MacDonald, 24 February 1933, MacDonald papers PRO 30/69/1/519.

129. Minute of W. D. Allen, 14 December 1934, PRO FO 371/17456.
130. E. G. Boxshall to Vickers, 9 April 1931, microfilm R213.
131. H. L. Wonfor to F. C. Yapp, 9 January 1935, microfilm R339.
132. Sir Archibald Montgomery-Massingberd, CIGS, to Lord Hailsham, Secretary for War, April 1933, PRO WO 32/3338.
133. Sir Austen Chamberlain, Memorandum on Foreign Trade and Finance, 16 February 1929. Prepared for circulation to the Cabinet as C.P.64 (29) to contribute to discussion of final report of the Balfour Committee on Trade and Industry, but withdrawn later. *DBFP*, ser. 1a, vol. 6 (London, 1975), pp. 131–44.
134. Sir Malcolm Robertson, Annual Report on Argentine Republic for 1927, PRO FO 371/12737; H. O. Chalkley to Department of Overseas Trade, 26 March 1927, PRO FO 371/11957; J. Walker, memorandum on Barings and the Argentine naval loan, October 1930, PRO BT 60/26/7.
135. Department of Overseas Trade memorandum on armaments exports, 4 October 1930, PRO BT 60/26/7. The Ottoman Bank's refusal to discount the bonds is particularly significant as the bank's London chairman, Sir Herbert Lawrence, was also chairman of Vickers.
136. Despatch 79 of Sir Malcolm Robertson, Buenos Aires, 24 March 1928, PRO FO 371/12737.
137. Arthur H. Pollen, memorandum on BSA selling organisation, April 1921, University of Warwick Mss 19A/1/2/43. But for a sympathetic description of Wilkins, the Anglo-Russian who was BSA's European bagman after the First World War, see diary of Sir Eugen Millington-Drake, 8 April 1922, MLDK 11/8, Churchill College, Cambridge.
138. Dudley Docker, *Economist*, 7 February 1914.
139. Correlli Barnett, *Collapse of British Power* (London, 1972), p. 242.
140. Trebilcock in Best and Wheatcroft, p. 95; J. D. Scott, *Vickers* (London, 1962), p. 81.
141. Vickers to D. A. Budisteanu Budeassa, 27 March 1912, Vickers 1010.
142. W. J. Keswick to F. C. Yapp, 7 February 1933, PRO T 181/84.
143. Evidence of Yapp and Craven to Royal Commission, 7 May 1936, ibid.
144. Vickers to Atkinson, 10 November 1930. Vickers papers, box of agreements AN-AR. Papers relating to Atkinson in China, including a diary of 1931–2 which he gave to Birch, are in microfilm K162.
145. Vickers to Rudkin, 2 January 1920, box of agreements R.
146. Caillard to H. B. Donaldson, 22 Feb. 1910, Vickers 1005; cf. Donaldson to Vickers, 22 July 1911, Vickers 1008.
147. Bridge to Atkinson, 12 March 1931, microfilm R309.

148. Livingston, *Hot Air in Cold Blood*, p. 220; Bridge, December 1928, microfilm R309.

149. Sir John Corcoran, minute of 9 April 1925; Sir Herbert Creedy to Sir George Barstow, 18 November 1925, PRO WO 32/5660; PRO FO 371/10975, 17181; Davenport-Hines, *Docker*, pp. 220–1.

150. Sir Joseph Addison to Gerald Hyde Villiers, 4 March 1929; Sir Frederick Yapp to Foreign Office, 3 April 1929, PRO FO 371/13982.

151. Caillard to John Noble, 23 April 1909, AW 167; Sir James Whitehead to Foreign Office, telegram 10 January 1910, PRO FO 371/982.

152. Sir Thomas Hohler, quoted Department of Overseas Trade memorandum of 4 January 1926; Dawson to Dept. of Overseas Trade, 31 December 1925; Sir Edward Crowe to Vansittart, 30 January 1926, PRO FO 371/11122.

153. Schneider to Vickers, 27 March 1907, microfilm R307; cf. Arthur Vere to Albert Vickers, 10 July 1907, ibid.

154. Birch, memorandum of 15 November 1928, microfilm R338.

155. The title of two articles by Caillard, in *Monthly Review* 18 (1905); cf. R. P. T. Davenport-Hines, 'The Ottoman Empire in Decline: the business imperialism of Sir Vincent Caillard', in R. V. Turrell and J. J. van Helten, eds, *The City and Empire* (London, 1985).

156. Charles Seymour, *The Intimate Papers of Colonel House*, I (Boston, 1926), p. 200.

157. Philip Noel-Baker, 'The Private Manufacture of Armaments', unpublished typescript, II, ch. 5, p. 4, United Nations Library, Geneva.

158. Tennyson-d'Eyncourt to Royal Commission on Private Manufacture of Armaments, Q. 407, *Minutes of Evidence*, p. 37.

159. M. D. (25) 01. Memorandum by Hankey on Limitation of Armaments and Unemployment, 9 February 1925, PRO Cab. 63/37.

Index

Aberdeen and Temair, 3rd Marquess of (1883–1972) 129

Acland, H.E. Peter Dyke (1884–1953): of Vickers Aviation 165

Adair, Admiral Thomas (1861–1928): courtmartialled 157

Addison, Sir Joseph (1879–1953)
  believes the English gentleman is best in the world 12; but is a 'bounder of the deepest dye' 108
  an expert on Baltic bribery 178

Admiralty 146–7, 150–4, 179

Advertising
  of tea and coffee 20
  too costly for Rowntree 21, 26
  Rowntree's motor car; stunt 27–8
  Benson's campaigns for Rowntree 28–31
  Elect cocoa advertising 36–7
  'indispensable' in USA 69
  neglected by Sheffield hardware manufacturers 70, 72
  of pharmaceuticals 82, 84, 89, 92
  of woodscrews 137–8

Ainscough, Sir Thomas (1886–1976): on trade in Szechuan 11, 110–1, 120

Air Ministry 152–3, 156, 165

Allen & Hanburys 94

Allgemeine Elektrizitats Gesellschaft: a German electrical giant 102
  sends agent to Chungking 110

Alston, Sir Beilby (1868–1929): 'society poodle' 109

Andrew, J.H. (1824–1884) 60

Argentina 93, 111, 161, 174

Armstrong, Oliver (1859–1932) 121–2, 129, 157

Armstrong Whitworth & Co.

seek Chinese contracts 109, 179
  also Chinese trade concession 121
  sign warship construction treaty 150
  join armour plate ring 153
  merge with Vickers 154, 157
  escapades of their Greek agent 170
  seek Greek orders 174
  Chilean orders 179
  saved from extinction 181

Arnhold Karberg: German traders in China 106

Arrol, Sir William (1839–1913): joins Representation for British Manufacturers 120

Askwith, Sir George (1861–1942; 1st Baron Askwith) 108–9

Associated British Engineers: of Calcutta 167

Atkinson, Sir Edwin de Vere (1867–1947): Vickers' bagman in China 177–8

Aubry, Luis: Peruvian bagman 168–9

Australia 42–3, 66–7, 95, 135

Austria 175

Babcock & Wilcox
  sell boilers in Szechuan 110
  join BEA 113
  propose British-China Trade Corporation 121

Backhouse, Sir Edmund (1873–1944): 'morally unsound' 107

Bacon, Sir Reginald (1863–1947): joins Coventry Ordnance 151

Balfour, Arthur (1873–1957; 1st Baron Riverdale)
  his committee on industry and trade 69

lambasts German penetration of
China   118
Balfour, 1st Earl (1848–1930)
signs Washington naval treaty   153
deplores War Office
improvidence   159
Baring Brothers   176
Barnes, James (1890–1955): 'completely
mad'   170
Barton, Sir Sidney (1876–1946): his
'social incompatibility'   109
Beardmore, Sir William (1856–1936; 1st
Baron Invernairn)
enters warship construction
alliance   150; but Admiralty
cancels orders   153
member of armour plate ring   154
reduces capacity   156–7
recruits managers   157; but stifles
them   167
loses Chilean orders   179
Beckett, Edward   65
Beecham, Sir Joseph (1848–1916)   20,
26
Belgium   94, 160, 164, 175
Bells   94
Bensdorp   24
Benson, Samuel (1854–1914)
his Rowntree advertising
campaigns   28–9, 33, 36–7, 39
their equivocal value   31–2, 47, 49
immortalised by Dorothy Sayers   41
Benzon, Ernst   62
Berthier, General: machine gun
designer   164
Birch, John   167
Birch, Sir Noel (1865–1939)
hectors War Office   160
urges industrial mobilisation   161,
164
laments foreign prices   166
derides arms embargoes   174
deprecates international
conspiracies   179
Birmingham Metal & Munitions Co.:

joins BEA   118
Birmingham Screw Company   133–5,
138
Birmingham Small Arms Company
poor overseas marketing   11
joins BEA   118
buys Sparkbrook factory   150
sues government   156
deals in second-hand arms   156
American marketing effort   167–8
supply Russia   172
selling organisation   176
handle War Office surplus
stocks   178
Bland, John Otway (1863–1945):
'disastrous'   121
Board of Trade, Committee on Commercial Intelligence   13
'insular and antiquated'   102
advise Vickers   108–9
send commissioner to China   110
foster South American markets   111
coordinates rearmament   159
mentioned   171, 179
Bofors   162, 171, 179
Bolivia   164, 166, 170–1, 174–5
Bonner, Colonel   167
Booth, Charles (1840–1916):
philanthropist   34
Boxshall, Edwin (1897–1984): spy   164
Bradford Dyers Association   110
Brazil   166
Brenan, Byron (1847–1927): on British
merchants in China   105
Bridge, Charles (1886–1961)
career with Vickers   161–2
cooperates with military
intelligence   164
and with diplomats   167
and with brasshats   173–4
observes Chinese and Polish
cumshaw   178
Bridge, Sir Cyprian (1839–1924)   162
British Aluminium: joins BEA   113
British & China Corporation

contractor 107
Peace, W.K. (c. 1822–1898): on Sheffield insularity 75
Pekin Syndicate: employs neurotic negotiator 107
Peru 10, 161, 168–9
Petter, Sir Ernest (1873–1954) 129
Pile, Sir Frederick (1884–1976): progressive soldier 162
Piry, Theophile (d. 1918): his daughter debauched 108
Plaza, Admiral: 'ill-chosen' 167
Pokotilov, Dmitri (d. 1908): 'overwrought and unmanned' 108
Poland 166, 174, 178
Portugal 166, 175
Power Gas Corporation member of BEA 113
Pricing Policy
   cocoa 16, 22–3, 33, 39–42
   hardware 65–6, 68–74
   pharmaceuticals 92
   China 116
   woodscrews 132–5, 137, 139
   armaments 147–56, 166
Projectile Company: shell manufacturer

Ransome, Stafford (1860–1931)
   early career 113
   splenetic opinions 113–5, 117
   complacent 115–6
   'interested in meretricious publicity' 118
   replaced 120
   plausible but disappointing 123
Ransome & Marles: semi-bankrupt 155–6
Rea, George Bronson (1869–1936): lambasts BEA 117, 119
Remington, Eliphalet (1793–1861): knifemaker 70
Rendel, George (1833–1902): joins Admiralty 147
Rendel, 1st Baron (1834–1913): on Armstrongs' Admiralty

relations 157–8
Ritchie, Charles (1838–1906: 1st Baron Ritchie of Dundee): his 1903 budget 44
Robertson, Sir Malcolm (1877–1951): despairs over stamp duty 176
Rodgers: of Sheffield 62, 69, 71
Rolls-Royce: claims against government 156
Romania 120, 167, 170–1, 175, 177
Roosevelt, Franklin (1882–1945): imposes arms embargo 175
Rowntree, Arnold (1872–1951) 28, 48
Rowntree, Henry (1838–83) 16
Rowntree, Joseph (1836–1925)
   product orientated owner manager 3
   'justly honoured' 16
   introduces cost accounts 20
   deprecates advertising 21
   seeks fair prices 22
   improves product range 23–4
   adopts logo 26
   builds model factory 27
   buys motor car 27–8
   sceptical about marketing 29–31
   distributes free samples 32–3
   market research 34
   stock discounts 35, 45
   considers advertising standstill 39
   efficacy of his strategy 40–2
   unhappy about exports 42–3
   eschews Cocoa Trust 44
   refuses Army contracts 47
Rowntree, Seebohm (1871–1954) 48
Russo-Chinese Bank 34, 48, 104
Rudge Whitworth: 'shut down' 155–6
Rudkin, Brigadier William (1875–1930): Vickers bagman 177
Russia 12, 118, 141, 158, 166, 173, 177
Ryan, Rupert (1884–1952): joins Vickers 161–2; proves his expertise 164

Sainsbury, John (1844–1928):